Creating Christian Indians

Creating Christian Indians

NATIVE CLERGY IN THE PRESBYTERIAN CHURCH

BONNIE SUE LEWIS

UNIVERSITY OF OKLAHOMA PRESS : NORMAN

Also by Bonnie Sue Lewis

(ed., with Patricia Lloyd-Sidle) *Teaching Mission in a Global Context*
(Louisville, Ky., 2001)

Publication of this book is made possible through the generosity of Edith
Kinney Gaylord.

Library of Congress Cataloging-in-Publication Data

Lewis, Bonnie Sue.
    Creating Christian Indians : native clergy in the Presbyterian Church /
Bonnie Sue Lewis.
        p.   cm.
    Includes bibliographical references and index.
    ISBN 978-0-8061-3516-8 (hardcover) ISBN 978-0-8061-9001-3 (paper)
    I. Title.

2002035799

Contents

Illustrations

MAPS

PHOTOGRAPHS

Preface

In 1873 John Williamson, missionary to the Dakotas, wrote a letter to John Lowrie, secretary of the Presbyterian Board of Home Missions. He included an "incident . . . which cheered me like the rising dawn." He told about a group of Yanktons who had just come from a visit to the distant Hunkpapa Sioux. While there, the Yanktons had been amazed by the news of a returning Hunkpapa war party who claimed to have heard a camp of Indians among their enemies "singing *Missionary Songs* all night." The war party was dismayed, but Williamson and the returning Yanktons rejoiced. Believing the singing camp to be Nez Perce Christians, he wrote to Lowrie to "let our good brother [missionary to the Nez Perces Henry] Spalding, whom we know only by name, to take courage and in the name of the Lord light up another peak of the Rocky Mountains."[1]

The story of the Oregon mission is a familiar one. It is often cited by historians as one of the most renowned examples of missionary failure among American Indians.[2] In 1847, after more than ten years of labor among the Plateau Indians, Dr. Marcus Whitman, his wife Narcissa, and a dozen others at the mission station were slain by disillusioned Cayuses. All mission personnel were pulled from the field, and the mission was closed.[3] Of the twenty-two Indians who had joined the mission church, only one was Cayuse.[4]

The Oregon mission story did not end in 1847, though. Christian Indians, particularly among the Nez Perces, who had received glimpses of the gospel message even before the arrival of Whitman's coworker Henry Spalding, continued to pray, sing, and practice what they had learned.[5] In time, a number of them became ordained Presbyterian ministers and established Native churches throughout the Pacific Northwest. The Dakotas supported an even larger number of their own Presbyterian clergy and congregations.

Between the years 1865 and 1935 the distinguishing feature of the missions to the Nez Perces and the Dakotas was the large number of American Indians trained in the ministry and ordained into the Presbyterian Church: nearly sixty pastors. Rivaled only by the numbers of Native pastors among the Episcopalians, Methodists, and Baptists, the Presbyterians still accounted for about a quarter of the ordained Protestant Native clergy during this era, despite more rigorous ordination standards.[6] Half of the Presbyterian Native ministers came from these two tribes alone. Although membership in the Protestant Christian community rarely moved above 10 percent of the Native American population, the denominations willing to ordain Native clergy in significant numbers were usually rewarded with higher levels of church membership.[7]

The motivation for this book came through the discovery among the correspondence of Sue McBeth, Kate McBeth, and Mary Crawford, Presbyterian missionaries in Idaho from 1873 through 1932, of nearly fifty letters written (in English) by Nez Perce pastors.[8] This relatively untapped source of primary documents piqued my curiosity.[9] Not only were there large numbers of ordained Native clergy in the Presbyterian Church a hundred years ago, they also left a paper trail! I went looking for other Native Presbyterian ministers who had done the same.

In Minnesota, among the correspondence of the Dakota missionaries were the letters of a number of ordained Dakotas, from which the story of their extensive Indian ministry began to emerge.[10] The Nez Perce and Dakota ministers' correspondence formed the basis of my research. Their stories are linked in many ways—by their similarities in training and in ministry, and by their sheer numbers.

The first Nez Perce pastor, Robert Williams, was ordained in 1879. By 1932, when the McBeth Mission, or Lapwai Training School, was closed, sixteen Nez Perces, a Makah, and a Spokan had been ordained. In 1865 the first Dakota, John B. Renville, was ordained. Thirty-nine other Dakotas were ordained by 1935. By contrast, in other Presbyterian stations during this same period, only one Native Alaskan, five Pimas in Arizona, and a handful from other tribes were ordained.[11] While never a large group, ordained Native pastors were responsible for leading more than their share of converts to the ranks of the church.

A similar pattern of development in the Dakota and Nez Perce churches fostered the growth of a Native ministry. In the early part of the nineteenth century the mission work at both stations revolved around the missionaries. As the twentieth century dawned, however, Native pastors who preached in their own churches and sent their own missionaries to other bands and tribes assumed the bulk of the work. When the spark of revival had ignited both the Nez Perces and the Dakotas in the 1860s and 1870s, the missionaries among them cooperated, and a Native leadership emerged empowered with the authority of ordained clergy. The rapid growth that followed in the organization of Native churches was the result of nearly a century of missionary labor and Native determination.

Historians who have written of Christian Indians have tended to focus on missionary efforts to save the "savages" and settle them on self-sustaining farms. This concentration on missionary activity came easily to historians, whose topics are necessarily tied to source materials. As Robin Fisher has noted, the paucity of written Indian sources makes it difficult to write an Indian history and has induced historians to write on Indian-European relations instead.[12] The drawback to concentrating on the missionaries, however, is that Indian agency—Indian leadership—is often overlooked. The emergence of ethnohistory in recent decades has gone far to refocus the inquiry by providing a methodology that makes greater use of anthropological and ethnological materials in understanding a culture or a people.[13] This new approach recognizes the importance of Indians as "active participants in the mission situation."[14] It has resulted in such notable works as William McLoughlin's *Cherokees and Missionaries*, Barry O'Connell's edited work *On Our Own Ground: The Complete Writings of William Apess, A Pequot*, Clara Sue Kidwell's *Choctaws and Missionaries in Mississippi, 1818–1918,* and Michael McNally's

Ojibwe Singers: Hymns, Grief, and a Native Culture in Motion. Despite these gains, however, histories of missions remain constrained by the lack of a written record and tend to focus on missionary action and Indian reaction.

With exceptions, the stories missionary histories tell are sad and predictable: the theme is the destructive impact of missionization on Native culture and institutions. As James Ronda notes in his study of the seventeenth-century Huron response to the Jesuits, "[M]issionaries promised heaven, but brought devastation."[15] Missionaries may not have always made an outright assault on Indian ways, but their often uncompromising attitude toward much of Native culture and their desire to change Native behavior became major sources of disruption in Indians' lives. Fisher claims Christianity was so destructive because "the demands of the missionaries could not be incorporated into existing Indian society."[16] James Axtell charges missionaries with "launching their own subversive invasion within" to bring down Indian culture.[17] Portrayed as cultural destroyers by many historians, missionaries have not fared well in much of the literature.

In this literature, missionaries more often than not destroyed without building, for their own missionary activity failed to establish Christian communities. Robert Berkhofer's classic work, *Salvation and the Savage*, recognizes that Indians were more than victims of white aggression, but their agency was confined largely to resistance. Berkhofer concludes that missions to Indians were doomed from the start because of missionaries' "own cultural assumptions, the racial attitudes of their compatriots, and the persistence of aboriginal culture."[18] Clara Sue Kidwell comes close to echoing this conclusion in her study of missionary activities and the Choctaws' cultural persistence. In the end, she claims missionaries failed because Choctaws, as "agents for their own survival," co-opted the church in order to remain "stubbornly, culturally Choctaws."[19] Historians such as Kidwell, Berkhofer, and Fisher assume that where missionized Indians remained Indians, the efforts of the missionaries had failed.

It could be argued, however, that where Indians remained Indians and yet became Christians, missionary efforts succeeded. Today it is a given that the "Christian faith never exists except as 'translated' into a culture."[20] What nineteenth-century missionaries often failed to recognize was the necessity of an inculturated Christianity in order for the faith to survive crossing cultural boundaries. A Native ministry, however, could encourage the kind of contextual work that would lay a foundation for securing the gospel within a Native community despite missionary diatribes against the culture. In the case of the Nez Perces and the Dakotas, that is what, to an extent, transpired. Where Indians became Christian and yet incorporated their cultural and behavioral patterns and constructed institutions and practices reflecting both identities, there is no story of failure. The development of an indigenous ministry among the Nez Perces and the Dakotas played a major role in establishing Indian Presbyterianism—a unique blend of cultures, beliefs, and institutions both Native and Christian.

This book draws from an Indian history penned in an Indian hand. It does not ignore ethnographic or missionary sources but uses them to flesh out the written record. In so doing, the focus remains primarily on the Nez Perces and the Dakotas themselves. From their own words comes a picture of cultural vitality and dynamic exchange that qualifies the claim of cultural and institutional destruction. Christian Indians formed a small but significant part of nineteenth-century American Indian history, due in large part to the leadership of Native pastors.

Few have recognized the important role of Native ministers, especially during this era of Indian missions.[21] As active members and leaders of their communities they saw in Christianity a universal message of hope and the appreciation of values that were at the heart of their own cultures. Native pastors and their congregations creatively preserved Native institutions and expanded Native influence in a time of rapid change. They appropriated those elements of nineteenth-century evangelical Protestantism that gave meaning to their lives. With the authority of ordination, Indian ministers maintained traditional leadership roles and cultural values. Their status as ordained Presbyterian ministers also enabled them to participate with their white brothers and sisters in the larger church community. Not simply assistants to white missionaries, the Native pastors became themselves partners in mission. As Nez Perce pastor James Hayes once wrote, quoting Paul's emphasis on cooperation in ministry for spreading the gospel, "Dear Miss McBeth you [know] what Paul says, I have planted, Apollos watered but God gave the increase."[22] By encouraging Indian ministerial leadership with the potential power and authority of white ministers, the story of missionization among the Nez Perces and the Dakotas did not end in total disaster for church or tribe.

Within the last decade a growing body of American Indian scholars and theologians has challenged both the academy and the church to reassess the missionary era, its assumptions and its actions. These scholars' insights and interpretive frameworks have invigorated discussion of the history and the present realities of Native Christianity and Native congregations. Among the more recent are James Treat's anthology *Native and Christian,* which presents the views of "self-identified Native Christians" on what it means to be both Native and Christian in an attempt to begin a "Native Christian narrative discourse."[23] Jace Weaver's collection of essays, *Native American Religious Identity: Unforgotten Gods,* brings into dialogue Indian Christians, traditionalists, and others who share a "Native post-Christian experience" to explore issues of religious identity. The contributors share a variety of religious perspectives but affirm the close relationship between Native culture and religious tradition in Native communities. They also share the common heritage of recent missionization.[24] As this book was going to press, I was given a copy of *A Native American Theology,* written by Clara Sue Kidwell, Homer Noley, and George Tinker. They have attempted to compose a Native religious theology "inclusive of all Natives (traditional, Christian, neo-traditional, syncretic)."[25] It is a valiant effort that should serve to promote discussion, if not about what it means to be Native and Christian, certainly about what it means to be Christian.

The recent contributions of historians, theologians, and religious practitioners who speak with Indian voices highlight the diversity of opinions regarding the effects of missionization on the Native community. They also indicate the importance within the Christian community of hearing from the recipients of Christian evangelization. Their experiences, insights, and wisdom lead to a fuller understanding of Christianity and how it has been appropriated in Native communities. By focusing on Native voices in conversation with the larger church at a time when both American Indians and American Protestant Christianity were undergoing transition and change, this book also contributes to that understanding.

A word about language is necessary. Both "American Indian" and "Christian" are labels given to diverse peoples and must be understood as such. The term "American Indian," one of the greatest misnomers in history, was applied by an outsider, who had lost his way, to all Native North Americans, a people who never considered themselves "found" much less a single entity. What indigenous peoples called themselves was not the name usually given by outsiders. Thus, the Nimipu, or "real people," became the "Nez Perces," or pierced noses, when French traders sighted some wearing pieces of decorative shell in their noses, although this was not a common practice by the 1800s. "Sioux" is a name derived from the French "Nadouessioux," which came from an Algonquian word that could mean "snake," given to them by the Ojibwas (Chippewas), who considered the Sioux enemies. They called themselves the Dakotas, meaning "friends."[26] The Sioux comprise three distinct social groups with their own specific dialects: the Santees of the East, the Tetons of the West, and the Yanktons-Yanktonais in between. Due to differences in dialect, the Santees and Yanktons call themselves Dakotas while the Tetons prefer to be called Lakotas.[27] However, due to the limitations of language, I have chosen to use common and specific appellations whenever possible, such as Nez Perces, Dakotas, and occasionally Sioux or Lakota, as required by context; I have used American Indian, Indian, and Native interchangeably.

If the term "American Indian" represents a diversity of cultures and languages, the term Christian has almost as many variations. The era considered here, roughly 1835 through 1935, saw Protestant Christianity in the throes of debates over the liberalization of Calvinistic Trinitarian doctrine, the roles of women in the church, and millennial expectations, to name just a few issues.[28] The founders of the American Board of Commissioners for Foreign Missions in 1810, followed by the New School Presbyterians, who took up the reins in the middle of the century, held to an evangelical Protestant understanding of Christianity that helped shape their views of the church, women in mission, and Native cultures. They upheld a concern for a purity of doctrine, for gender specific roles in the church, and for salvation of the "heathen," if possible, "in this generation." The missionaries were not typical of most Americans but did represent many of the leading ideologies of the day.[29]

I have reproduced quotations as written in the original sources. Errors in spelling and punctuation, variant spellings of proper names, capitalization, and emphasis are as shown in the original documents unless otherwise indicated. Interpolations and changes in capitalization and punctuation are marked with brackets.

American Indian ministers of the Presbyterian Church translated into their own cultures and languages what was meaningful from what some claimed was a "white man's gospel" and provided spiritual and material leadership for their people. In doing so, they created a more authentic gospel, one not tied to the cultural trappings of nineteenth-century evangelical Protestantism. While Native Presbyterianism reflected certain more visible aspects of missionary culture, it became rooted in Nez Perce and Dakota lives because it addressed Nez Perce and Dakota needs, upheld Nez Perce and Dakota values, and was expressed in Nez Perce and Dakota voices.

Acknowledgments

This is a story with many authors. It was pieced together from many strands of others' lives, some living and some living on in memory. I am indebted to so many for sharing their histories, their homes, and their hearts with me as I have undertaken this project. A thank you hardly seems adequate to express my gratitude and appreciation to the many who have contributed to my personal journey and understanding as well as my professional growth.

This project began with the support, direction, and encouragement of a great many people at the University of Washington. One of the greatest was my dissertation chair, Richard White, whose patience, guidance, and availability was unequaled. To Richard, John Findlay, and Lewis O. Saum I give my thanks for making a historian of a confirmed high school teacher.

The research behind a work of this magnitude would be unmanageable were it not for the help of a bevy of archivists, librarians, and others. Among those to whom I am most indebted and most grateful are Frederick Heuser, Kristin Gleeson, Beth Bensman, and the staff of the Presbyterian Historical Society (which published a version of chapter 3 in its *Journal of Presbyterian History,* fall 1999); William Tydeman, Judy Austin, and Carolyn Bowler of the Idaho State Historical Society; Elizabeth Gutch of Augustana College; Alan Schreiber of the San Francisco Theological Seminary; Mark Thomas of the Charles Cook Theological School; Ruth Bauer of the Minnesota Historical Society; Carla Rickerson and Karyl Winn of the University of Washington; Laura Arksey of the Eastern Washington State Historical Society; Erika Kuhlman of the University of Idaho

Library and Archives; Robert Applegate and the staff of the Nez
Perce National Historic Park and Archives; and University of
Dubuque Librarian Joel Samuels and his wonderful staff. Special
thanks go to Jo Ann Reece, Shelia Buckley, Barbara Siegemund-
Broka, and the helpful folks of the University of Oklahoma Press.

Research is also costly. I want to thank the University of Washington Department of History for matching funds with the Presbyterian Historical Society for translation purposes. I am grateful to
William Beane and the members of the translation team of the
Dakota Letters Project of Flandreau, South Dakota, for sharing the
fruit of their labors with me. I am indebted to the Louisville Institute for the Study of Protestantism and American Culture, a Lilly
Endowment Program for the Study of American Religion based at
Louisville Seminary, for a generous grant supporting a year of
research. To the University of Dubuque Theological Seminary
Dean, Bradley Longfield, and my faithful colleagues I am most grateful for a sabbatical to complete the manuscript.

This book owes its greatest debt, however, to the men and women
who inspired it: American Indian Presbyterians. Not only did they
open their doors to me, but also patiently taught me about their cultures, invited me to worship with them in their churches, and
showed me the hospitality and friendship for which they are most
noted. I received valuable help and insights from a number of
church ministers and elders including Cecil Corbett; Sidney Byrd;
Walter Moffett; Josephine Dickson; Clifford Canku; the late Lynus
Walker; the late Richard Halfmoon and Nancy Halfmoon, his
widow; Edith Strombeck; Lydia Angle; Jeannie Wheeler; Corbett
Wheeler; the late Charles (Pete) Hayes; Mylie Lawyer; Beatrice
Miles; the late Fred Jose and Jo Ann Jose, his widow; Ralph Scissons;
Earl and Beverly Crum; the late Ada Patrick and her son, Lawrence;
the late Helen Peterson; Shirley Johnson; John and Edith Hottowe;
Isabella Brady; Sophia Porter; Walter Soboleff; and Henry Fawcett
and his wife, VeNita, who also provided a home away from home for
me. Other church leaders, ministers, and students also extended
their friendships and contributed to my understanding of Native
Presbyterianism: Sallie Cuaresma, Buddy Monahan, Elona Street-

Stewart, Floyd Hart, Ron and Danelle McKinney, and Irvin Porter and the Theological Indian Student Association of the University of Dubuque Theological Seminary. All proceeds from this book will go to providing scholarships for the Native American Program of the University of Dubuque Theological Seminary for the continued training of a Native clergy.

There are also many others I have met in the course of my study who have enlarged my understanding of Native communities because of their relationships within those communities. For their friendships and what they have taught me, I want to thank Hunter and Barbara Keen, Hank and Mary Sugden, Otis Halfmoon, Lafe and Gertrude Stock, Bill Ailes, Jeffrey and Dana Bullock, Michael Lewis, Steve Hillis, Armand Minthorn, Steven Crum, Raymond DeMallie, Ted and Caryl Hinckley, and Margaret Connell Szasz. To all of these, the wonderful friends of Talmaks, and many more I am deeply and profoundly grateful.

While many have given me of their time and their wisdom, I hold none of them responsible for any errors of omission or commission found here. They also cannot be held responsible for my interpretation of the materials discussed in this book. For any I have offended by my words or deeds, I ask forgiveness. Learning to walk in another culture is both delightful and disarming, providing great opportunity for both forming profound friendships and jeopardizing others.

Finally, there are those who have blessed me in this undertaking by their unwavering encouragement, support, love, and prayers. To family and friends from Seattle to Cincinnati, I give my heartfelt thanks. To my sister, Linda Holmes, and my brother, Weston Lewis, who gave me courage to keep at it, thank you. To those to whom I owe the most—who gave me life and taught me to return it to One greater—I lovingly dedicate this work: my parents, R. Spencer and the late Geraldine T. Lewis.

Creating Christian Indians

Introduction

Our Chief Moses says long time ago . . . we will be Christian in Presbyterian Church . . . I want to be a Christian but not now.

SPOKAN CHIEF TIYAWASHAT

Nez Perce pastor James Hayes, D.D., addressed a congregation of New England Presbyterians and supporters of mission work among American Indians in 1927. He began with a sermon: "Jesus have power to save to every one that believed on Him no matter if a Chinaman or Negro or Indian or White." He ended with a history lesson: "[O]ur Chief command us do not kill anybody who come to our Camp. This man who became first Chief among Nez Perce Indians he was great Chief[.] [T]his mans grandson Speaking Eagle goes St. Lou[is] after Book of Heaven."[1] Hayes wanted his audience to know that although the Christian God had no favorites, the Nez Perces were particularly suited to receiving God's favor. Traditionally, they were a people that so esteemed the holy that they would not harm creation; and when they heard about a holy book, they went searching for the Christian Bible, hoping it would reveal more about the sacred and confer power on the worthy.

While the details vary, three Nez Perces and a Nez Perce–Flathead journeyed to St. Louis in 1831–1832. They were Eagle (Tipyahlanah, or Kipkip Pahlekin), Rabbit Skin Leggings (Hi-yuts-tohenin), No Horns on His Head (Tawis Gee-jumnin), and Man of the Morning (Ka-ou-pu).[2] The four were seeking their friends, Meriwether Lewis and William Clark, to ask them for "black robes" with the "Book of Heaven" that the Spokans had received through the chief's son, Garry, when he attended an Anglican mission school in the Red River Valley. The Nez Perce delegation touched off the first large missionary migration to the West when eastern missionary journals picked up a version of the story.[3] Hayes, a Nez Perce Presbyterian minister, reflected the pride that the Nez Perces took in being a people who sought after the holy and the powers offered to the deserving.

American Indian people historically are known for a deep spirituality permeating all of life that long preceded the arrival of Euro-Americans. Native respect for the Creator, a sense of shared kinship with all of creation, and reverence for the mysterious and the unknown or unknowable broke down any barriers between the sacred and profane. Ritual activity sought to maintain balance, promote harmony, and keep peace with all parts of the created order. The welfare of the community was everyone's responsibility. That meant not only living honorable lives but also securing spiritual power to assist in the community's good. Because the lines between the material and the spiritual worlds were blurred, that power could come through visions or dreams, from human or nonhuman objects, or by fulfilling one's obligations to the community through prescribed means. The Nez Perces believed that each person could seek a personal spiritual power or guide, known as a "weyekin," for personal and thus communal protection. Similarly, the Dakotas looked to "wakan" beings—spiritual beings—to imbue them with personal power through the hanbleciya—"crying for a spirit"—for their community's safekeeping. American Indian lives were especially attuned to spiritual realities and open to manifestations of the holy.[4]

The interest in the sacred, such as the wakan (encompassing all that is mysterious and incomprehensible) of the Dakotas, predisposed many American Indian people toward any who came to them speaking of or representing the holy. Missionaries, associated as they were with the realm of the spiritual, were initially sought by many tribal leaders for their potential benefit to the good of the community. The "medicine" they practiced might bring health, protection and victory over enemies if shared with a person or tribal nation. And so it was that some Nez Perces went looking for missionaries to come among them and that certain Dakotas welcomed the first ones to enter their territories.

It was the summer of 1835 when two Presbyterian medical doctors went west as missionaries of the American Board of Commissioners for Foreign Missions (ABCFM) responding to the call of the Nez Perce delegation to St. Louis. One was Dr. Marcus Whitman, who joined Rev. Samuel Parker to scout out a mission station to which he brought his bride, Narcissa, the next year. They were joined by Rev. Henry H. Spalding and his wife Eliza and eventually settled in Oregon Country to serve among the Plateau peoples. The other, Dr. Thomas S. Williamson, was an ordained Presbyterian minister as well as a medical doctor. He came from Ohio with his wife, Margaret, and infant daughter to live among the Dakota Sioux on the Minnesota River. Both families, accompanied by other missionaries and assisted by Native interpreters, began work immediately to learn the local dialect in order to preach and to translate the Christian scriptures. Within a year the Dakotas had a Presbyterian church among them, and two years later the first Nez Perces joined the First Presbyterian Church of Oregon. The Book of Heaven and the black robes had arrived.[5] The relationships begun among the Nez Perces and the Dakotas with the Presbyterian Church, despite a tumultuous history, helped produce more American Indian pastors in the Presbyterian Church in the next generation than at any other time in the church's history.[6]

To the mission board, the initial stage of the Nez Perce and Dakota missions was not promising. The missionaries gathered only a handful of Native converts. Although they organized churches, translated some biblical texts, and opened occasional day schools, these missionaries did not equip a Native leadership for carrying on

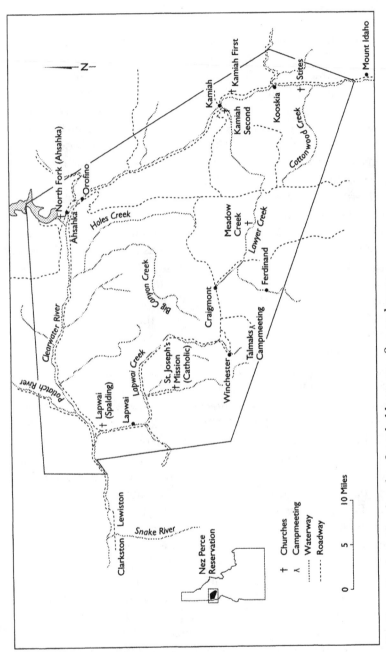

Nez Perce Presbyterian churches founded between 1871 and 1903.

the work of the churches. When conflicts between Indian communities and encroaching settlers erupted in both regions, the work was brought to a standstill. In 1847 the death of the Whitmans at the hands of the Cayuses, devastated by diseases brought through overland wagon trains, ended the ABCFM Oregon mission. Fifteen years later the Dakota war, brought on by starvation and broken treaties, disrupted the mission work among the Sioux. However, a foundation for future Christian leadership had been laid to lead future generations of Presbyterians.

While missionaries were at the forefront of bringing Christianity to American Indians, it was the Indians themselves who established Christianity among their people. A second stage or wave of Christian fervor among the Dakotas and the Nez Perces arose on the heels of these conflicts, led by Native converts. In the aftermath of the 1863 treaty that diminished the Nez Perce Reservation to nearly a tenth of its original size and drove a wedge between bands that had signed the treaty and those that had not, Yakima Methodist minister George Waters (sometimes spelled "Watters") visited his relatives among the Nez Perces. He touched off a religious revival that brought Spalding back to the reservation to assist. Similarly, following the Dakota war of 1862, while nearly four hundred Dakotas were incarcerated and driven from their homelands, Dakota Presbyterian elder Robert Hopkins of the Hazelwood Church provided the catalyst for a religious revival among the prisoners. These Native-led efforts got the attention of the missionaries, who responded to the religious enthusiasm by helping to train indigenous leaders to carry on the ministry.

In the years between the Civil War and the Great Depression, Nez Perce and Dakota pastors worked alongside missionary personnel to consolidate gains and expand the reach of the Presbyterian Church among the tribes. Ministers and missionaries worked together, for the most part, to put church structures into place to train new leaders, establish new churches, and provide Christian nurture for growing congregations. The relationship between Native pastors and missionaries was not without tensions and even open hostilities, which at times threatened the very work of establishing

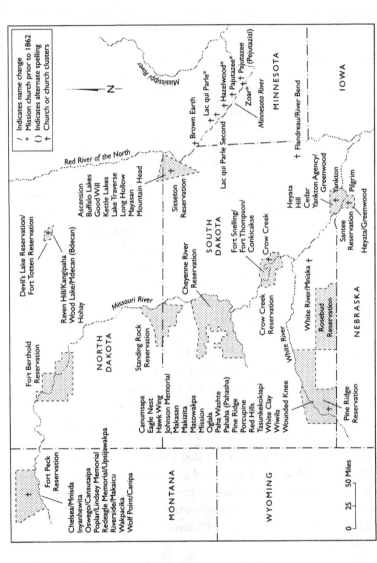

Dakota Presbyterian churches founded between 1835 and 1950. *Note:* Several churches existed outside the area depicted: the Pahacokamya/Middle Hill, in Fort Ellice, Manitoba; and Scouts

Native congregations that both parties desired. Despite these difficulties, the numerical growth of Native pastors and church membership rose steadily until the 1920s.[7]

Understanding the events surrounding the growth of indigenous
churches among the Dakotas and the Nez Perces begins with understanding the missionaries that took up residence among them. From
its inception in 1810, the ABCFM charged its missionary personnel
with inculcating the gospel among the tribes to which they were
sent. For Eliza Spalding, like most of her co-workers, the benefits of
that gospel were far-reaching. Upon gaining the Nez Perce mission
field, she wrote, "O may this people soon have the word of God in
their own language to peruse, & embrace the truth to become a
people, civilized, Christianized & saved."[8] Spalding's enthusiasm for
the benefits of the Christian gospel among the Nez Perces clearly
indicated her belief that both their spiritual and material worlds
would be recognizably changed. "Civilized and Christianized" meant
a Christianity dressed not in Native garb but in the guise of the
"superior" Western culture from which she had come. She failed to
see that a gospel in their own language would be one of the most
effective tools to enable the tribes to dress Christianity in their own
cultural garments and so ensure that the faith became their own.
Although desiring the Christian conversion of the tribe, she could
not envision it in any other clothing than her own.

Eliza Spalding's concern for both the civilizing and the Christianizing effects of the gospel was shared by most Protestant missionaries of the early nineteenth century, who saw themselves as
both receivers and dispensers of God's salvific grace and good gifts.
Inspired by a "Calvinist concern for a practical faith and morals,"
and empowered by the fervor of the Second Great Awakening and
the urgency of millennial expectations, these missionaries sought
"the salvation of souls both in this world and the next."[9] In this
world their Enlightenment view held that all cultures were evolv-
ing toward the Western ideal they represented. American Indians,
they thought, were at the bottom of the spiral, needing both the civilizing effects of Western culture as well as the soul-saving effects of
the Christian gospel to bring them not only into the Kingdom of

Heaven but also into the American mainstream. Failure to do so, they believed, would ultimately result in the demise of the Native peoples.

The humanitarian aspect of the missionary mindset called forth a desire to "save the Indian—the hunted, despised and unprotected Indian—from entire extinction."[10] The enemies, as the missionaries understood it, were avaricious whites, "primitive" living conditions, and little understood tribal customs and practices that appeared to endanger the very existence of the Native peoples. They believed that assimilation into the dominant culture was the only sure way to prevent wholesale destruction of a people. Regardless of the means chosen, assimilation remained the dominant policy of both the missionaries and the American government that assisted in their mission.[11]

Discussion within the ABCFM during the early years of its existence over whether civilizing or Christianizing should come first was tilting toward the latter by the time the missionaries to the Nez Perces and the Dakotas went west to the mission field in 1835. Concern for the salvation of Indian souls was gaining the upper hand over concern for "cultural uplift."[12] The disastrous loss of mission compounds, personnel, and Indians during the Cherokee and Choctaw removal of the 1830s convinced the ABCFM that the danger of extinction for American Indians was real. A heavy investment in boarding schools and large farming communities had not only failed to save many souls but had also nearly bankrupted the board. With that in mind, the ABCFM gave the missionaries to the Plateau and to the Plains a clear mandate to focus on preaching the gospel—in the Native language as soon as possible to reach the most Indians as possible—and to consider civilizing a secondary goal. Upon leaving St. Louis, ABCFM Secretary David Greene charged the Oregon missionaries to concentrate on evangelization, "especially the introduction of Christian knowledge among them and the salvation of their souls," and "be as life from the dead to the benighted tribes of the remote west."[13]

Both missions soon discovered the difficulty inherent in trying to "keep their secular activities in balance with their religious work."[14] The Oregon mission found it particularly difficult to meet the demands of the board to focus primarily on religious matters. It was nearly impossible to be devoted to language study and evangelism among nomadic Indian tribes while carving out a living on the frontier. In addition, Marcus Whitman spent much time on horseback attending to the medical needs of both missionaries and American Indians. Elkanah Walker, one of the eight in a reinforcement party sent out in 1838 who went to Tshimakain among the Spokans, summed up the difficulties in a letter to the board: "It is impossible for us to do much in the appropriate work of a missionary, so long as we are compelled to do so much manual labor . . . It is impossible for me to do much at studying the language when I am worn out with labor."[15]

The Oregon missionaries received a little help from Hudson's Bay Company, whose jurisdiction over the area remained quite real despite the joint occupation agreement with the United States reached in 1818. Dr. John McLoughlin, chief factor of Hudson's Bay Company at Fort Vancouver, received the missionaries kindly and provided for many of their needs. It was not in the company's interest, however, to assist in turning lands or Indians into farms or farmers; and their aid, though often life-sustaining, was minimal in that regard.[16]

Forced by circumstances to make farming the center of their activities, the Oregon missionaries succeeded at it wonderfully. They harvested more crops than souls. Farming was a familiar activity to most of the Oregon missionaries; they were, after all, more accustomed to it than to transcribing Native languages or preaching to those with little concept of Christian religion. Soon, to the dismay of the board, the priorities of the mission seemed to have been reversed. Despite the board's admonitions, the missionaries succeeded in establishing large and prosperous farms, hoping to induce the Natives to do likewise.[17]

Strong personalities further complicated much of the work of the Oregon mission. Narcissa Whitman penned to her parents, "[i]f this mission fails, it will be because peace and harmony does not dwell among its members."[18] Upon arrival Whitman and Spalding promptly divided the mission into two stations largely due to the discord that had plagued their journey.[19] The Whitmans settled among the Cayuses, and the Spaldings among the Nez Perces, although both tribes spoke variations of the same language. The arrival of four more missionary couples, all newly married, contributed to the tensions and further divided the mission into three and then four separate stations, and two distinct language groups.[20] The inability of the missionaries to cooperate impaired the administration of the mission and made language acquisition more difficult.

Failure to learn the Native languages was due as much to a lack of talent as a lack of time. Only Asa Smith appeared to have any bent in this direction, and his disagreeable nature and short tenure with the mission made it difficult to accomplish much more than an established orthography of the Nez Perce language.[21] When the Hawaiian mission sent a printing press and a Hawaiian couple to run it, few publications emerged outside of a couple of primers in both the Spokan and Nez Perce languages and a Nez Perce hymnal and gospel of Matthew.[22] These items, however, gave the Nez Perces the means of becoming literate, helped preserve the language, and in time, contributed to the development of an indigenous Christianity.

The Oregon missionaries began to focus their attention on teaching the American Indians to farm, justifying their actions by claiming that until the Indians settled down to farm, their roving tendencies would prevent them from receiving either religious or educational instruction.[23] Spalding wrote to the board, "[W]hile we point them with one hand to the Lamb of God which taketh away the sins of the world, we believe it to be equally our duty to point with the other to the hoe, as the means of saving their famishing bodies from an untimely grave & furnishing the means of subsistance to future generations."[24] Lacking plows, Spalding literally beat the Nez Perces' old guns into hoes and furnished the seeds for planting. Within two years of his arrival, close to one hundred families were farming around the mission station in Lapwai.[25] He had more difficulty getting them to move into frame houses. Of all the American Indians in the Oregon mission, only one—Tamootsin, the Nez Perce chief later renamed Timothy—could be induced to build one, and then he insisted on using it for storage while his family remained in their original abode.[26]

When Spalding requested help for the mission, he put as much emphasis on material as spiritual advancement, requesting an additional "thirty ordained missionaries, thirty farmers, thirty school teachers, ten physicians and ten mechanics with their wives (220 people) . . . including 100 ploughs and 600 hoes as well as iron works and milling machinery."[27] Already financially strapped, the board refused, admonishing the missionaries, "[Y]ou have not in all cases reflected with what difficulty money is obtained by the board for its several missions."[28] Furthermore, the ABCFM, which was inclined to "begin with a sermon and end with the plow," perceived that the missionaries would "begin with the plow and end with the sermon."[29] This conflict over priorities and budget, as well as the antagonism evident between the missionaries, did not endear those of the Oregon mission to the board nor help sustain the mission itself.

The ABCFM maintained the same expectations of the Dakota missionaries as those of Oregon. The missionaries were to first and foremost harvest souls and so, according to Stephen R. Riggs, who joined Williamson in 1837, "it had been impressed upon us by Secretary David Greene, that whether we were successful missionaries or not depended much on our acquiring a free use of the Language."[30] He noted, therefore, that "our first business was to learn the language . . . to make known to them the most important truths of [C]hristianity."[31] Riggs, however, did not neglect the second duty of the missionaries, and in the next line penned, "At the same time we did what we could to improve their temporal condition—by inculcating habits of industry by our own example as well as by precept."[32] In contrast to the Oregon situation, however, more harmonious relations, an aptitude for language acquisition, and the help of others, native and non-Native, already on the scene aided the missionaries in making greater headway toward the board's objectives.[33]

The Dakota missionaries benefited from the agricultural work commenced by the government in the 1820s under the leadership of U.S. Indian Agent Maj. Lawrence Taliaferro. Supplying the plows,

hoes, and seeds, as well as the instructors, the agency was beginning
to convince some bands of the efficacy of large-scale farming. A
growing shortage of game and extreme winters helped to persuade
them.[34] Although little more successful in the long run at inducing
the Dakotas to become large-scale farmers than the Nez Perces, the
government did reinforce the missionaries' agricultural goals. Government aid also eased the burden of agricultural instruction for
the missionaries, allowing them more time for other pursuits such
as language acquisition.[35]

Two self-proclaimed missionary brothers who eventually came
under the auspices of the ABCFM, Samuel and Gideon Pond, assisted
the Dakota missionaries in their study of the language. They had
arrived the year before Williamson and begun to put the Dakota
language into writing, drawing on word lists compiled by various
military personnel and traders in the region.[36] The missionaries also
had the invaluable assistance of Joseph R. Renville, a French-Dakota
fur trader. With his help, the missionaries not only gained entrance
into Dakota society but also had the advantage of a knowledgeable
teacher and willing collaborator in translating the French Bible into
Dakota.[37] With the Pond brothers' and Riggs's strong aptitude for
languages, Williamson's perseverance, and Renville's cooperation
and idiomatic grasp of the language, the mission team made a significant contribution in the history of the Dakotas. Together they
helped preserve the Dakota language, publishing several of the
gospels, primers, and a hymnal by 1841; a grammar and dictionary
by 1852; a monthly newspaper, the *Iapi Oaye*, by 1871; and the complete Bible by 1879.[38] The missionaries' longevity in the field definitely contributed to completion of these projects, but cooperation
among themselves and with influential Dakotas as well as linguistic
aptitude were also significant factors.

As "people of the Book," both the Nez Perce and the Dakota missionaries made literacy a large part of their mission work. Riggs wrote
that "to teach them to read in their own tongue the wonderful works
of God, was what brought us to the land of the Dakotas."[39] Schools,
therefore, were instrumental in the work of the mission. To avoid
the expense of building boarding schools, the ABCFM encouraged

the missionaries to maintain day schools for all ages and both genders. The missionaries taught basic skills in reading, writing, math, and geography to children and adults. They also gave instruction in Euro-American forms of singing and domestic crafts such as weaving, sewing, cooking, blacksmithing, and farming methods.

The women of the Dakota and Oregon missions participated in the educational work alongside their spouses. Former schoolteachers, such as Narcissa Whitman, Eliza Spalding, Mary Walker, and Mary Riggs, served the missions as teachers while also fulfilling other duties.[40] At one point, Henry Spalding noted there were 225 Nez Perces attending their school, and "only Mrs. Spalding, with her delicate constitution and her family cares, for their teacher."[41] Holding classes in their homes until schoolhouses could be built, missionary wives cared for children and household responsibilities while contributing more directly to the work of the mission. Many, however, felt as Mary Riggs did, who wrote, "I sometimes feel that I am doing nothing & can do but little for their [the Dakotas'] benefit. The various little domestic duties, which seem to claim attention, take up more time than I anticipated."[42] Eventually these domestic duties proved too cumbersome for the missionary wives, and others arrived to carry on the work of the schools. The Dakota mission, particularly, benefited from the labors of a succession of single women and Native teachers.[43] The decision to teach in Native languages proved instrumental in providing both American Indian parents and their children the opportunity to become literate.[44]

Initially, both missions received an enthusiastic response to schooling from the Indians, but interest waned as time went on and the novelty wore thin. Hampered by uneven attendance and then outright opposition, schools suffered in both tribes, and many were closed in this early mission stage.[45] The difficulties facing mission schools were myriad. Attendance was always sketchy, at best, particularly during hunting and gathering seasons. Having very limited teaching materials and minimal Native language skills, missionaries began to offer inducements to bring in students. This sometimes had the adverse effect of leading Indians to expect payment for attending school. According to Mary Riggs, one Dakota chief told her that "if we would make much corn & potatoes for them, they would learn faster."[46] Food and clothing were used at various times to keep up attendance.[47] Even incentives, however, proved ineffectual. By 1852, after nearly twenty years of mission work, Gideon Pond reported that there were only a little over forty Dakota men and women who could read the Bible in their own language.[48] By the time the Oregon mission closed in 1847, classroom education had all but come to a standstill.[49]

Despite the missionaries' emphasis on the "civilizing" aspects of the mission, conversion remained foremost in their minds. From the inception of the Oregon and the Dakota missions, the missionaries held daily religious services for the Native populations and extended services on Sundays. The Oregon missionaries encountered, to their surprise, a people already "very strict in attending to their worship which they have regularly every morning at daybreak & eve at twilight, once on the Sab. They sing & repeat a form of prayer very devoutly after which the Chief gives them a talk."[50] Early Catholic traders, as well as the returned sons of tribal chiefs who attended Anglican schools in the Red River Valley under the auspices of Hudson's Bay Company, encouraged these observances among the Plateau tribes.[51] Indeed, it was the American Indians' interest in learning more of the Euro-Americans' medicine and securing more of the material and spiritual benefits of having missionaries among them that almost brought the Nez Perces and Cayuses "to blows" during the fur rendezvous of 1836. Each tribe felt entitled to receive the newly arrived missionaries and were only somewhat mollified when the missionary party split up to settle among each.[52]

The breakthrough in evangelistic work for both missions was gaining converts among the tribal chiefs. Although that accomplishment did not in itself translate into large numbers joining the church, it did make an entrance for missionization. Failure to win over Spokan chiefs Old Chief and Big Star was one of the factors that resulted in nine years of mission work at Tshimakain without a single convert.[53] The first Native converts to be baptized in the First Presbyterian Church of Oregon were Nez Perce chiefs, Teutacus and

Tamootsin, renamed Joseph and Timothy.[54] Several missionaries noted the piety of Timothy who, while praying occasionally "burst into tears and almost wept aloud."[55] A Nez Perce interpreter, Kentuc, noted that one man "prayed with his lips, but Teutacus [Joseph] prayed with his heart."[56] The sincerity of Joseph and Timothy undoubtedly encouraged their people to accept the new religion. By assisting Spalding in leading services and preaching to other tribes, they paved the way for acceptance of the missionaries and the message they brought. Native leaders also ran interference for the missionaries with those who opposed them.[57]

The Dakota missionaries enjoyed a similar relationship with Joseph Renville. After becoming their first convert, Renville held services, taught the Dakotas gathered around him, smoothed the way for the missionaries, and helped with translation work.[58] The former Catholic trader had, according to missionary Riggs, "acquired an unbounded influence over many" in the Lac qui Parle region of what was to become Minnesota.[59] To the consternation of the missionaries, however, this influence often spilled over into the administration of church policy. When one of Renville's daughters was denied church membership, Renville, his family, and the Dakotas in the area boycotted the church. The daughter was admitted to church fellowship.[60] That the missionaries capitulated to Renville indicated the degree to which they were indebted to their benefactor. As Mary Riggs wrote, "[i]f Mr. Renville should leave, his family & relatives will of course follow, & what will be the fate of this little feeble church we know not."[61] Even with Renville's assistance, however, the Lac qui Parle Church consisted largely of women and mixed-bloods, many Dakota men ridiculing the "church of women."[62]

Simon Anawangmani and Joseph Napesni were in 1841 the first full-blood Dakota men to join the church, after years of association with the mission primarily through its school. Anawangmani, a chief among the Wahpetons, and Napesni, related to Mdewakanton chief Little Crow through Joseph Renville's wife, opened the way for Dakota men's entrance into the church.[63] Their wives and children joined with them, and within the year several other men joined as well. Enraged Dakotas ridiculed and assaulted them and even killed their animals.[64] Anawangmani succumbed to liquor and left the church, returning seven or eight years later. Despite the difficulties of becoming and remaining Christian, both eventually became church elders; and Anawangmani was one of the first Dakotas licensed to preach after the Dakota war of 1862.[65]

Even with the help of tribal leaders, the actual number of converts remained low. In its nearly ten years of existence, the First Presbyterian Church of Oregon admitted only twenty-two Native converts, none of whom were Spokans—only one Cayuse and the rest Nez Perces.[66] The Dakota mission fared little better. By the time of the Dakota war, there were only about one hundred church members among three mission stations.[67] The meager success of their evangelistic work coupled with the constant dissension among the Oregon missionaries prompted the financially strapped board to call for a drastic reduction of the personnel and stations of the Oregon mission in 1842.[68] Only Whitman's harried ride that winter to ABCFM headquarters in New York saved the mission.[69] Although the Dakota mission was reduced financially to only eleven hundred dollars over five years, there was no attempt to close down any of its stations.[70]

Many factors contributed to the Indians' poor response to these initial attempts at Christianization and civilization in both the Plateau and Plains missions. A strict Calvinism that preached the depravity of humankind, the wrath of God toward sinners, and predestination (which precluded the ability to bargain with God for his favor) certainly made evangelization more difficult among a people who viewed their gods as somewhat malleable and fairly benign.[71] Narcissa Whitman wrote to her father that the Cayuses liked to learn about "something new and marvelous—scripture names and history, or any subject that does not touch the heart," but they objected to Marcus Whitman's preaching, which, she alleged, did not gratify their "pride and vanity."[72] They "call it bad talk, mutter and often tell him to stop for they have heard enough," she penned. Instead, she continued, "they wish us to teach two or three of the principal chiefs and let them teach the people, as they used to do . . . before we came."[73] The Whitmans did not agree to the suggestion. The

Walkers and the Eellses at Tshimakain encountered the same problem. Perhaps it is not surprising that no converts were made among the Spokans when the primer used to teach them contained such messages as "Our God is the best [kindest]. We Indians are bad. It is his wish that we are alive."[74]

The Dakota missionaries came up against a similar situation. Williamson attributed tensions with Renville to the fact that, among other things, "I think it my duty to teach many things which he had never said anything about and some which are contrary to what he had been in the habit of teaching."[75] Besides undermining Renville's position of leadership among the fur-trading Lac qui Parle community, the missionaries' Calvinist doctrine often seemed to contain more of God's wrath and less of his grace, repelling rather than attracting the Dakotas.

The paucity of Native converts to Christianity was also due, in part, to the timing of the missionaries' arrival. Indian people were in the midst of rapid and extensive cultural change and blamed missionaries for many of their misfortunes. In the 1830s both Plateau and Plains Indians still retained enough of their freedom to remain fairly mobile, causing missionaries to despair of being able to preach to such an unsettled population. The Nez Perces and the Dakotas also retained significant power to contest attempts to force changes on them. The pressure of western settlement, an increasingly intrusive government, and missionary impetus to persuade Indians to change their habits, though, numbered those days. By 1840 both the Nez Perces and the Dakotas, threatened by the growing encroachment of Euro-American society, stepped up acts of aggression against all non-Indians in their areas.[76] This usually took the form of killing cattle or destroying crops or buildings at mission stations, as Riggs learned when he once tried to prevent a war-party moving against the Chippewas (Ojibwas) to avenge deaths of the previous year. Failing to stop the braves, he said he would pray there would be no killing. The unsuccessful party returned; and blaming Riggs's prayers for their poor luck, turned on his cattle in anger "and took off the edge of their disgrace by killing another of our unoffending animals."[77] Mary Riggs wrote home that the Dakotas

did not consider it "theft . . . but justified by their code of honor
that demands retaliation, if one would be deemed a brave man."[78]

As conditions deteriorated among Plains and Plateau Indians,
missionaries continued to be the focus of their unrest. The Cayuses
attributed the severe winter weather of 1847 to settlement of non-
Natives among them.[79] The Dakotas held the missionaries responsible for increased raids by the Ojibwas.[80] Many accused the missionaries of frightening off all of the game. One Dakota woman said
of the missionaries, "[B]efore you came there were a great many
deer, but afterward, none." She feared that "now we have made
some sugar, but you have come, and perhaps we shall make no
more."[81] Due to their relationship with the spiritual world, missionaries were particularly vulnerable to accusations of manipulating power to the detriment of the Natives.

Encouraged by mountain men and eastern tribesmen who had
seen American Indians pushed from their lands by the onslaught
of settlers, some Indians tried to exact compensation from the missionaries for land use. By demanding payment for timber, water,
and rent, both Plateau and Plains peoples hoped to gain some
material benefit from the missionaries if they could not persuade
them to leave. A grieved Spalding wrote the board, "We are now
called upon to pay for the water we use, the wood we burn, the trails
we travel in, and the air we breathe."[82] When Whitman refused to
meet such demands, he literally had his ears pulled by an irate
Indian and his hat thrown in the mud.[83] The Dakota missionaries
faced similar importunities. Accused of trespassing on Dakota lands,
Riggs lamented, "We had helped them get larger corn patches by
ploughing for them, we had furnished food and medicines to their
sick ones, we had often clothed their naked ones, we had spent and
been spent in their service, but all this was, in their estimation, no
compensation for the field we planted, and the fuel we used, and
the grass we cut, and the water we drank. They were worth a thousand dollars a year!"[84] Although willing to pay for lumber and workers, the missionaries would not pay rent. Such encounters did not
endear them to their would-be landlords, who often took reprisals
in the destruction of mission animals or property.

Government policies exacerbated Native anger and suspicion toward missionaries. In 1842 Spalding collaborated with Elijah White, Indian agent to the Oregon Country, to impose a set of laws on the local tribes to stem the tide of ill will against the missionaries. It did more harm than good, however, leading to more violence when the Indians discovered that the laws did not protect them from violations perpetrated by whites. Furthermore, the Indians themselves were expected to mete out punishments to their own people, often for actions they deemed justifiable.[85] The government laws served only to drive a deeper wedge between the missionaries and the American Indians they hoped to convert.

Some of the Dakotas suffered the ill effects of a treaty promise in 1837. In return for lands ceded to the government by the Santee Sioux, they were promised, among other things, an education fund. When few goods and moneys materialized, discontented traders spread rumors that the missionaries were hoarding the funds. This led to a general boycott of the schools and growing animosity toward the missionaries.[86]

When subtle forms of resistance failed, both Plateau and Plains Indians pursued more strident forms. Ultimately, the Cayuses' fear and frustration came to a head in 1847 when a virulent measles outbreak followed the arrival of a particularly large emigrant train to Oregon. Posturing, threats, and the destruction of mission property seemed to have had little effect in bringing relief from the epidemic. In desperation, two Cayuse leaders turned on the missionaries they believed were responsible for their misery, killing Marcus and Narcissa Whitman and a dozen others at the Waiilatpu station. The deaths resulted in the closure of the Oregon mission. The Spaldings and two other missionary families located among the Spokans were ordered to leave the area, and the mission grounds were eventually left to the American Home Missionary Society.[87]

The Dakota missionaries were spared the same fate in 1862 only because of a larger government and settler presence in Minnesota, which received the brunt of the anger unleashed in the Dakota war. Nevertheless, the war in Minnesota brought the destruction of the mission stations and nearly caused the closure of the entire mission.

The missionaries escaped with their lives only due to the protection of Christian Dakotas. When the Plains mission resumed, the missionaries, like their counterparts on the Plateau, found themselves responding to Indian initiative.

It is at this point in the narrative that the following story picks up. Despite the failure of Protestant missionaries to distinguish between biblical truth and their own cultural milieu, "dispensing a gospel of soap alongside a gospel of grace," American Indians became Christians.[88] And by the end of the nineteenth century, many had become Christian ministers. In the trans-Missouri West the Presbyterian Church could claim nearly forty ordained Native pastors.[89] While Native initiative was evident throughout the initial stage of mission work among the Nez Perces and the Dakotas, the second and third stages, in which an indigenous Christianity took root, would not have happened without their leadership. In the 1860s and 1870s conversions numbered in the hundreds among the Dakotas and the Nez Perces. Native leaders were instrumental in the harvest of souls. Indigenous efforts were so successful that mission agencies were forced to recognize the potential of Native leadership and to begin to utilize Native personnel by cooperating in the education and consecration of Native leaders. The birth of an indigenous Christianity among the Dakotas and the Nez Perces allowed a means of responding to change while affirming Native identity in these two tribes.

CHAPTER 1

The Conversion of American Indians

Now I want to repent. . . . I want the Session to take me into the church.

FISH HAWK

In 1899 Fish Hawk was a sick old man. His penchant for alcohol had landed him repeatedly in a Pendleton, Oregon, jail cell. When he sobered up, the marshal would return him, without ceremony, to the Umatilla Indian Reservation. Eventually the marshal tired of arresting Fish Hawk and hauling him back to the reservation. One day when he dumped Fish Hawk off at the reservation, he threatened to have him locked up for good if he ever returned to town for another drinking binge. Abandoned by the side of the road, the lonely old Cayuse fell to the ground and began to dream: "A giant figure, holding an immense bottle, was coming toward him. The horrible creature had eyes as large as saucers. He was a terrifying sight. . . . Then sweet voices—a flock of white geese . . . a maiden with golden hair and a white robe . . . 'Are you ready to go?'"[1]

Shaken, Fish Hawk related his dream to a friend, Parsons Motanic, a member of the Presbyterian church on the reservation. Interpreting his vision, Motanic said it was Fish Hawk's dead sister telling him he had not long to live. Fish Hawk swore off liquor. Shortly after

that he contracted tuberculosis. Motanic brought the white missionary, the Nez Perce ministers, and the elders of the church to
pray for him. Fish Hawk sent them away. He said he was not ready
to repent.

Two years later Fish Hawk, now quite ill, sent word to Motanic to
bring the Nez Perce minister, Enoch Pond, and the church elders.
"Now I want to repent of my sins. I want the Session to take me into
the church."[2] When they arrived, Fish Hawk held up several bundles of sticks. He said each bundle represented the crimes he had
committed; a stick for each robbery, each man killed, each criminal
act. Then he pushed them from him to indicate his desire "to
renounce his sins" and said he wanted "the Lord Jesus Christ for his
Savior."[3] In a brief ceremony, recorded in the church records shortly
before he died, he was officially married to his wife, baptized, and
renamed Abraham.

The conversion story of Fish Hawk is compelling. As his narrative indicates, the decision to become a Christian Indian was a complex one. The identification of American Indian culture with a way
of life considered pagan meant that to most Protestant and many
Catholic missionaries, conversion was not complete until the hair
was cut, the blanket shredded, and the new convert entirely torn
from the evil influences of the Native environment.[4] Such a wholesale renunciation of one's past and community made it difficult for
many Indians to consider Christianity a viable alternative to Native
ways. Those who embraced the new ways most fully and adapted to
the required changes recognized that even in becoming a Christian, they did not have to sacrifice being Indian. Christian Indians
may have transferred their "primary religious identity," but they did
not relinquish who they were.[5]

Twentieth-century historians and anthropologists tended to support the position that American Indian culture and Christianity,
especially as advocated by nineteenth-century missionaries, were
incompatible. Much of the early historiography and the more
polemical literature of the last century would lead one to believe
that "Christian Indian" is somewhat of an oxymoron. Writing in the
1950s Lucullus McWhorter claimed the Nez Perces "could not

understand the god of the whites. He differed so drastically from their own deity, whose heart was kindly disposed toward all people."[6] He blamed Christian Nez Perces for not only turning away from all that was Indian but also giving away all that belonged to the American Indian. Alvin Josephy, in his 1958 biography of "patriot chiefs," excluded any who had become Christian, noting that those presented were the "greatest heroes of the Indian peoples."[7] A decade later, even Robert Berkhofer, in his seminal work on Protestant missions to Indians, claimed that "to become truly Christian was to become anti-Indian" and leave all semblance of Native life behind.[8] To these historians it was difficult to imagine American Indians living in two worlds that seemed at such odds.

While the existence of Indian Christians could not be denied, the genuineness of their conversions could be. Berkhofer believed that more Indians converted to share the "loaves and fishes" than the "blood of Christ."[9] Neal Salisbury, writing of an earlier period, claimed that Christian Indians abandoned their "traditional Indian personality patterns" if they became Christians because Puritan missionaries "demanded that Indians no longer be Indians."[10] Most historians agreed that only when tribes lost their autonomy could Christianity even begin to make inroads into a tribe, because Indian Christians accepted "cultural suicide" if they accepted the "English Protestant version of Christianity."[11] Missionary correspondence and journals certainly provide ample anecdotal evidence that Indian beliefs and practices were considered "heathen" and that Christian Indians were expected to divorce themselves completely from them.[12] If Christianity destroyed the Native culture, as was asserted, it most certainly destroyed the American Indian in the process as well.[13]

Only recently have historians begun to explore the role of Indian agency in Indian-white relations. Increasingly, American Indians are being viewed as more than just the victims of white cultural aggression. While James Ronda and James Axtell suggest that "Indians accepted only as much 'civilized Christianity' as they deemed necessary," Axtell does concede that the longevity of Indian congregations testifies to "bona fide" Indian conversions.[14] Drawing on anthropological studies and a trend toward ethnohistory, recognition of Indian agency has brought about a shift in focus to ways in which Indians remained Indian, despite missionization.[15] It has also provided insights into ways Indians became and remained Christians, creating either an "indigenized Christianity" or a "Christianized indigenous religon."[16] As historian James Treat asserts, however, "[t]o disregard Indian Christians, either as Indians or as Christians, is to deny their human agency, their religious independence, and—ultimately—their very lives."[17]

A growing number of historians have begun to show an appreciation for Native ingenuity in shifting cultural boundaries to gain their own ends. The permeable divisions between Jesuit and Algonquian cultures created a "middle ground" that allowed both parties to manipulate those boundaries to their own advantage, as explored in Richard White's landmark volume *Middle Ground*.[18] William McLoughlin illustrated how the Cherokees used Christianity to revitalize their own religious and political lives. He noted that, in essence, "Cherokees converted Christianity to their own needs and values" by melding Christian and Cherokee elements.[19] When Raymond DeMallie examined Black Elk's conversion to Catholicism, he acknowledged the sincerity of the Lakota shaman's conversion but reasoned that Black Elk remained Indian insofar as he used the resources of the Christian church to fulfill traditional Indian leadership roles.[20] As Clyde Milner and Floyd O'Neil noted in their study of Protestant clergy and western Indians, they did, indeed, exhibit a "complex layering of responses to attempted Christianization."[21] The emergence of a "new Indian history" that sees American Indians as multidimensional has finally led to the recognition that, in fact, Indian conversion to Christianity was an open-ended social process actively involving choices and change.

American Indian Christianity was based on a conscious choice.[22] Where Indian religion no longer offered hope or solace, the new religion acted as an alternative. Where similar values were discovered, such as respect for family ties, an emphasis on charity toward one's neighbors, and strong taboos against immoral practices, Indian Christianity built on parallels. In response to personal or social crises, Indians used Christianity to shape their own solutions and transform their lives. However, even when Indians claimed to have renounced Indian religious culture in favor of the missionaries' Euro-American Christianity, American Indians went on to construct Christian Indian communities, with Indian leadership and vigorous Indian institutions that took pride in Indianness. Despite the cultural trappings of the new religion, Indian Christians recognized an essential Christian doctrine: the universality of the Christian faith.

Fish Hawk exemplifies the complexity of the process of religious change. He illustrates how one American Indian found in Christianity a viable religious alternative, with parallels to his own cultural values and a solution to his personal crisis. Throughout, however, he remained Indian even as he became Christian. Fish Hawk was willing to relinquish some control over his life and submit to the church leaders' ministrations because he was concerned about his future. The new faith promised a good end and rewards for moral behavior. Sobriety, kindness toward others, and adherence to religious rituals were valued by both Christian and non-Christian Cayuses, so Fish Hawk had no difficulty accepting conformity to these standards, although he may have failed to live up to them. He came to believe that Christianity offered the only medicine strong enough to transform his personal failures and help him secure his future.

Fish Hawk's dream taunted him with visions of death. When death came near, and not before, he signaled his interest in the Christian faith. He wanted to be assured he would go to the land of white geese and sweet maidens, where his sister dwelled, not the land of terrifying giants wielding immense liquor bottles. His friends in the mission church assured him that he could avoid such a catastrophe by confessing his wrongdoings, putting his faith in the power of Jesus Christ, and casting his lot with his Christian friends. He understood that entry was gained through an act of repentance.

Fish Hawk chose his moment, repenting in his own way and before his chosen audience. The white missionary was not invited. When the Nez Perce minister and the elders arrived, Fish Hawk was

the master of ceremonies. He laid out before his friends his version
of repentance: he cast away bundles of sticks representing his "sins"
and claimed he wanted what Jesus Christ offered—peace of mind
over his future. As the shaman would cast out an evil spirit in the
form of a small stick or stone from one who was sick, Fish Hawk used
the Indian ritual to express a Christian doctrine.[23]

Fish Hawk expanded a traditional ceremony to convey his decision to receive the new medicine.[24] The sticks he cast away did not
represent an alien force causing his illness but rather his own past
actions, his moral transgressions. Further, he needed to identify
someone else as the healer. He, in essence, abdicated his own position of authority over the spirits by naming another, Jesus the Christ,
as the one who brought healing. He did not, however, abandon all
of his power.

By doing it his way, Fish Hawk created a ceremony that incorporated what was important to him. The old Cayuse rejected what were
considered behavioral offenses by both cultures, and yet, by expressing his choice in his terms, kept the autonomy prized by American
Indians feeling more and more subject to a dominant culture. He
bridged both cultures by choosing actions recognized in both as
cleansing or purifying.[25] He creatively used the elements at hand and
his knowledge of traditional medicine to create a middle ground
whereby the church leaders and he could maneuver to reach a conclusion satisfying to both.

The church members accepted his gesture as an indication of
a changed heart, and Fish Hawk was welcomed into their fellowship. He was initiated into their denomination by Christian ceremonies of marriage, baptism, and the conferring of a new name
to mark this significant event in his life. Fish Hawk could now die
in peace. He chose his path, made his concessions to the new ways,
and yet preserved ownership over who he was by expressing his conversion in terms and in timing that were, in essence, both Cayuse
and Christian.

Unfortunately, Fish Hawk did not live long after his conversion.
Although deathbed conversions were not rare among Christian Indians, of those who left records, most converts came to the church in

adolescence or early adulthood. The few church records uncovered indicate that one common pattern of conversion followed family or kinship lines. Children and extended family members usually entered the church on the heels of one or both parents.[26] However, most American Indians discussed in this book came to Christianity through a second route: Native churches or schools. No matter how they came, all were drawn to Christianity for a variety of reasons. They considered Christianity a legitimate religious alternative because they believed that its spiritual authenticity rivaled that of Native religions, or because of its parallels to indigenous cultures and beliefs, or because it offered creative solutions to personal crises, or because of a combination of these factors.

The discovery of Christianity as a legitimate religious alternative came in a variety of ways. Old Eve was one of the first Dakota women to join the mission church at Lac qui Parle, in 1835.[27] Her four sons, including Paul Mazakutemani, were among the first students to attend Dr. Thomas Williamson's day school. Although twenty-nine years old when he commenced schooling, Mazakutemani claimed that it was knowledge gained by reading the "Sacred Writings" (portions of the Bible translated into Dakota) that convinced him that the Christian faith had something to offer him.[28] While his mother's influence should not be underestimated, the son claimed, "I came to understand from the Sacred Writings . . . that for all my past evil deeds I must die . . . that I was even now dead, but the Great God was merciful, and had given his only begotten Son to die for us . . . that through His sufferings we might live."[29] He concluded from his own reading of the scriptures that "the Great God brought to us Wild men the knowledge of the way of Life" that would save him from death.[30]

Mazakutemani's understanding of that message was influenced by "the sacred men" who brought the book and on whose "good advice . . . I acted in accordance therewith."[31] He adopted their dress and their agricultural orientation, eventually becoming a church elder and elected "chief" of the Christian Dakotas of the Hazelwood Republic, an experimental farming community near the mission. He continued to maintain his chosen path even when challenged

by Little Crow's party in the Dakota war of 1862. At great risk to himself, he sought the release of the white and mixed-blood captives.
Although threatened with death, he defended his position as a
Christian Indian and a friend of the white community. He reminded
the warriors that "[n]o one who fights against the white people ever
becomes rich, or remains two days in one place, but is always flee-
ing and starving."[32] He was not blind to the material benefits of following the path the missionaries laid out, but satisfaction with his
choice came from several sources.

For Mazakutemani, as for others, before becoming a Christian
and adopting the lifestyle of those who taught him about Christianity, he studied the new religion, as put forth in the Christian
scriptures, and got to know the missionaries. He wrote of God, "I
knew He was mighty. He made my heart strong."[33] He called the missionaries his friends and claimed that he rescued them at the outbreak of the Dakota war "to keep my sacred men from being killed
. . . to save alive my friends."[34] When the Dakota warriors took white
women and children captive during the Dakota war, Mazakutemani
pleaded for their release and admonished the braves to fight against
soldiers "but don[']t fight with women and children."[35] To Mazakutemani, the Christian faith offered a religion he could compre-
hend, a power he could appropriate, and an ethic he could esteem.
Christianity did, indeed, provide a genuine religious alternative.

Recognition of Christianity as a legitimate religious option came
to James Dickson, a younger Nez Perce contemporary of Fish Hawk's,
in his teens. He claimed that he grew up "under heathen influences
. . . a wild, ignorant boy" on the same reservation in Oregon as the
old Cayuse.[36] At age fourteen he moved from the Umatilla to the
Nez Perce Reservation in Idaho to be with his father. Curious to "see
what they did," he and several friends occasionally attended the Presbyterian churches on the reservation, which were under the leadership of Nez Perce pastors. "We were the wild ones and as is the
custom among the Nez Perces we sat away in the back seats, giggling
and laughing as the services went on."[37]

According to Dickson, one Sunday in 1896 as Nez Perce pastor
James Hayes was preaching from the third chapter of John, "[i]t

was the 7th verse that the Holy Spirit used to touch my hard, heathen heart, 'Marvel not that I say unto you, ye must be born again.'"[38]
As Dickson listened, the pastor went on to explain from the six-
teenth verse of the chapter that the love of God and the promise of
everlasting life extended to "whosoever" believed, whether "Indian
or white man and was for old or young, rich or poor."[39] Dickson
claimed, "It was then for the first time that I [knew I] was lost without the Savior Jesus Christ."[40] When "some of the young people testified to their faith in Jesus Christ" and some of the "old men who
used to go on the war-path rose and spoke of how glad they were
that the Lord had called them into the Christian warfare instead,"
Dickson decided "that the message was for me."[41] He went forward
to stand with the new believers at the front of the church.

Dickson had grown up to revere his grandfather, a shaman whose
power and wisdom were well respected. As he told his companions,
"My grandfather was a medicine man and I had great respect for his
teaching . . . I would rather follow the teachings of my grandfather
than the teachings that comes to us from the white man."[42] The
young man's concern, however, was not the old medicine man's spiritual power or ability to effect cures but his teaching. The superiority of his grandfather's words over those of any white man was
simply that they were Indian. They reflected a Nez Perce understanding of life and, therefore, far surpassed any other viewpoint. It
was only when Dickson heard that Christianity was intended for both
Indian and white, and witnessed Indians teaching and responding
to that message, that he considered it a valid alternative to his grandfather's teachings.

Dickson did not say why he was looking for an alternative, but
perhaps his recent move had loosened familial bonds and affections,
as well as influence, leaving him more open to other views. Perhaps
he felt alienated from his roots and the suggestion of a community
within the church appealed to him. Most likely, he was not looking
for a change at all, but something in the service resonated with him.
For whatever reason, James Dickson noted that his conversion
angered his father, "who called me a coward fro turning away from
their old teachings."[43] He gained the acceptance and approval of

church members, however, who came forward to shake hands with him "as the tears rolled down their faces."[44] According to his testimony, they "spoke words of encouragement and help to me."[45] They became for him an alternative family, even as Christianity became an alternative faith.

Dickson did not reject the family of his birth. Although church membership separated him "from many of my heathen friends, even my father," he still felt a deep affection for friends and family, especially for the older man. He wrote to missionary Kate McBeth while away from home that "I am glad to know that you had seen my dear Father[.] I believe in God and I know He will save my relatives."[46] When his one sister among the Umatillas and a brother and sister with the Nez Perces also became Christians, he noted that he was "helped and strengthened" by it.[47]

Fish Hawk, Paul Mazakutemani, and James Dickson were of different tribes and different eras but of the same mind. They were attracted to Christianity by its power to engage the intellect, to change lives, and to provide a spiritual as well as a physical home. At times against great odds, they continued in the faith they had chosen, and it sustained them throughout their lives. Although Fish Hawk did not live long after his conversion, Paul Mazakutemani lived as a Christian Dakota for more than forty years. He claimed, "I am not a preacher. . . . But for eighteen winters I have been and am an elder, and I love to labor in this work. I cannot do much, but I try to carry a candle into the dark corners. Where I go I speak of the Saviour and the way of salvation."[48] He held the office of ruling elder in the Presbyterian Church until his death in 1885, being "[p]rominent in civil and religious affairs throughout his life."[49] James Dickson became a Presbyterian minister and served Nez Perce churches as well as churches among the Umatillas of Oregon and the Shoshone-Paiutes of northern Nevada. He remained a pastor for forty years, until his death in 1948.

Besides its religious reliability, there was a second reason for considering Christianity a genuine alternative to Native religions: its similarities to Indian religious practices and parallels to indigenous culture and beliefs. Scholars such as Ronda and McLoughlin have made note of some of the Native Christian practices and values of eastern and southern tribes that "did not represent a radical break with the traditional past."[50] This was also true for the Nez Perces and the Dakotas. Similar cultural values of hospitality and charity expressed in the Christian Bible and in both Nez Perce and Dakota society made the move toward the Presbyterian Church seem, at times, merely an extension of Native practice. When entrance into the new faith resembled known paths of religious activity, it made the move even easier.

To Nez Perce Mark Arthur, becoming Christian was in keeping with familiar habits. Christianity came to him in a recognizable form and invited a Nez Perce response. Arthur was a small boy during the 1877 flight of Chief Joseph, when the Nez Perce were forced by the U.S. government to abandon their homes in the Wallowa Valley of eastern Oregon and settle on the Nez Perce Reservation. His father was killed in the war, his mother captured and sent to Oklahoma; and he, having become separated from his mother, joined Sitting Bull in Canada. He returned to the Nez Perces in Kamiah, Idaho, after the war and earned his keep by taking care of horses. It was while he was pasturing horses in the hills above the community, and dreaming of a trip to Montana that summer, that he heard the church bell of the Indian Presbyterian church in Kamiah. He described his reaction:

I felt like I was in great danger, standing on the edge of a precipice or high place and felt as though I might drop down. Of course my tears ran down. I never before was praying but I prayed there on the top of that butte and said, "My Maker, my Father, if you give me life until the evening, then I will repent and go to show myself before the session of the church. Whatever they will say to me I will do it.["] Not long from that hour my sorrow went away, but there was feeling in my heart for I am thinking "I am wrong in sin."[51]

Arthur's epiphany drove him to the church, whose bell had summoned the experience, to learn what he had to do to find peace. A wary Nez Perce minister and church elders asked this stranger to their services, "Who told you to go repent?" When he answered, "Nobody," and then related his experience while out on the mountain with the horses, they responded with understanding: "That was the Holy Ghost speaking to you." Upon examining him further, they baptized him the next Sunday.[52]

It did not seem strange to Arthur, nor to the Native Christian leadership, that a Ghost, Holy or not, should speak to him. And it did not seem unlikely that it should get his attention in such a manner. To the Nez Perce mind, steeped in a culture that revered the sacred and its manifestations, such experiences were not unexpected. Most Nez Perce boys and girls were sent on vision quests at an early age to receive spiritual help from a guardian spirit who might appear to them while they were alone, fasting and praying.[53] Arthur's ordeal was not unlike the supernatural visitation experienced on a vision quest. That he was on a hilltop alone when it came also suggested a spiritual vision.[54]

A middle-aged Dakota at the time of the Dakota war of 1862 also explained his conversion in terms of a vision experience. While incarcerated, Artemas Ehnamani claimed that he "saw a great light" and concluded "it was Jesus." Then, like the New Testament apostle Paul, he responded with "I saw I believed."[55] Visions and unexplainable phenomena were recognized as powerful influences in the Bible as well as in most American Indian cultures. Visions were often sought but sometimes came unexpectedly. They could appear as human or nonhuman forms, male or female, and be audible or inaudible. In all cases visions were to be taken seriously and acted on, for the good of the individual and the community.[56] Like Arthur, Ehnamani concluded that his vision was a supernatural visitation; and he credited it to the Christian God, who seemed to exhibit the most power in his sordid prison surroundings, where Dakota spirits seemed to have abandoned him. He believed in its message and then, in Dakota fashion, took it to the community, eventually becoming one of the first of the Dakota pastors in 1867.

In the same way, Arthur's Nez Perce background prompted him to recognize the importance of his experience and to respond. He followed what were Native understandings of spiritual encounters

Dakota minister Artemas Ehnamani, co-pastor of Pilgrim Church with
Titus Ichaduze. Photo courtesy of the Presbyterian Historical Society,
Philadelphia.

on his route to conversion. When he looked for someone who could explain his experience, the church elders obliged. Themselves Nez Perces, they were struck by the dreamlike quality of his calling, not at all foreign to Nez Perce experiences of the transcendent world, and they led him to the altar. There he was adopted into a new family, and the well-known rules of kinship obligation and duty were applied to his new relatives. Following the instructions of the church leaders, Arthur soon followed in their footsteps as well, becoming a Presbyterian minister in 1899.[57]

New converts found many parallels in the Presbyterian Church to cultural values with which they had grown up. James Dickson found that the "new teachings" actually embodied much of the teachings of his grandfather, ultimately convincing him of the legitimacy of the Christian faith. Nez Perce and Dakota cultures both placed great importance on the care of kin. In the church, this kinship circle was extended to include the entire body of Christian believers. Hospitality, generosity, and charity were expected of good American Indians as well as good Christians. And biblical customs, such as praying, fasting, and feasting had parallels in both Dakota and Nez Perce cultures. These perceived similarities attracted Native converts and served as the foundations of their churches.

Kinship rules governed both Nez Perce and Dakota societies so that all might "get along together harmoniously and with a measure of decency and order."[58] Whether in the more elaborate system of formal "address, attitude and behavior" prescribed in Dakota family interaction, or in the more informal relationships among the bands of the Nez Perces, family obligations "demanded of relatives that they not harm each other."[59] Further, kin were expected to stand by family members, provide for them if in need, and participate with them in celebration as well as mourning. A person could be related, especially in the Dakota culture, by blood or by choice.[60] Either way, the relationship required that those involved be committed to the welfare of the other, despite the cost or inconvenience.[61] The Christian commandment that a man or woman must be willing to lay down his or her life for a friend was readily accepted in these American Indian cultures because it was an ideal to which they already adhered.

The Nez Perce minister James Hayes, who so influenced James Dickson, illustrated the way kinship values were transferred from one culture to another. A member of the White Bird band during the Joseph war of 1877, Hayes came to Kamiah as a very young man. In relating his own conversion story, he noted the important role of the Native pastor: "I could not see the light. Then, through the preaching of my red brother, Robert Williams, my blind eyes began to open. He took the blanket off my shoulders, put a coat on me—cut off my hair—then led me to Miss McBeth's school, where I began to study the Bible."[62] Robert Williams was the first Nez Perce to be ordained. When Hayes became a member of the church, Williams extended to him the hand of Christian fellowship and he became a member of a new family. The minister opened his home to the young convert and encouraged him to attend the mission school. He even took pains to ensure that Hayes would be accepted at the school by personally dressing and preparing him for his new role as student.

Williams gave Hayes his extra coat. It was one the missionary, Sue McBeth, had salvaged from a missionary barrel to make him "presentable among the white ministers" at the presbytery meeting. When she saw Hayes attired in the coat intended for Williams, she was chagrined. Williams looked surprised and responded, "Miss McBeth he is a Christian now. I want him to be a schollar of yours. You would not allow him to sit in your School in a blanket. [H]e had no coat and I had two. The Bible says, 'He that hath two coats let him impart to him that hath none.'"[63] She could not argue with his reasoning on either account. The requirements of kinship were akin to those of the Christian gospel. Providing for a brother's need was expected of Nez Perce and Presbyterian alike.

Ella Deloria, linguist and anthropologist who studied under Franz Boas and herself a Dakota, noted that "because [Christianity's] social message was already partially familiar, there was a sound foundation for the structure of Dakota Christianity."[64] This was certainly the case for Paul Mazakutemani. Following the Dakota war, Mazakutemani offered his services as a scout to the U.S. Army in order to help bring in noncompliant Dakotas. While on a mission with them, his son sickened and died. Concern for his two remaining daughters prompted

First Nez Perce minister, Robert Williams. Photo courtesy of the Department of Interior, National Park Service, Nez Perce National Historical Park, Spalding, Idaho. Photo number NEPE-Hi-0796.

him to write to missionary Stephen Riggs, "[I]f thier is anathing hap-pins to me on this expediedition I wish you will take . . . good care of my children."[65] Later he wrote to Riggs reminding him that "I have always regarded you as a friend and you know that I have always tried to carryout to my best ability every thing that you have asked me to do."[66]

His relationship with Riggs enabled Mazakutemani to expect Riggs to provide for his family, in the Dakota way of kin, should his children ever be in need. He could have reminded Riggs of the obli-gation of a Christian brother to care for the widow and the orphan but chose instead to write in terms of his friendship. Among the Dakotas, "friendship was of no trivial consequence."[67] Christian brotherhood and the Dakota kinship system, with its "laws of inter-personal responsibility and loving kindness," were so similar that to call one a brother or a friend in the Dakota world, as in the Christ-ian, would immediately suggest a reciprocal obligation.[68]

Winnebago society, likewise, reflected similar values and further illustrates the way biblical and Native values complemented each other.[69] Henry Roe Cloud grew up in a wigwam on the banks of the Missouri River in Nebraska. In the early 1890s he was sent to a gov-ernment boarding school with other Winnebago children, where "the greatest event of my life took place."[70] The students all marched to the Presbyterian church every "Cross Day" (Sunday), the school band leading the way. Young Henry played his cornet. When about fourteen years of age, he was asked in a Sunday school class what he would do with Jesus and answered, "I would like to be His friend."[71] That prompted a visit from the missionary. "We sat down upon the grass, and Mr. Findley told me, for the first time, about Jesus Christ, as one who had a real claim upon my friendship. I felt a strange con-straint to accept this new spirit-friend."[72]

Roe Cloud esteemed the concept of friendship. To him, it was a "meaning-full and a very formal act among Indians. . . . So I under-stood that when I took Jesus that night to be my friend, we were to stand by each other through this life and through the 'land of the setting sun.' He was to defend me and I was to defend Him."[73] Roe Cloud became what the Indians called a "Preaching Listener" and stopped fighting with others, despite ridicule. His grandmother did not forbid his actions but cautioned him, "[I]f you want to be forever a wanderer in the other world, you can continue in the road you have taken."[74] Despite the "severe soul-struggle" that followed, Roe Cloud was baptized, claiming he would obey Christ, even over parents and relatives, and as he explained it, "testified my belief in the reality of the 'Friendship.' It was stronger than the desire to go to any particular place in the world beyond the grave."[75]

As a young student, away from home, Roe Cloud needed friendship. Christianity, to him, offered far more than salvation and life in the hereafter.[76] It meant having a personal friend whose "family was mine, and mine was his."[77] Christianity invited a Winnebago response to the person of Jesus—a relationship with him. Roe Cloud knew the value of having a friend powerful enough to stand by him in a foreign situation. The missionary was astute enough to recognize that friendship with Jesus was one aspect of the divine nature, and encouraged the young student to pursue that understanding of faith. By so doing, Roe Cloud could appreciate the Christian deity while acting out of a basic American Indian concept of relationships. He was ordained in the Presbyterian Church in 1913, eventually serving as minister, educator, and even Indian agent.

Not only did Native Christians find recognizable kinship relationships within the church, they also found social values esteemed in the Native culture. Kindness, hospitality, and generosity were traits exhibited by respected Nez Perces and Dakotas. Luther Standing Bear, who grew up in the late 1800s, the first son of a Lakota chief, noted that generosity was "a mark of bravery" and thus a subject for instruction of the young Sioux warriors.[78] Charles Eastman, a contemporary of Standing Bear who became a medical doctor, remarked that "Winona," the name given to a couple's first-born girl in Sioux society, meant "charitable, kind, and helpful," traits admired by the larger community.[79] Pi-lu'-ye-kin (Albert Moore), a Nez Perce who studied for the ministry in the early 1900s, noted that his mother "would give meat to her friends, and they would give her camas and kows. That's the way it used to be. Indians didn't sell; they just gave to each other."[80] It is not surprising that Indians noted and affirmed Christianity's endorsement of selfless generosity.

Flandreau, a Dakota Christian community that homesteaded in South Dakota in 1869 even before the Dawes Allotment Act of 1887, displayed the parallels between Dakota and Christian ideals.[81] Reporting their church and community news in the Dakota mission's monthly newspaper, the *Iapi Oaye*, members of Flandreau frequently commented on the qualities that made good Christians—the same as made good Dakotas: "If we are wise we will look for the good. The Bible says to think over everything well and hold unto it tightly, flee from all bad/evil sorts/names," wrote one churchman.[82] Another wrote, "Jesus tells us to do good, and help each other. Jesus said: 'Have mercy.'"[83] Commenting on the strength of the Flandreau community, one man affirmed, "[T]hese people are like one family. There is no opposition. . . . God put love in their hearts."[84]

Although Indian social values and Christian ones were not identical, the Flandreau Christians chose to build on the similarities. Active reinvention is evident in the obituary of Mrs. S. D. Hinman, a white woman and the wife of the Episcopal priest. When she died in 1876 her virtues, which would have been quite familiar to Dakotas, were praised in the *Iapi Oaye:* "This woman was very much depended upon. She had a fine house and whoever came they cared for them and they greeted them joyfully. She took pity on the poor. And when very bothered, she was never ill natured. She was never heard to speak bad words/gossip nor jealously. Women would like to have seen her continue to live, this women was very well respected."[85]

The description of Mrs. Hinman sounds a great deal like the formal instructions given to Dakota women upon coming of age. According to Ella Deloria, they were taught, in the words of the Buffalo Ceremony, that "[a] real woman is virtuous and soft spoken and modest and does not shame her husband and neglect her children. She is skillful in the womanly arts and hospitable to all who enter her dwelling. She remains at home ready to receive guests at all times. Her fire burns permanently cheery and smoke curls prettily upward from her tipi head."[86]

Mrs. Hinman, like a good Dakota woman, was "kind, generous and loyal."[87] She showed hospitality to the visitor, did not neglect the needy, and was a good housekeeper. Those same values, ingrained in Dakotas from childhood before coming into the Christian church, continued to inform Dakota lives after Christian conversion.

James Hayes perhaps best exemplifies Christianity's appeal as a reflection of Nez Perce values. In 1927 the local presbytery sent James Hayes east as a representative to the General Assembly, the highest governing body of the Presbyterian Church. Hayes addressed a white audience. After apologizing for his poor, though perfectly comprehensible, English, he then proceeded to preach to them from the second letter to the Corinthians, "about Jesus Christ and Him crucified because there is nothing else but Jesus Christ is our Saviour."[88] Following his two-page sermon was a three-page story "about the Nez Perce Indians"and their welcome of Lewis and Clark. Hayes told the audience how the chief had commanded the people to keep the Kamiah Valley, never to kill their wives, and never to kill an enemy who came into their camp, thus saving Lewis and Clark from certain death. Hayes ended by proudly relaying the story of the chief's descendant who went to St. Louis after the "Book of Heaven," thus initiating contact with Christian missionaries.[89]

The bulk of Hayes's narrative recounted the kindness and humanity of the tribe prior to the coming of the white people. The rest of the story was secondary; his point was that the Nez Perces had been worthy of receiving the Book of Heaven that followed. Hayes used the Nez Perces' goodwill toward Lewis and Clark to show that Nez Perce cultural values paralleled Christian ones. In so doing, he placed Indian and white cultures on the same level. Both needed the salvation offered through Christ, both were equally incomplete without him; but both valued the same elements of hospitable social relations, making each culture worthy of receiving the Christian message. A good Christian was also a good Nez Perce.

In addition to genuine religious alternatives and significant parallels to indigenous culture, Christian conversion was attractive for a third reason: it could provide creative solutions to personal or social crises. Fish Hawk discovered this in trying to avert the horror of living out his dreams. He creatively repented of past behaviors offensive to both cultures and gained entrance into a new community. Other American Indians also discovered a transformative power in entering upon the Christian road. As McLoughlin has noted, "Christianity is a religion of hope, of miracles, of divine support for the weak and oppressed. When a tribe had reached the point of despair, Christianity provided a way out. It offered spiritual power for personal and tribal revitalization on new principles. It made God's power available to Indians, not only to the white man."[90]

Ehnamani's conversion to Christianity, which occurred during his incarceration, enabled him to cope with his deprivations and redirect his future. Prior to the outbreak of the Dakota war, Presbyterian missionary activity among the tribe had been going on for nearly thirty years, with relatively little success. Several small Dakota churches existed, made up primarily of women and mixed-bloods and led by the missionaries and a handful of male elders.[91] However, the Dakota war prison camp became an incubator for religious activity.[92] In the words of Francis Frazier, Ehnamani's son, the Dakotas "felt the need of a great power which would save them from their particular predicament. They turned to the old Medicine man and to their religious beliefs for help but to no avail. Then came the time when they began to think that the old Gods had deserted them."[93] Ehnamani, following his vision of the light, became one of the early converts.

In the wake of the tragedy and carnage around them and facing an unknown future, the prisoners found themselves bereft of belongings, family, and home. They needed a hope to which they could cling. Ehnamani found it in the promises of the Christian message, that "with [the] word of Jesus we heal our sorrows & fears . . . [who] has my word n[o]t see death."[94] As he understood it, "Jesus shows up the evil and folly in the world that we may escape it. He comes to call us so we may live with Him in heaven."[95]

While still in prison, Ehnamani began to share his experience and urge his friends and family members to "throw away the bad mind. Throw away sorrow. The light has come to all. Has come to us."[96] The power Christianity offered did not depend on wealth, bravery, or nobility. It was, as Ehnamani noted, not "the grand & mighty" who were called, but "the poorest little boy here is one to . . . whom Jesus came down."[97] It was a message for the impoverished and the downtrodden, for a people who no longer had a home or a homeland.

Inspired by the hope the Christian message offered, Ehnamani found a transforming power for his life. The former hunter and warrior gathered his band around him and stirred them with his enthusiasm. To missionary Riggs he wrote, "God had mercy on me and my people to whom I have preached, all listened carefully and have become wise."[98] When the prisoners were released in 1866 to rejoin their families on the Santee Reservation on the Niobrara River in Nebraska, Ehnamani and Titus Ichaduze, another Dakota who had been imprisoned with Ehnamani, were licensed to preach. They became the first Presbyterian ministers of the Pilgrim Church, made up of nearly three hundred former prisoners and their families. Like Fish Hawk, Ehnamani found that Christianity offered a means of transforming his life. He accepted the challenge and remained pastor of the Pilgrim Church until his death in 1903.[99]

Despite the contention that "a native Christian identity is both historically and culturally problematic," the term "Christian Indian" is not an oxymoron.[100] Christian converts such as Fish Hawk, Paul Mazakutemani, and Artemas Ehnamani experienced an infusion of power in their lives that left them no doubt that the God of the white people could also be their God. As McLoughlin has noted, a good missionary "enable[d] Indians to see that the Christians' God was not culture bound but that his power was available to all people."[101] Christianity, as it was appropriated, proved a genuine alternative to Native religions because Native Christians found it reliable. Further, Christianity coincided with many indigenous values and could offer, at least in part, creative solutions to both personal and communal crises.

Although at times called "heretical, inauthentic, assimilated, and uncommitted," Dakota and Nez Perce Presbyterians today come from a long line of Christian converts who found the Christian faith, as they assumed it, an alternative capable of "satisfying new emotional needs and intellectual hunger."[102] Christian scriptures engaged the minds of American Indian peoples even as spiritual power assured them of God's presence. Presbyterian missionaries believed

Nez Perce minister Mark Arthur, circa 1924. Photo courtesy of the Department of Interior, National Park Service, Nez Perce National Historical Park, Spalding, Idaho. Photo number NEPE-Hi-3313.

that one of their primary tasks was to transmit the written word of their God to those they wished to convert, in the Native language if necessary.[103] Scriptures and sermons in their own tongue gave Indians greater opportunity to draw their own conclusions about Christianity. Although the Nez Perces never had an entire Bible translated into their language, the early Indian ministers spent much of their training in translating large portions of it for study and for sermons.[104] The Dakotas had the New Testament in their language by the time of the Dakota war. The Old Testament was completed by 1879.[105] Even in crossing cultural boundaries Christianity retained its power to rival Indian religions; and Christianity invited evaluation firsthand through the written or spoken word.

When read or heard by Native peoples, the Christian Bible recounted tales of a tribal people, of encounters with a greater power, and of a God who freed captives. The Christian scriptures resonated with the stories of people who were tied together by kinship relationships, who revered the transcendent world and its temporal manifestations, and who could identify with the oppressed or imprisoned. Reading the stories convinced Paul Mazakutemani. Hearing them convinced Sidney Byrd. A retired Dakota pastor, Byrd became a Christian through listening to his "beloved grandfather," Samuel K. Weston, a Dakota missionary, preach at a campmeeting among the Lakotas.[106] As a third-generation Presbyterian, Byrd has stated that although he is Dakota by birth, he is Christian by choice.[107] Both the number of Native Christian converts and the permanence of their faith testify to the legitimacy of such a choice.[108]

CHAPTER 2

Revival

PASTORAL PREPARATION

*Native helpers were raised up of the Lord. John B. Renville, Robert Hopkins,
Artemas Ehnamani and others were filled with the Spirit, and prophesied.
One after another were ordained to the ministry.*

JOHN P. WILLIAMSON

In June 1870 the Nez Perces gathered on the Weippe prairie on
the eastern side of the reservation to harvest the kouse roots and
the camas bulbs that sustained their diet throughout the year. This
annual event had long been a time to celebrate winter's end, social-
ize with family and friends from other tribes, and participate in sto-
rytelling, games of chance, and horse racing.[1] Arriving in time to
join in the festivities were four Yakimas whose leader, George
Waters, had married into the Nez Perce family of Henry Spalding's
first convert, Tamootsin, called Timothy. Waters was a Methodist lay
preacher who began to hold Christian worship services in the camp.
Response to his preaching, according to missionary Kate McBeth's
account written forty years later, was so intense that the site became
known as the "Place of Weeping."[2] Such a strong religious awakening broke out that the Presbyterian Indian agent of the Nez Perces,
John B. Monteith, called for Presbyterian missionaries to return to

the reservation so that the new converts would not join the Methodist Church. Henry Spalding, eager to return to his "beloved Nez Perces," responded to the call to "gather in the sheaves" and baptized over six hundred new converts before his death in 1874.[3]

A similar experience of Native-led religious revival occurred almost simultaneously among the Dakotas—on the prison grounds where nearly four hundred men were incarcerated following the 1862 Dakota war. Nearly fifteen hundred of their family members were held in another camp. From all accounts, it appears that Robert Hopkins, former elder of the Pajutazee (Pajutazizi) Church, led the prison inmates in the men's camp in religious activities.[4] Missionaries Thomas Williamson and Stephen Riggs, who continued throughout the Dakotas' imprisonment to visit the prisoners several times a week bringing supplies, messages from loved ones, and words of encouragement, noted the leading spiritual role Hopkins played. Williamson informed the Presbyterian mission board that Hopkins led the prisoners in morning and evening worship: "He reads a portion of Scripture sings a hymn and either himself or one of the others who were church members before the massacre leads in prayer . . . after adding a short exhortation."[5] Hopkins looked to the missionaries to provide the sacraments and bring Bibles and books. He wrote to Riggs, "I want to take something sacred [communion]. For that reason, I want very much for one of you to come. . . . Iron Thunder wants a songbook, and he also wants one of the new Holy Bibles that they make for a half dollar. . . . Bring as many songbooks as you can. . . . Also, bring one of the yellow alphabet books."[6]

Williamson's assessment was that "the Holy Spirit enabled Robert the ruling elder to speak in a manner highly appropriate and edifying far beyond what could have been expected of one of no more education and experience in public speaking." Furthermore, he was convinced that although the missionaries were on hand, "the work has seemed to be carried forward chiefly through the instrumentality of him and his fellow Christian prisoners."[7] Riggs called Hopkins the "ruling spirit in that prison—he is the spiritual bishop there. . . . Hopkins has been there all the time and he stands spiritually, as he does physically, head and shoulders taller than the rest of the

Group of Dakotas at the home of Chaska (who might have been Robert Hopkins), *center right*, near Pajutazee mission church in 1862. Photo by Whitney's Gallery, courtesy of the Minnesota Historical Society, St. Paul. Photo number E91.7U/r1.

people."[8] Even months later Riggs was still impressed by Hopkins's continuing leadership. He wrote, "The Indians all look to him as the head in religious matters and the soldiers speak of him as 'The minister.'"[9] These missionary observers clearly believed that God had enabled certain Christian Dakotas to assume leadership roles not previously exhibited.

Hopkins was one of less than a dozen Native church elders in a total church membership of about seventy from three mission churches prior to the outbreak of the war. The Christian Dakotas sprinkled throughout the camp came forward to join Hopkins in religious meetings with, at times, 90 percent of the prisoners.[10] Riggs noted that prayers were at first made only by former church members, those "who were accustomed to pray; but others soon came forward and did the same."[11] He and Williamson were amazed at the number who "prayed with such copiousness and fervency as to make it manifest that they are taught of God's Spirit. They pray not only for themselves and absent families but also very appropriately for the soldiers who guard them, the officers, the President of the U.S. and also for those who are angry at them and seek their destruction."[12] Frequently they prayed for "*A country, a sanctuary and religious teachers in that land*. . . . And I don't know that it is wrong for them so to pray."[13]

Even more amazing was that the Dakotas' prayers were being answered. Williamson commented that although the prisoners' guards did not know that prayer was being offered up for them, "an amazing change in their feelings toward these Indians" was taking place. "Instead of looking on them with scorn and contempt, and rejoicing in their sufferings, they now manifest a disposition to make them as comfortable as possible."[14] Shackles were being removed, greater freedom to move around in and even out of the camp was being allowed, and the Dakotas' prayers continued to flow. Hopkins believed that participation in public prayer indicated Christian conversion.[15] Following up on Hopkins's initiative, the missionaries, with the help of the elders, baptized the new converts, who numbered over three hundred.

Neither the Methodists nor the Presbyterians were strangers to religious revivals. Both denominations had been involved in the series of lay- and clergy-led outbreaks of religious enthusiasm that marked the Great Awakenings of the eighteenth and nineteenth centuries. Hallmarks of these revivals were intense religious fervor and a rapid increase in professions of Christian faith. Mass religious meetings led by ministers and laity often elicited emotional responses from those in attendance that included weeping, fainting, singing, and praying, especially in the more lively and less decorous atmosphere of the Methodist meetings. By the 1860s revivals had become recognizable and respectable even in the more restrained gatherings of the Reformed and Presbyterian churches.[16] If the missionaries were surprised by the revivals that erupted among the Dakotas and the Nez Perces, they certainly saw them as a work of God. That they were Native led, however, motivated a redirection of the entire mission strategy. A focus on the ordination of a Native clergy resulted.

The Nez Perces and the Dakotas were also not strangers to religious awakenings. For the Nez Perces, a prophetic tradition had arisen to meet cultural stresses since the latter part of the eighteenth century. These events were usually led by individuals who claimed to have returned from death and were accompanied by a call for dancing to bring about the predicted release from their oppressors.[17] The most recent religious revival had arisen among the non-treaty Nez Perces and centered around a Wanapum shaman named Smohalla. Eventually referred to as Dreamers for their reliance on dreams to direct them, Smohalla and his followers practiced certain rituals and dances to hasten the departure of the whites and their world and usher in a reemergence of the traditional Nez Perce world and the return of their dead.[18] The Dakotas would experience one final prophet-led revival in the 1880s with the coming of Wovoka and the Ghost Dancers.[19]

Following as they did on the heels of cultural, economic, political, and religious disaster, the mass conversions of the Nez Perce and the Dakota revivals were not without precedent. In fact, in light of such declension, revival was, perhaps, to be expected.[20] In the 1850s and 1860s land loss, broken treaties, and the privations and uncertainties surrounding reservation life contributed to the general malaise that enveloped both tribes. The Nez Perces lost nearly 90 percent of their reservation through the treaties of 1855 and

1863. The Treaty of 1863, never signed by the Joseph or White Bird bands, severed their beautiful Wallowa Valley in northeastern Oregon from the reservation, deepening the division between treaty and nontreaty Nez Perces. Gold strikes on the reservation, fertile soils, and excellent grange lands in the Wallowa Valley brought thousands of miners, farmers, and ranchers to Nez Perce territory and wreaked havoc on the Nez Perces. They became a people whose past was disparaged, whose present was tenuous, and whose future was uncertain.

In this same era, the Dakotas found themselves in a very similar situation. The 1851 treaties of Traverse des Sioux and Mendota placed the Dakotas on reservations and an annuity system, and handed over nearly all of the present state of Minnesota and a small part of South Dakota to white settlement. Delayed payments, drought, and government mismanagement added to the woes of the long-suffering Dakotas, who were told by one disgruntled trader that if they were hungry they could eat grass. He was one of the first casualties of the Dakota war in 1862, the mouth of his corpse found stuffed with grass.[21] The subsequent loss of lives and livelihood, the incarceration of many who had been among the "friendly Indians," and banishment from their homelands further eroded the spirits of the imprisoned Dakotas. Life for the Dakotas and the Nez Perces could not have declined more dramatically in the years before the religious awakening.

The response of the Nez Perces and the Dakotas to the spiritual awakening that came upon them prompted their leaders to call for evidence of faith and changed allegiances. The Yakima preacher Waters called the people to put their trust in the Christian God and rid themselves of the symbols of their former loyalties. As missionary McBeth later told it, "Then and there, they threw away their bottles, their pipes, the feathers and tails of animals, and their wives."[22] The destruction of medicine bundles indicated the converts' confidence in their newly discovered God's ability to meet their needs. The issue of multiple wives, however, became the source of many grievous decisions. In a faith that stressed monogamous marriages, converts were required to let go of extra wives. The willingness to make such a sacrifice, which meant hardship for many families, confirmed the seriousness with which the new converts took their religious experience.

The Dakotas also responded to the signs of revival among them by courageous acts of devotion that astounded the missionaries. Word of the spiritual awakening among husbands and fathers in prison soon reached the members of the Dakota family camp, who were rocked by rumors of impending disaster to their incarcerated loved ones. According to Riggs, the small group of Christian Dakotas meeting regularly with missionary John Williamson, who had taken up residence with the Dakota families, soon expanded to include many in the camp. No longer convinced that their "charms and medicine sacks" were powerful enough to "prevent misfortune," many burned them.[23] As Riggs interpreted it, "confessions and professions were made; idols treasured for many generations with the highest reverence, were thrown away by the score. They had faith no longer in their idols. They laid hold on Christ as their only hope. On this ground they were baptized, over a hundred adults, with their children."[24] The missionaries were amazed at the willingness of so many Nez Perces and Dakotas to cast away their formerly sacred bundles.

Most remarkable to the missionaries, however, may have been that this revival took place solely under the leadership of American Indians. As missionary Kate McBeth exclaimed over the Nez Perce revival, "[T]here was no Mr. Spalding there, and no white missionary. Just God and their guilty souls."[25] Although the missionaries recognized that conversions "have been influenced by *mixed* motives, and that *deliverance from that chain* has been one of the motives," they also believed that "no religious man can go there and spend a week in the prison, attend their meetings morning and evening (and noon sometimes) and hear them sing and talk and pray and come away feeling that there is not a great deal of reality there."[26] Missionary teaching had continued, albeit sporadically among the Nez Perces, for at least thirty years; but the revival had definitely been instigated by Native converts, even if at the prompting of the Holy Spirit. Thus it is not surprising that the religious enthusiasm that

Waters fostered among the Nez Perces took Indian Agent Monteith aback. He was unable to envision a Christian mission without a white missionary to superintend it, preferably a Presbyterian.

Although he received help from the missionaries, in the Dakota camp Hopkins took the lead in providing spiritual services for the prisoners as well as nurturing their faith and overseeing their care. Williamson wrote that Hopkins "spent some whole nights conversing and praying with the anxious."[27] Soon he and others appointed to the task committed themselves to "the work of education and establishment in the faith of the gospel," since the missionaries "could not properly watch over and care for these people, as *they* could watch over and care for each other."[28] Religious instruction included the academic, as Hopkins and others tutored in reading and writing the many who wanted to send letters to loved ones and to read the sacred texts that had been translated into Dakota. Riggs called the camp "one great school. Go in almost any time of day and you will see from ten to twenty groups or circles reading."[29] As their detainment continued for the next several years, the women, like the men, began to oversee daily tutorials and prayer meetings and even the children held meetings "conducted by themselves."[30] The missionaries saw this as a sign of the "Holy Spirit . . . breaking . . . the herculean chains of Paganism" and fitting the people to carry on the work of the church among themselves.[31]

When American Indian leaders came forward to lead their people in the Christian path, the missionaries had to reappraise the role of Native leadership. Of necessity, the vast numbers baptized into the church meant that the missionaries had to turn to Indian helpers to minister to their constituents. These helpers could have remained in secondary positions if the missionaries had insisted on using them only to buttress their own leadership positions. In the case of both the Nez Perces and the Dakotas, however, missionaries rejected this option. It appears that the decision fully to equip Native leaders with ministerial credentials was opportunistic; it was less a planned policy than a recognition of capable Christian Native leadership, arising when most needed and just as a new generation of missionaries took up the reins of the missions.

Henry Spalding was the last of the Oregon missionaries to labor among the Nez Perces. When he arrived on the scene of the Yakima-led revival, he immediately assumed his former position as spiritual leader of the Nez Perces. Under the leadership of Timothy and several others who had joined the original church in the 1840s, the reservation Nez Perces had continued Christian practices of daily prayers, hymn singing, and Sabbath observance. Now that leadership, including George Waters's able guidance, gave way to the elderly Spalding. Gathering a handful of the leaders around him, the missionary began a circuit of preaching fields that ultimately included the Spokans to the north, the Yakimas to the west, and the Umatillas to the south. Spalding built on the labors of faithful converts in all these areas, baptizing hundreds, "assisted by Bro. George Waters . . . native preacher & most efficient."[32] Spalding's method of ministry took the lead from the Indian leaders and, had he lived longer, Native pastors may never have evolved.

The American Indian spiritual leaders' willingness to give Spalding such a position may have been more than a matter of respect for the older man. Chief Spokan Garry, educated by the Anglicans of the Red River Valley in the 1820s and the catalyst for the Nez Perce trip to St. Louis in 1832, had refused to support the Presbyterian missionary activity among the Spokans in the 1830s and 1840s, during the tenure of Elkanah Walker and Cushing Eells. The missionaries had objected to Garry's Episcopal form of Christianity, and the Spokans may have ridiculed his preaching.[33] When the missionaries were pulled from the field in 1847, however, Garry continued his preaching. During the Yakima revival, Garry found the Spokans also caught up in the religious awakening. Only reluctantly did he now turn to Spalding and request a visit. His apparent intent was to prevent the loss of Indian property to settlers and to forestall Catholic activity on the reservation. Christian baptism and marriage would allow Indians to inherit property and would keep the Spokans in the Protestant folds. Assisted by preachers William Three Mountain, an Upper Spokan, and Ama-mel-i-kan, a Middle Spokan, Garry did not need another preacher. He did need an ordained one, though, or no church or government in Washington Territory would recognize the new converts. Spalding's visit in the company of a nucleus of Nez Perce Christians resulted in several hundred baptisms and many marriages as well as the foundation of two Spokan Presbyterian churches a decade later: the Deep Creek and the Wellpinit Presbyterian Churches. Both had their origins in Chief Spokan Garry's preaching.

The 1860s and 1870s were major transition years for the Dakotas and Nez Perces. When revival broke out among them, the former missionary teams that originated the two missions in the 1830s were aging. Henry Spalding, the only surviving member of the Oregon mission, was in his seventies. Although he managed to travel long distances to baptize hundreds of Nez Perces, Spokans, and other Plateau Indians, by 1874 he could ride no more. Ministering to him at his deathbed was the young Susan L. McBeth, recently hired by the government and appointed by the Presbyterian Board of Foreign Missions to teach at the government school in Lapwai. McBeth assumed the mantle Spalding laid down. For nearly twenty years she carried on the work of educating and training the small group of men Spalding had used as assistants. Neither ordained nor the recipient of a theological education, she nevertheless helped ten Nez Perces to achieve ordination. McBeth recognized the Nez Perces' competence to lead and the importance of ordination to their task. She was a new breed of missionary.

The Civil War years were instrumental in forming this new breed of missionary. McBeth's missionary career began among the Choctaws in 1860 but was interrupted within a year by the war. Wanting to continue in service, she worked among the wounded as a chaplain with the U.S. Christian Commission. The expansion of women's roles during the war allowed women to gain "administrative and technical knowledge, confidence in their stamina and abilities, security in working outside the home, and respect for one another."[34] By the time of her appointment to Lapwai in 1873, McBeth felt well equipped to perform the task before her, and society was better prepared to accept her contributions.[35] She had acquired the tenacity to stand against board members who criticized her for teaching theology, Indian agents who chastised her for opposing their policies, and even American Indians who complained at times of her heavy-handedness. She had also learned that the marginalized must take every advantage to gain entrance and acceptance into the dominant culture. Ordination for Indian pastors gave them that advantage, even as it enhanced her status and influence in the church.

John Williamson was also a new breed of missionary, but it was not gender that shaped this development. He was a second-generation Dakota missionary who had been born and raised on the mission field and who had the advantage of being "acquainted with the habits customs and language of the Dakotas."[36] He had learned these in his childhood playing with Dakota friends, among them John B. Renville, youngest son of translator and church leader Joseph Renville.[37] Growing up among the Dakotas gave Williamson an understanding of and appreciation for Native abilities and an egalitarian spirit that fostered trust in Indian leadership.

Both Thomas Williamson and Stephen Riggs became convinced, after witnessing the spontaneous Christian leadership of the Dakotas during incarceration, that the Indians were ready to take responsibility for their churches. Both men, however, were facing advanced years and had retired to the comforts of larger towns. It remained for the younger Williamson carefully to shepherd the new leaders that were emerging. Just prior to the outbreak of the Dakota war, John Williamson had completed his education and been ordained as a missionary to the Indians with whom he had been raised.[38] He lived with the Joseph Napesni family, the Christian Dakota family he had known as a boy in Lac qui Parle, and began construction of a church building. He had just left for a trip east when he read the news of the uprising and turned around without finishing his business. Hearing that the "Indians with whom I was acquainted were in [the prison] camp," he "determined upon visiting them" and remained in the family camp during their entire incarceration.[39]

Williamson relied on the Christian experience and wisdom of the Dakota Christians in ministering to those in the camps. He wrote to the Presbyterian board that whoever wanted to unite with

the church was "examined personally as to their piety and knowledge . . . as thoroughly as I have been accustomed to see in any of
our churches."[40] He did this with four former Dakota church elders
and himself, along with "Mr. Riggs, when present."[41] When the Dakotas were reunited after the war, he proposed that the Pilgrim Church
choose for ordination two of their own leaders as pastors.[42] His confidence in the Dakota leadership was later reflected in his practice
of instructing the church session on disciplinary matters while let-
ting them "know that they were responsible for the decision."[43] He
was not ashamed to admit that "[s]ometimes when they have decided
contrary to my advice, I have thought afterwards that their decision
was the best."[44]

    Williamson worked beside the Native pastors, not over them. He
attended to pioneering work among unreached Sioux tribes while
encouraging the Christian Dakotas' pastoral and missionary work
to other parts of the tribe. He advised, encouraged, and maintained
faith in the Indian leaders to guide their own people. In 1867 Williamson led the fight to secure an all-Indian presbytery for the Dakotas so that they could participate in decision-making as did the white
ministers.[45] The result was the formation of the Dakota Presbytery,
made up primarily of Dakota ministers and elders, with the power
to ordain its own ministers. When the Flandreau Indians wanted to
homestead, Williamson appealed to the government on their behalf
to allow "that independence without which civilization is naught."[46]
He implored Washington, D.C., not to put an agent over the young
community. Assigned as a special agent to them, for which he took
no pay, he insisted on treating them as "men and citizens," in contrast to "the common agency regime which is founded on the idea
of their being paupers or wards."[47] When the government placed
an agent over them anyway, Williamson noted the discouragement
of the leaders: "[T]hey have started out to be men, and they are not
going back to pupilage."[48]

    At Williamson's death in 1917, the highest tributes came from
those Indian pastors with whom he had worked so closely. John Eastman was most struck by Williamson's willingness to identify with the
Dakotas. He eulogized in his Native tongue at the graveside:

Whatever I am at this time I owe to him, and I think of him as my father. Whatever I have wanted to know, I have asked of him, and he has told me. Whom shall I inquire of now?

He more than any one else had compassion on the Dakota people. He went with them in the early days, carrying his pack as they did theirs, oftentimes hungry and thirsty and tired, but he remained with them because he wanted to tell them the Good News.[49]

Francis Frazier, son of Artemas Ehnamani and a Congregational minister, in his funeral address noted the way Williamson came alongside those he taught:

He was the first one I heard preach the Gospel and was my first teacher. I was one of the young men whom he gathered around him and treated as younger brothers, so I have always loved him and regarded him as an older brother, and not myself only, but all of us older Santee men and women always remember how he lived with us and taught us to pray and to read, and we are very thankful.[50]

Although the praise was effusive, the real testimony to Williamson's effectiveness as a missionary were the nearly forty Dakotas who had been ordained to the Presbyterian ministry since he had begun work among them. They were in charge of their own churches and their own presbytery, allowing the well-established ministry to continue to flourish despite Williamson's passing.

Both Sue McBeth and John Williamson began their missionary work at a crucial time. American Indians had taken the lead in presenting and responding to the gospel message and desired instruction so they could further take the word to their people. The missionaries could have fostered Indian dependence on white ministers by insisting that the Dakotas and Nez Perces remain lay-workers without authority to lead in the sacred offices of the church. Instead, McBeth and Williamson—one prevented from ascending to the pulpit by her gender, and the other so at home among the Dakotas he recognized their potential to lead—worked to give Indians every advantage for perpetuating the growth of the church by preparing them for ordination. This farsightedness, coupled with the American Indians' determination to guide their people in their chosen path, preserved Native autonomy and strengthened the establishment of the Presbyterian Church among both Nez Perces and Dakotas.

During the 1880s through the 1920s Native-led churches sprouted among the two Plains and Plateau tribes. Education for the ministry focused on aiding in the evangelization of Native peoples and development of the churches. The missionaries continued active participation by teaching and encouraging the growth of the church and its leadership, but they did so more as partners than as employers. American Indians set the tone and often the pace of development.

Much of the strength of the Native pastorate was its preparation. Marked by a concern for an educated clergy, the Presbyterian Church had long been involved in establishing institutions of higher learning.[51] Education was one of the missionaries' basic tools in their efforts to convert and "civilize" the American Indians.[52] Advanced theological education for Indians did not become an issue until large groups of American Indians wanted to become ministers of the gospel. When this happened on the Nez Perce and Dakota reservations, both McBeth and Williamson found it imperative to help fashion a system whereby Indian ministers could be fitted locally for the office.

Due to the limitations imposed on her by the church because of her gender, McBeth's role in the classroom was enlarged even though her presence in the church was minimized. She was restricted not only because she lacked ministerial credentials but also because a physical disability impaired her mobility; and as the years passed, she found it more and more difficult even to attend church.[53] She therefore closeted herself with her students and, as Gen. Oliver O. Howard observed, "gather[ed] her disciples, a few at a time, around her, and having herself learned their language so as to speak and understand them, she instruct[ed] and [made] teachers of them."[54] Her students included church elders and Sunday school teachers, as well as potential ministers, "for the sake of their church duties and influence . . . that they may be good and intelligent Elders."[55]

This "sort of Theological Seminary," as the board grudgingly referred to it, provided the means for Christian leaders to gain enough knowledge of church doctrine and scripture to pass ordination exams given by the white presbytery.[56]

Perhaps due to illness that made her look older than her forty-five years, Sue McBeth's students called her "Pika," or "mother," and afforded her the respect given elder members of the tribe.[57] Kate McBeth wrote, "No journey was ever undertaken, not even from Kamiah to Lapwai, or Mount Idaho to Kamiah, without kneeling beside this mother to ask the Father's care. Little notes came back to her if detained, and then as soon as possible after their return they reported to her. How they trusted her!"[58]

If the Nez Perce pastors looked to Sue McBeth as guide, counselor, or friend, reporting to her regularly and conferring with her frequently, her inability to follow them into the church preserved an element of autonomy that enabled the Native pastors to be more than simply missionary assistants in the eyes of the community. When she tried to assert greater influence over the workings of the church by manipulating session meetings through her students, it was "her boys" who most objected by staying away from school.[59]

McBeth's teaching was quite pragmatic. While it covered studies of the church's doctrinal confessions and catechism, it concentrated on preparing the ministers for preaching on Sundays.[60] The students translated biblical passages into Nez Perce and practiced sermons the class had worked out together. McBeth was convinced that what the ministers needed to know they could learn in her classroom and in the pulpit. Little effort was made to encourage students to receive further training elsewhere. She failed to establish a connection with any institute of higher learning and even ridiculed one student's attempts to study under a minister in Portland. When the church began to require a college degree for its ministers, Nez Perce students had little experience of and little success among such institutions. The strength of the McBeth school, however, was its emphasis on practical ministry in the churches.

Williamson's relationship with the Dakotas was a more fraternal one than that of McBeth and the Nez Perces. He worked side by side

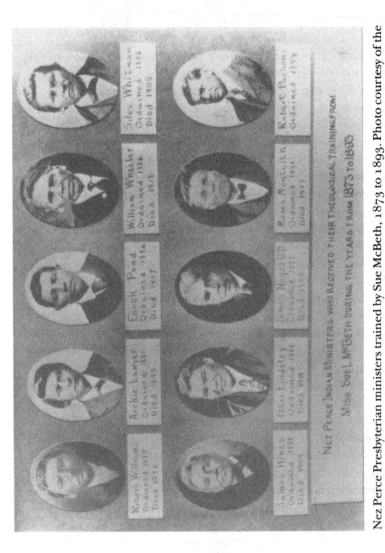

Nez Perce Presbyterian ministers trained by Sue McBeth, 1873 to 1893. Photo courtesy of the Department of Interior, National Park Service, Nez Perce National Historical Park, Spalding, Idaho. Photo number NEPE-Hi-1569.

with the Dakotas as a fellow preacher. Williamson might have been tempted to relegate American Indians to second-class positions as ministerial assistants because they lacked the seminary training he had received. Instead, Williamson worked to provide every educational advantage for the nascent pastors and encouraged their independence. He believed they must be enabled to share equally in the burden of caring for the churches. When in 1864 Tapitatanka, a church elder, told Williamson he proposed asking Simon Anawangmani to help preach to the Sissetons, Williamson encouraged him to do so with complete faith that the two could accomplish their task.[61] A year later, when there were, as yet, few Native preachers, Williamson believed that Robert Hopkins, the leading preacher in the prison camp, was the best one to go to the Yanktons because there would be "pretty strong opposition there and I doubt whether there is any one else here who will stand up under it without a white man to hold him up."[62]

Believing, as he did, that the "first supply of Native preachers" would "come principally from those now in jail and the young men who came home from there," Williamson strove to provide adequate theological training for them.[63] He envisioned a boarding seminary for the older, "most promising scholars from the day schools" to prepare them to teach and preach to their people shortly after the Dakotas were incarcerated.[64] Upon their release, he continued to plead with the mission board for funding and personnel to provide a school for training pastors. He began a boarding school on the Santee Reservation at Bazile Creek, Nebraska, "in the hope of preparing some of the larger boys for useful positions among their people."[65] By 1870 Williamson had encouraged another missionary son, Alfred L. Riggs, to return to the field and take over the educational aspect of the mission.[66]

Alfred Riggs began the Santee Normal Training School at Santee, a few miles north of Bazile Creek on the Santee Reservation, to carry on Williamson's vision of "raising up teachers for the Dakotas and other tribes."[67] With the help of John Williamson and the two older missionaries when available, Riggs began holding short

intensive theological classes for church leaders every winter.[68] Soon
Native ministers were also helping to do the teaching. Williamson
noted that "a number of them are already ordained, and a number
of the others may never be," but it was hoped that it would "prepare
the young men who are coming up to the work to fill the places of
the fathers, with a higher grade of scholarship, and especially with
a more thorough knowledge and appreciation of Bible truth."[69]
Williamson and Riggs emphasized theological education in the context of doing ministry. They did not expect that ministers would
complete a prescribed course of study before being ordained. They
looked on education as much in terms of enhancing already acquired
pastoral skills as in preparing for ministry.

Just after the Santee Normal Training School was started, the mission split between the Congregationalists and the Presbyterians. The
school went to the Congregationalists. Williamson, although continuing to encourage Native leaders to attend Santee, implored the
Presbyterian Board to fund its own theological school.[70] He wrote,
"I have always advocated the 'preaching of the Word' as the first duty
of missionaries. In connection therewith it is usually necessary to
have schools for such instruction as may be necessary for an understanding of the Word, for the raising up of Christian workers and
for the advancement of Christian life."[71] Williamson encouraged
that "such a Training School be started in connection with Pierre
University . . . with its standard gradually advancing to meet the wants
of the Indian Christians."[72] He succeeded in this endeavor in 1878
by becoming one of the founding members of the Board of Trustees
of Pierre University in Dakota Territory, which in 1898 became
Huron College, located in Huron, South Dakota. This is where, eventually, Dakota pastors came to be educated.[73] Alfred Coe, ordained
in 1899, was the first Dakota to go on from Santee to receive an education at Pierre University and then at Omaha Seminary.[74]

While McBeth and Williamson pushed for the education of the
clergy, Native leaders were building up the churches. Although
McBeth was unremitting in viewing the Nez Perces as "her boys" and
in trying to secure a position of power despite her gender, Nez Perce
leaders minimized her control by absenting themselves from the

"little mother" when she made them uncomfortable. They would not let their congregations view them as being led by a woman. It was to their advantage that she seldom darkened the door of the church itself because of her physical disability and that her lack of position in the church kept her from sharing the pulpit with them. Her one-woman theological seminary, while providing an extraordinary basis for an ordained clergy among the Nez Perces, did little to prepare students to pursue an education beyond that which she provided. When the McBeth mission was closed down in 1932, it took a number of years before future pastors were able to adjust to and enter institutions of higher education as a part of their regular education.

Williamson's push to link theological training to an institute of higher learning proved more farsighted. Williamson prepared students for the eventuality of a church-required educational level, which came to pass in the 1920s. His students were able to move into the new regime more easily than McBeth's. Williamson's use of localized institutions so that pastors would not have to go too far afield to receive their education was also fortunate. Ministers in training could maintain ties in their Native communities where their leadership was confirmed.

In an effort to conform to changing times in the larger church, however, the focus for training Indian pastors became the classroom, not the pulpit. Potential leaders were taken out of the proving ground of local Indian congregations, where Dakotas and Nez Perces placed the greatest emphasis for confirming such leadership. While Williamson and McBeth both valued the experience gained by practicing ministry in the churches, they also endorsed the need for an educated clergy. Unfortunately, the models they inspired of combining the two did not transfer to the new realities in ministerial training.

It was due to the leadership of the Nez Perce and Dakota converts that Christianity actually took root in these tribes. Had the revivals led by George Waters and Robert Hopkins not transpired it is doubtful the earlier missionary work could have produced much fruit. When the Dakota and Nez Perce elders were "filled with the

Spirit and prophesied," a new era emerged in these two mission stations. Converts and missionaries became partners in mission, although they were charged with different duties. Together they built up a church that was both Presbyterian and American Indian.

CHAPTER 3

Presbyterian Indian Ministers

*These Indians were very glad when I came here and they listen to me when I
preach to them and some of them they want to be Christian.*

JAMES HAYES

The vitality of American Indian Presbyterian churches during the
late nineteenth century owes much to the leadership of its Native
ministers. As James Ronda found among the Wampanoags of the
seventeenth and eighteenth centuries and William McLoughlin has
shown among the Cherokees earlier in the nineteenth century,
Indian pastors formed the most essential component for the growth
of Native Christian churches.[1] They communicated the gospel message, bringing words of hope and power, without needing to be
trained in the Native languages or given a cultural orientation. They
provided ongoing leadership and guidance for their people. They
were adept at discerning and meeting the spiritual and communal
needs of their congregations. Native ministers maintained traditional roles of community leadership by shaping the church pastorate to fulfill those roles.

The experience and understanding of both Native and Christian
ways, coupled with the authority granted them as ordained church

ministers, equipped American Indian pastors to demonstrate to their people the possibility of being both Christian and Indian. They were an example to others that Christianity was not just the white man's religion. They were, in effect, both the messengers and the message.

Presbyterian missionaries and observers often marveled at the ability of Native pastors to bring Indians into the church.[2] After going on a preaching circuit in 1865 with newly ordained Dakota pastor John Renville, missionary Riggs wrote to the mission board, "I am more and more satisfied that Native preachers may be more effective than we ever were or ever could be."[3] In 1924 Mary Crawford, missionary to the Nez Perces, defended the ordination of Native ministers: "We have always believed that the Indians in general will never be brought to Christ until the Indians themselves lead them to Him. The Indian knows the Indian as no white man can ever know him."[4] Perhaps this was the Indian ministers' real advantage: they knew Indians. They knew the Native languages, customs, and cultural values, which enabled them to present the Christian message in terms that made sense to other American Indians.

Indian ministers spoke with an authority among their own people that came of shared circumstances as well as a shared language. When James Hayes arrived in Kamiah in the later 1870s, a poor, homeless young Nez Perce, he claimed that it was hearing the gospel from the lips of one of his own countrymen that led to his conversion in the Kamiah Presbyterian Church. Hayes found in Robert Williams a "kind, helpful, trusted 'Elder brother,'" one who spoke Nez Perce, understood Nez Perce thinking, and could offer the young man the support of a Nez Perce family, though he was not kin.[5] As Sue McBeth explained, "Robert found him, led him to the Saviour, took him to his own house & instructed him for a time, then brought him to me—in his first 'civilized garments'—some of Robert's own clothing, which he could then illy spare."[6] Christianity, when explained and championed by another Nez Perce, made sense to Hayes. With the nurturing of the older man, whose home provided a welcoming and supportive setting, the message took root.

Nez Perce ministers William Wheeler, *left*, and Silas Whitman, *right*, and their wives. As with most of the Nez Perce ministers, they served churches among the Spokans, Umatillas, and others as well as Nez Perce churches. Photo courtesy of the Department of Interior, National Park Service, Nez Perce National Historical Park, Spalding, Idaho. Photo number NEPE-Hi-2480.

Nez Perce minister James Hayes, D.D., and family, with James Dickson, *standing*. Photo in the public domain.

Several years later, Hayes's preaching had the same effect on the young James Dickson, who was struck by the Indian pastor's explanation that Christianity was for all peoples regardless of race, age, or economic circumstances. He said that he "felt that the message was for me."[7] Dickson responded to the word preached by one who, if he was no longer young, knew what it was to be poor. And as Robert Williams had done before him, James Hayes took the young man into his own home and provided for him as one of his own.

The sense of the universality of the Christian message, particularly its call to the old, the weak, and the poor, strongly appealed to American Indian peoples, impoverished by the treaty and reservation system. They were set back even further when dispossessed of their land through land allotments in the 1880s.[8] These measures placed most of the Nez Perces, once one of the wealthiest Plateau nations, in the same straitened conditions.[9] The Dakota war of 1862 had a similar leveling effect on that tribe, reducing most to basic subsistence living.[10] Indian pastors, particularly when in desperate circumstances themselves, spoke eloquently on the theme of finding favor in the Lord's eyes because they were so in need. When Artemas Ehnamani preached that the Lord was sent not to call the "grand & mighty," but the "poorest little boy here," he spoke as one of the poor and lowly.[11] Ehnamani and his people could identify with the indigent, especially following the Dakota war, just as Hayes and his people could. Not only did they find comfort in a gospel for the poor, but also by sharing in that plight with their countrymen, Native pastors often gained credibility among their listeners.

The trope of "poor and lowly" was a culturally familiar concept among many American Indians, who used it to call on spiritual powers for help. Both the Nez Perces and the Dakotas approached the spirit world humbly. Both believed in the existence of guardian or tutelary spirits that men and women could seek to serve "in the role of guide or protector."[12] Usually taking the form of a special animal or force of nature, such power came to an individual in a vision. As one Nez Perce explained it, American Indians could appeal to these powers in the same way that Catholics might appeal to a patron "saint to help with something where you probably are stalled."[13]

Extreme caution had to be used when invoking one's weyekin or wakan powers, however, as failure to approach with the necessary regard and ritual could result in turning it against oneself.[14]

In Dakota, a petition for help from a greater power was often prefaced with "Wakan Tanka, pity me."[15] The prayer of the Kit Fox Society among the Oglala Sioux ended with "Have pity on me. Help me to defeat others."[16] Charles Eastman noted that one on a "hambeday," or "religious retreat" seeking "the motive power of his existence," stood stripped before the Great Spirit, "[w]ishing to appear before Him in all humility."[17] As historian Raymond DeMallie points out in his study of Lakota religion, the word "wacekiye," meaning "to pray," means literally to ask for help.[18] As among the Algonquians and other Woodlands tribes, the Plains Indians petitioned the help of transcendent powers with the plea "I am pitiable" or "I am poor" and in extreme cases used self-mutilation to underscore the point.[19] Becoming pitiable was expected to move the higher beings, the wakan, to grant one's petition out of compassion for one's need.[20]

There is, however, a noticeable lack among the precontact Nez Perces of "pity me" prayers, perhaps indicating a slightly different attitude toward the spiritual. Nonetheless, approaching spiritual powers required supplication. As in the case of the Dakotas, the Nez Perces believed themselves inadequate to approach powerful spirits without preparation. The goal, however, was less abjectness than purity. According to Ruth Underhill's observation of Plateau Indians, the "way of spirit favor, in this land of streams and pools, was fanatic cleanliness."[21] Ritual cleansing, as practiced among the Dakotas in the sweat-bath ceremony, or "Inipi," was also necessary to the Nez Perces to gain a hearing in the spirit world. It was even more extreme in that it included, along with ritual fasting and vision quests, the use of cold baths, mud baths, sweat baths, and emetic sticks (twigs inserted into the stomach orally) for total body purification.[22] According to Nez Perce Albert Moore, ministerial candidate and student of the McBeth mission, such cleansing and purging was "preparation for anything; getting ready for hunting, fishing, gambling, for the girls also."[23] It not only strengthened the supplicant, but also allowed him to find favor in the presence of those spirits with power believed to ensure success.

Spiritual power must be approached with humility—as exhibited by the Plains Indians, who began their prayers with "O Great Mysterious Power, I stand here, humble and needy, Praying to Thee."[24] Among the Nez Perces, the very nature of the purification process was humbling. "Poor and lowly" language toward the Dakota Wakan Tanka[25] and the Nez Perce hanyawa-t[26] carried over to Native understanding of the supplicant's position before the Christian God and his emissaries, both sacred and secular. When Nez Perce minister Archie Lawyer requested funds from the mission board to build a church among the Spokans, he quoted Cornelius, one of the elders, to underline the need. According to Lawyer, when Cornelius was told that they did not yet have sufficient funds to buy lumber, he got "kind of mad. He said to me, how Board will not help you when you send to us! We are poor Indian."[27] Lawyer's message got through to the board, which sent the necessary cash and also published his letter in their journal as an American Indian mission success story.

Identification with the pitiable was expressed not only in petitions to mission boards but also appeared in requests made of government personnel. Thus, many who approached the president of the United States or his emissaries reverted to "pity speeches" to obtain their favor. Rain-in-the-Face, a Dakota who had fled to Canada after the Battle of the Little Big Horn in 1876, requested an audience with President McKinley twenty years later. He wanted to assure the president he was still loyal to him and wrote, "Great Father, We are poor, we want your protection and help, we want to see your face."[28] In a similar way, Nez Perce Chief Lawyer, father of Archie Lawyer, addressed Governor Isaac I. Stevens at the Walla Walla Indian Council in 1855, entreating the government to act in good faith by reminding the governor that "from the time of Columbus, from the time of Lewis and Clarke, we have known you, my friends; we poor people have known you as brothers."[29]

By identifying themselves with the poverty of their people, Native pastors gained credibility for the message they brought of a God who cared for American Indians.[30] To be effective, though, leaders needed also to be successful. Native communities responded to leaders who knew their suffering, but Indian traditions celebrated leaders who relieved suffering. Such leaders were often not rich, but they were liberal with what they possessed and successful in securing material goods and favors for their people.[31] In pre-reservation times, those who possessed the means to ensure the welfare of the band were most likely to be considered for leadership. Although hereditary claims to leadership positions were an asset, behavior mattered most in determining who advanced to leadership. For the Nez Perces, a leader had to act "at all times in a moral manner, to make sound decisions, and to be generous" in order to be worthy of leadership.[32] Among the Sioux, those who were chosen to lead showed bravery, hospitality, and liberality.[33] Whether one's largess was due to having a big herd of horses, or, in later years, a government-appointed or mission-related job with regular pay, a leader established a position of authority within his community not only by his wisdom and courage but also by his generosity.[34]

Although nineteenth-century missionaries could not fault the cultivation of such characteristics among the Native pastors, they were often at odds about how best to implement them. With the twin goals of "civilizing and Christianizing" American Indians, missionaries insisted Native pastors maintain small subsistence farms and be model farmers in addition to their pastoral duties. This created tensions between the Native ministers and the missionaries over whether a pastor's duty to his farm or his congregation came first. Indeed, pastors themselves often struggled internally between the Native emphasis on serving the community and the need to support themselves and their immediate families. Sue McBeth noted that those preaching would "need every dollar they can raise from their crops for support of themselves & families the coming year."[35] She expressed concern when she learned that Robert Williams "lately among the Spokanes [preaching] . . . had barely time to cut and thresh his harvest, and no time to sell any of it before starting to Presbytery, so could not raise money for his expenses."[36] To McBeth, farming and family were high priorities for Christian ministers.

As Dakota pastor John Renville discovered, however, such work took an immense amount of time and did little to provide for the immediate good of the community. He had other priorities. In a letter to the mission board in 1871, Renville wrote of the difficulties of being a model farmer while attending to the spiritual needs of his people. He wrote that in "four weeks I preached 27 times besides breaking my land. Tired I was, the more so not being used to using oxen or breaking new land."[37] In that time, he also succeeded in building a "comfortable log house" for his family for the winter.[38] It was hard to provide an example of a self-supporting farmer and fulfill the duties of caring for his congregation as well. That Native pastors often made farming secondary to ministerial duties reflected both a lack of enthusiasm for farming and what they regarded as the stronger obligation to work for the good of the community as a whole.

Native pastors' concern for their parishioners' needs caused additional conflict with missionaries. Because of the community's expectation that its leadership be generous, Indian pastors needed to receive enough compensation, whether in money, goods, or services, to fulfill that role. Sue McBeth showed unusual insight into Native culture when she pleaded for larger salaries from the mission board for the Nez Perce ministers, especially those going among other tribes. She noted that an "Indian minister has only one room & he cannot eat without asking the others, hungry standing around watching."[39] George Deffenbaugh, missionary to the Nez Perces, backed her up by writing to the board that "it is considered an almost unpardonable breach of hospitality for a man to sit down to eat and not invite to his table all who may be present—and usually they are all hungry."[40] Furthermore, he noted of Indian pastors that "[t]hese brethren have to be very hospitable in order to retain of the good will of the people with whom they labor."[41]

Church officials created both obstacles and opportunities for Native pastors to provide adequately for their people. As ministers within the missionary department of the Presbyterian Church, Native pastors had unique access to people and to a benevolent organization disposed to contribute generously to American Indian missions. Native ministers called on their church connections to enhance the material lives of their congregations, asking for everything from missionary barrels of used clothing sent from eastern churches to the construction of new schools or church buildings.

Although Deffenbaugh recognized the importance of liberality in helping a minister stay in the good graces of his church, the board frequently saw individual petitions for aid as self-serving and was reluctant to grant such requests. In 1866 Mary Renville, writing on behalf of her pastor husband John, was concerned about the support of several young girls they had taken into their home to teach. She was not embarrassed to pen to the mission board, "I do wish that some of the rich would send us boxes of second hand clothing ... for our salary is to[o] small our faith to[o] weak not to ask anything."[42] In the end, she and her husband were encouraged by the board to discontinue the practice of boarding students because it was not cost-effective. When Renville wrote requesting payment for extra preaching duties at the Yellow Medicine (Pajutazee) and Redwood (Zoar) churches, he claimed he had "received 3 pairs of Mogacins from Sister Madeline is all I have got for my preaching up here but Dr[.] you know it[']s impossible to expect anything from families when there children are crying for food and many of them were when I was among them."[43] This request was also denied.

A petition for money, however deserving, was even less apt to be awarded by the board, as Archie Lawyer discovered. In light of his work as a messenger of the gospel whose goals he believed mirrored those of the church, Lawyer felt it not unreasonable to request additional funds. He wrote to the mission board, "I received $200 from Bo[a]rd now [b]ut all to Bank[.] I need money very bad Dear brother when winter coming ... I like to hear from you if willing to send to me all my wages for six month[s] for work for Christ sake."[44] Lawyer noted that he had spent "plenty money" for traveling to prayer meetings every Thursday, twelve miles south of his church. There is no record, however, that the board gave him an advance on his wages, despite his reminder that it was the Lord's work in which he was engaged. Lawyer could not convince his co-laborers that it was to the advantage of his church work that he should receive the necessary funds to maintain his expected role as a provider for his people.

Erecting churches, especially when the Native congregation showed a willingness to share in the financial burden or the construction, was another matter. While Archie Lawyer served as pastor to the Spokans at Deep Creek in 1889, he wrote that "there are many wild Indian round here, so they need good church," made of lumber and not of logs.[45] He noted that the Indians had raised some money and needed one hundred and fifty dollars more to purchase the lumber. The board published this letter in the mission journal of the church with a request from the readership for additional funds to meet the "touching" appeal. It reported several months later that funding had been provided and published another of Lawyer's letters acknowledging receipt of the moneys. In it Lawyer wrote that "we will collect for bell now."[46] Whether or not he received additional funds is not known.

When Renville pleaded for the board to help the Dakotas build "churches that will be useful and attractive" to compete with the Episcopal Church work going on in the same region, he initially met with the same response as Lawyer. Renville addressed the board by writing, "Christian Indians can't all be Bo't but when so much is done to Beautify the church and to relieve bodily suffering [by the Episcopalians] many will be over persuaded to leave our church and join others who to all outward appearances are so much more interrested in all their affairs."[47] The funds were forthcoming, but his success may have owed as much to protecting the field from the Episcopalians as from sympathy with Renville.

Beneath the conflict over finances lay a deeper struggle over the nature of the Native church. What the board thought of as merely self-serving was to Native pastors like Renville and Lawyer an attempt to enhance the appeal of the church. Dakota and Nez Perce Christians would be more apt to support the one who best provided for them. The Native leadership thought more in terms of what the church could do for the people than what the people could do for the church. Ministers used salary as other Native leaders used wealth: to create following and influence. Ministers could easily reconcile Christian mandates to spread the Christian gospel with the demands of American Indian leadership. Money was the means, not the end, of their efforts. Yet this belief cut against Presbyterian ambitions for their churches. In the effort to make Indian churches completely self-supporting, as were most white congregations, the Presbyterian Church expected that Native churches would subsidize at least a part of the Native pastor salaries and church expenses.[48] Church officials gave little recognition to the support American Indians provided the church and ministers in terms of food, gifts, and services.

Church officials only incompletely recognized that much of the Native pastors' success was due to their ability to use their roles within their congregations to fulfill the obligations of Native categories of leadership. As both government and mission policies sought to eradicate traditional leadership positions, power shifted to agency police forces or church leadership positions.[49] The church positions themselves possessed many of the same qualities as the positions they replaced. Historian Loretta Fowler has noted that among the Arapahos, political and economic changes in the tribe were more easily weathered because the Arapahos maintained their social organization of age-grade categories that mediated the changes and legitimized their acceptance.[50] The functions of these various age-based categories changed with white contact. The Arapahos adopted new practices in order to "appear progressive" but did so in ways that at once transformed and perpetuated the traditional leadership roles of chiefs, scouts, priests, and elders.[51]

In much the same way, if not nearly in so clearly defined a manner, the Dakotas and Nez Perces maintained traditional leadership roles by having the position of minister mirror older leadership positions. Native pastors rose to prominence by preaching, teaching, healing, and advocating for their people—recognizable roles traditionally filled by holy men, tribal elders, and chiefs. As had been in the past, Indian ministers were drawn from descendants of aboriginal leaders as well as those with no family history of leadership but recognized ability. They were strong orators, teachers, healers, and mediators who gained the respect of the people by their diplomacy, generosity, and devotion to them.[52] The revered Dakota pastor John Eastman, for example, was championed by his congregation because "he had mercy for the Lord and he can help real good."[53]

Tribal headmen and chiefs needed to be persuasive individuals. Eloquence gave "power and prestige" to chiefs who usually lacked coercive power and depended on persuading others to support their decisions.[54] Thus, in the aftermath of the campaign that followed Gen. George Armstrong Custer's defeat in 1876, George Sword, a Lakota of Pine Ridge, through his oratorical skills convinced first Crazy Horse and then Sitting Bull that, as kinsmen, they should come into the agency for the sake of unity.[55] In similar fashion, the Nez Perce Hallalhotsoot got his nickname, The Lawyer, among English-speakers because of his ability to argue and persuade. He owed much of his influence within the tribe to his proficiency in both Nez Perce and English.[56] The famed Nez Perce Chief Joseph prevailed on his band in the Wallowa Valley to seek peace, and when that was no longer possible, to at least refrain from war atrocities. Despite his reputation for eloquence among the whites, one member of the tribe noted that while "Joseph was looked upon as the head-man of his band . . . Alokut [Ollokot, Joseph's brother] had more influence because he was the better speaker."[57] The ability to speak well and persuade others was a valuable skill highly prized by both the Dakotas and the Nez Perces.

The importance of preaching in the Presbyterian Church paralleled the importance of oratory in both Nez Perce and Dakota societies. Rufus Anderson, mission theorist and secretary to the ABCFM, whose influence on Protestant missions in the mid-nineteenth century went far beyond his own mission board, noted that for missionaries, "[t]heir grand agent is oral instruction; their grand theme is the cross."[58] In other words, the preached word was the primary means of reaching a people with the message of salvation.

Cultivating strong preachers among Presbyterians stemmed from the church's Reformed tradition and John Calvin's admonition that "[p]reaching ought not to be lifeless but lively, to teach, to exhort, to reprove . . . that the Spirit of God ought to sound forth by their [the ministers'] voice, so as to work with mighty energy."[59] Missionaries took pains to develop their ministerial candidates' preaching skills. Sue McBeth noted that before giving the Sunday evening sermon, her students would "choose their subject from what we had gone over in the school room, study out what they could through the week, then, come to me for an hour and a half (or more) on

Sabbath morning (or afternoon). Then they would take their message fresh to the people."[60] As people of the Book, Presbyterian ministers needed to be adept at conveying its message, especially among
congregations that could not yet read.

Native pastors were quite conscious of the significance of eloquence in both American Indian and evangelical Protestant cultures
and honed their preaching skills. James Hayes, a preacher of note,
took particular pride in his young protégé, James Dickson. He
touted his preaching ability to missionary Kate McBeth in 1907:
"Jas[.] Dickson he doing nicely. I hear him last night he prea[c]hing
in a prayer meeting. [H]e preach the sermon very good, and I am
very glad of it. I am . . . happy with Jas[.] Dickson."[61] He was concerned to nurture this ability in the younger man, knowing it would
make him more effective as both a pastor and a leader among his
people. Good preachers, it was noted by one Dakota Christian, had
the power to "wake us up and renew our faith."[62] Another church
member noted of Joseph Rogers and Joseph Hillers, studying to
become Dakota pastors in 1887, that "I thought God told them and
they understood. We will get strength from these good words."[63]
Indian ministers used their skill in their pulpits to lead their people
in much the same way as their forefathers used their skill in council.

The power of the spoken word was not necessarily identical to
the wisdom and insight traditionally associated with age. When
Native pastors united the two, they became even more influential.
The role of American Indian elder was one that rested on proven
ability to advise and counsel and was usually reserved for those of
advanced years.[64] At his death in 1921, John Eastman's daughter,
Grace Eastman Moore, claimed he "was a great preacher in the
sense of the Dakota word for preaching—Wowahokonkiye—which
means not only in public speaking, but in council and giving of general and personal advice."[65] Eastman not only spoke well, but he
spoke with sincerity, conviction, and the authority of one esteemed
for his counsel. His standing gave authority to his message. Since
the Indian pastor served as a "bearer of the new wisdom and an
interpreter of that knowledge," he needed not only to be articulate,
but also to hold the respect of his audience.[66]

Nez Perce minister James Hayes, *left*, and Dakota minister Joseph Rogers, *right*, circa 1920. Photo courtesy of the Presbyterian Historical Society, Philadelphia.

Because of the importance placed on age, the earliest pastors usually came from among the mature members of the tribe. While she may have been pushing the issue a bit, Sue McBeth claimed that all of her pupils, except James Hayes, were "full grown heathen when the Gospel reached them."[67] Most of the first Dakota pastors were at least middle-aged; they had either proven their ability to lead as warriors or their competence in dealing with the new order ushered in by the Dakota war.[68] One of missionary John Williamson's main concerns in ordaining John Eastman and Albert Frazier in 1876 was that they were still considered young men by tribal standards and might not be accepted by the congregation. He wrote to his father that "[t]hose whom I talked with said—White men may be able to listen to a young man but a young man can't stand before this people."[69]

Generosity and eloquence were routes to power, and so, too, was the power to heal. In Dakota society as well as among the Nez Perces, this activity was usually the province of the healers that whites called shamans and medicine men.[70] A Nez Perce with the ability to effect cures was generally given the title "tiwet," and it was believed that his or her weyekin was especially strong.[71] Tiwets, or shamans, used a combination of methods to heal, including "herbs, physical manipulation, and special rituals they obtained from their tutelary spirits."[72] The Dakotas, in contrast, had "wicasa wakans" or shamans, who cured by spiritual power, and medicine men, who produced cures by the use of medicines and herbs.[73] It was expected that shamans were also medicine men, but not necessarily the reverse.[74] The Dakota and Nez Perce societies gave healers considerable respect. They were expected to maintain harmony between the people and the natural world as well as heal the sick.

Missionaries, at their kindest, referred to Native healing practices as the "vagaries of the magician." They held that those who practiced medicine were governed by "love of power" and that "the people through fear were constrained to unworthy practices."[75] While careful to avoid anything that smacked of shamanism, Native pastors, nonetheless, assimilated the role of the shaman into their duties as Presbyterian ministers. American Indian pastors brought to Christianity the same concern for health that had preoccupied their ancestors. Most saw in the person of Jesus Christ the source of all healing. Nez Perce pastor Joseph Cook spoke of the power of Christ to cure both "bodily disease" and "soul sickness" and encouraged the people to "[c]ome to him [Christ] and you will be satisfied and healed from your sin sickness."[76] What especially endeared John Eastman to his Flandreau congregation was his ability to heal and provide for those under his care. A grateful church acknowledged that he could "recognize most sickness, and when he helps, the people get better."[77]

There is little in the written record to indicate the methods or results of this aspect of the Native pastors' ministry. There is, however, plentiful evidence of the concern pastors had for the health of their parishioners. James Hayes frequently asked of the health of those at home when he was out on evangelistic trips and remarked on the health of those with him.[78] John Eastman and Dakota pastor Daniel Renville (grandson of Joseph Renville, Sr., of Lac qui Parle) were commended for visiting the sick. David Faribault, whose eighteen-year-old son, Soloman Samson, had just died in 1882, wrote to Eastman, who was also the boy's uncle, "you cared for my child and came to see him and that was a nice thing you did."[79] He was particularly grateful that the two ministers gave Soloman communion, claiming that "[o]n that day he was happy and he didn't worry anymore and he died peacefully."[80] When a parishioner was sick, he called on the pastor to offer prayers for healing, communion, and comfort.

The church did not condone anything that smacked of healing by "sorcery." It condemned drums, rattles, incantations, or invocations of one's spiritual tutelary. The elders of the prison church of the Dakotas concluded that "the system of conjuring brings men into contact with the spirits of evil, and tends to lead them away from Christ."[81] Attempts to muster spiritual power were anathema in Presbyterian circles, but belief in the efficacy of such power lingered among converts. When one member of the Lapwai (Spalding) Church was called before the church session in Lapwai and accused of practicing "the acts of the medicine man," he denied it. According to the session's records,

He admitted that he still retained the "charm" with which he used to practice as a medicine man. He was asked to give it up or destroy it. [S]aid he was afraid that he would die if he did so. But after being instructed in a better belief and assured that nothing of that nature could have any effect on his physical condition, as witness Wanan Walter Lowrie of the Umatillas, he took our hands, [s]aying that he would give up believing in his charm and trust only in God through Jesus Christ.[82]

Although the church did not allow Native forms of healing, it did invoke another source of spiritual power. The church held that prayer alone was an effective means of combating illness, especially that of "soul sickness." Congregations knew that the church's pastor and elders could be counted on to come to sickbeds and believed that, as "the prayers of the righteous availeth much" (James 5:16), they would be in good hands. A man in a Dakota church recovered from his illness only after the elders had prayed over him several times. Upon his return to health, the elders exclaimed, "Why, he ought to get well; for we have had four prayer-meetings with him."[83] It was usually only after a patient failed to show signs of recovery that some church members would consider calling in a traditional medicine man and thus risk the wrath of the church.

Whether or not pastoral visits to the sick included medicinal remedies can only be speculated. There is evidence that medical doctors were beginning to assume this function. The sad confession of one Native pastor who admitted to falling into alcoholism from "bitters prescribed by a physician" indicates the turn toward non-Native doctors.[84] James Hayes showed disdain, however, for cough medicine given him by a missionary. He claimed, "[H]ot water is better then every medicine."[85] If he prescribed that to his parishioners, however, there is no record of it. For the most part, it appears that pastors relied on their prayers to heal the sick.

Finally, to their roles as orators and healers, American Indian pastors added the role of mediator for their people. Native leaders had acted as intermediaries both between their community and other communities and with U.S. government agents. Now Native pastors assumed similar roles on behalf of the people. Educated in mission

schools and therefore able to write and speak English, and possess-
ing some authority among whites because of their ministry, many
were in a unique position to act as intermediaries. Native pastors
believed such mediation was part of their ministry. In recommend-
ing Nez Perce pastor William Wheeler to the Spokans, Deffenbaugh
noted, "He can speak English and can help you in your dealings with
the whites."[86]

Native pastors went before mission boards, the government, and
even the president of the United States, as spokesmen for tribe or
band. John Renville frequently petitioned the mission board on
behalf of his people, as "one who desires the welfare of the people
among whom I labor."[87] When he requested funds for building the
church he wrote, "[L]et the ABCFM join with them in the erection
of churches that will be useful and attractive. I speak with great
boldness for are not this people my people and has not God called
me to be one of their Shepherds[?]"[88] His role as spiritual leader
complemented his role as material provider for his people. Just as
in the famous Christian metaphor a shepherd sheltered and fed the
sheep and rescued those that were lost, so a Christian minister was
to mediate for the material needs of his people and help save their
souls.

In 1896 John Eastman, along with several others, including his
brother, Dr. Charles Eastman, went all the way to the president of
the United States to begin a legal battle in Washington, D.C., for the
restoration of the Santee Sioux annuities forfeited during the
Dakota war of 1862. The funds, in the amount of $129.30 per per-
son, were realized only after his death, but Eastman was credited with
the success of the fight. He supposedly cut a deal with Republican
National Committee Chairman Marcus A. Hanna to help defeat
Senator Richard F. Pettigrew in return for a Senate bill to restore
Santee funds.[89] Eastman saw his responsibility as extending to the
well-being of the entire community, Christian and non-Christian
alike. When this demanded his involvement in political circles, he
did not hesitate to mix politics and religion. His congregation wrote
a letter to thank him, noting that "he works for free and he helps
people very much so the people will live nice and not get confused

. . . that all the people will benefit."[90] Eastman, according to the church members, "worried about us and liked us, [but] he went beyond that. This man did a lot of good work for the people, he made them happy."[91]

Native pastors became cultural brokers.[92] They moved between American Indian and white worlds. Familiar with each and conversant in both, they became intermediaries and interpreters of one culture to the other. When used to the benefit of the tribe, this, of course, enhanced their own power and prestige. That this role was appreciated is evident in the praise of Eastman, the "much sought for adviser and close friend of old and young."[93] He developed the "friendship, respect and confidence of the Indian as well as the white man—and thus he was able to accomplish much for his people that otherwise would not have been possible."[94] James Hayes similarly gained the respect of both missionaries and Indian people and mediated between them. Wrote Sue McBeth, "I have not a more promising pupil than James, nor any, save Robert, whom I trust more."[95] From among the Nespelems in Washington, Hayes wrote of his encounter with Chief Tiyawashat, who told him, "I am very glad you come to visit us and tell us about Jesus our saviour. You tell us all true and good."[96] The ties of Indian ministers to both the white culture and their own, and the ability to bring some mutual comprehension through replication of traditional leadership roles, as well as providing material benefits to each, made them valued and powerful members of both societies.

The capstone of the ministers' effective cultural brokering, their authority both inside and outside the community, was ordination. Ordination historically allowed the Presbyterian Church to admit to the ministry those qualified to serve that the "sacred office may not be degraded, by being committed to weak or unworthy men."[97] It was granted to those who proved their worthiness by "satisfactory testimonials of . . . good moral character," as well as knowledge of the scriptures and the ability to preach.[98] Ordination protected the integrity of the office and provided the structure for maintaining the church. It also identified pastors, regardless of social, economic, or racial differences, as spiritual leaders and guides.

The presbytery, a judicatory composed of ministers and elders grouped by geographic location, had the authority to grant ordination. The candidate being considered for ordination came under the supervision of the presbytery for a designated time. This allowed the presbytery to set the terms of his probationary period, oversee his preparation, and then examine his piety, education, and ministerial abilities before sanctioning his ordination.[99] The Dakotas, through the recommendation of the missionaries in 1868, formed their own Dakota (all-Indian) Presbytery, greatly facilitating ordination.[100]

American Indian ministers were not exempt from the ordination process. Nor were they exempt from the examinations and educational requirements, except that of biblical languages, Greek and Hebrew.[101] If recommended by the missionaries who trained them, and able to meet all other standards set by the presbytery, they would be ordained. Thus, although missionary Deffenbaugh feared for Archie Lawyer's ultimate success as a pastor due to "slight pulpit preparations," an "*innate* taste for display," and an inclination "to be domineering," he regarded Lawyer as morally upright and "standing fairly and squarely in the faith as it is revealed in God's Word."[102] The Walla Walla Presbytery agreed. Lawyer met the spiritual, moral, and academic standards set by the church for ministry and he was ordained.

The importance of ordination cannot be overemphasized. It at once provided American Indian ministers with credentials that put them on par with their white counterparts, giving them equal standing in presbyteries, synods, and General Assembly, and it also constituted a mark of authority among their own people. It gave them official status within Indian communities to oversee such crucial activities as births, deaths, and other ceremonial events. Finally, it gave Indian ministers the autonomy and the means to establish other churches and expand the circle of their influence.

Native American Christian communities did not want to be without a minister. In 1878 Robert Williams lamented the loss of the white minister who had briefly served the Nez Perces, claiming "there will be no ordained minister on the reservation or Presbyterian Minister within one houndred miles."[103] He was concerned because

Second Nez Perce minister, Archie Lawyer, and family. Photo courtesy of the Department of Interior, National Park Service, Nez Perce National Historical Park, Spalding, Idaho. Photo number NEPE-Hi-0351.

just that winter eighteen people had become Christians, "but there was no ordained minister to recieve them into the church."[104] Only ordained ministers could baptize and extend church membership to new converts and their families. Only ordained ministers could offer communion. Only ordained ministers could join couples in Christian marriage. Without someone to perform these duties, the church had no opportunity to flourish, and the Christian community had no one to look to for leadership in the realm of the sacred.

Most missionaries agreed that if the church were dependent on white ministers to fill American Indian pulpits, Indians would, as one venerated missionary put it, "remain in a dependent condition, and make but little progress in spiritual attainments. The same congregation, under competent Native pastors would become more self-reliant, and their religion would be of a more manly, home character."[105] The missionary to the Nez Perces made the same observation, "that if you take away the independence of the Indian ministry and place him under the white man, you will break his spirit and he will allow the white man to do the work and pay the bills."[106] In the late nineteenth century, several farsighted missionaries among the Nez Perces and the Dakotas recognized the importance of developing a Native pastorate and granting them the authority of ordination.

James Hayes, John Eastman, and the nearly sixty other Nez Perce and Dakota pastors who were ordained between 1865 and 1930 provided leadership over flourishing American Indian Presbyterian churches for more than sixty years. They were effective because they spoke the people's language and knew the culture of those to whom they preached. They saw in Christianity a congruence of values that justified taking the gospel message to their people. Native pastors, whose theological training consisted primarily of biblical translation into the native language and study of that ancient text, saw strong corollaries between biblical and Indian values. Both cultures emphasized the importance of kinship, hospitality, morality, and a spirituality that permeated all aspects of life. Both cultures expected of their leaders the oversight and care of their people. This congruence allowed Native pastors to assume leadership roles familiar to

American Indian people, and these roles gave them the opportunity to present their message.

Nez Perce minister James Hayes told a white audience in 1927, "[L]ook at Jesus. He hang on cross. He was wounded for our inequity and he was bruise[d] for our sin. He give Himself and died for us ... Indians ... [we] understand because Jesus [h]ave power to save to every creature."[107] Hayes was convinced that the Christian faith would not kill the Indian within, for that was who he believed God had saved. He did not question that the Christian message belonged to all people.[108] It spoke of hope and empowered those who embraced it, minister or layman, white or Indian. As Hayes learned from his own pastor, Robert Williams, an Indian was no less Nez Perce or Dakota because he was Christian.

CHAPTER 4

The Birth of Indian Congregations

And now we have the bible and we have prayers; and the Dakota people have created seven organizations [churches]. And now whatever they do . . . they should hold strongly to God's words, I am here thinking.

JOHN C. WAKEMAN

In form, format, and matters of faith, nineteenth- and twentieth-century Dakota and Nez Perce Presbyterian churches replicated eastern Presbyterian churches, home to the majority of the missionaries serving among Indian tribes.[1] White, clapboard buildings with steepled belfries and high, narrow windows housed rows of pews faced by a pulpit and, if the congregation was fortunate, a small pump organ. Sunday morning worship services of hymn singing, prayer, and a sermon were usually followed by Sunday school services, separating children and adults. Midweek prayer meetings included "witness-bearing," or confession, more prayer, and more hymn singing. In the construction of the church building, the order of worship, the structure of the governing bodies, and the content of the services, there appeared to be little difference between American Indian and non-Indian Presbyterian churches.

Sisseton, South Dakota, however, was not Steubenville, Ohio; and neither were the Dakotas or Nez Perces Scottish immigrants establishing a church that reflected several hundred years of Presbyterian tradition. What emerged among Indian reservations led by Native pastors was neither an imitation Euro-American church nor a strictly American Indian organization but rather a unique institution responsive to the needs of Indian peoples in each particular locale. Presbyterian churches reflected the character and nature of their membership. Indian Presbyterian churches, in many ways, reflected Indian communities that perpetuated Indian values, support systems, and leadership.

Forged at a time of extreme cultural upheaval in Indian country, the churches offered a means of social cohesion as important to the various tribes as the message of hope and power preached from the pulpits. To the credit of the Native leadership, stability was often accomplished despite the complicated set of negotiated relationships entailed by membership within the larger Presbyterian Church. As active agents of change, Native churches combined tribal social and political structures with denominational structures; the result often sported features atypical of Presbyterianism. Interacting with missionaries, Presbyterian Church officials, U.S. government agents, American Indian church members, and non-Christian Indians, these same church leaders developed versatile and sometimes unusual church offices and lines of communication. When combined with the historical events in which they were set, Native churches that may have appeared to imitate their Euro-American counterparts were, in fact, quite distinctive.

One of the most influential forces in the shaping of Nez Perce and Dakota church organizations was the strong attachment to band membership. Bands, usually consisting of localized groups of related families, functioned in tribal society to protect their members from outsiders, while acting as a means of social control within.[2] The "tiyospaye" of the Dakotas revolved primarily around related families; however, membership was ultimately "determined by residence and choice, not descent."[3] Leadership was usually hereditary, but if the chief failed to measure up or if he "were a coward, then

First Presbyterian Church, Flandreau, and Dakota Presbytery meeting, circa 1900. Photo courtesy of the William L. Beane Private Collection, Flandreau.

his people would leave him" and follow another.[4] Within Dakota society, "band structure and names changed, sometimes often," allowing great flexibility in forming and re-forming alliances.[5]

This flexibility was not quite as evident among the Nez Perces. Divisions between bands were more pronounced, and the treaty system was more divisive. Band divisions among these eastern Plateau peoples were most strongly related to specific geographical locations, and bands were made up of autonomous villages centered on several extended families.[6] There were at least four major band divisions in four different regions separated by "dialectical, ecological, and economic differences."[7] These, in turn, were broken down into smaller bands or village groupings. Leadership consisted of councils of headmen chosen from each village, primarily on the basis of achievement—especially in war—rather than by heredity.[8] Reflecting the growing influence of Plains tribal organization, bands united under a common leader usually only in the time of war.[9] Loyalty to band members in both the Dakota and Nez Perce tribes was fairly strong because of kin relationships, although political structures surrounding band formation were loose.[10] It was the loyalty to members of one's band, and particularly one's village, that most affected church formation.

At the time the Dakota and Nez Perce churches began to flower in the 1870s, band organization remained strong but had come under attack. President Ulysses S. Grant's Peace Policy was in effect. Seeking to break up tribal relations, the government encouraged individuals to forsake their bands completely, move on to individual land allotments, and farm.[11]

The Nez Perce missionaries sided with the government, claiming, "the power of the chiefs over the people must be broken."[12] The McBeth sisters believed that "the seed royal at Kamiah would not down" and that band loyalties to these chiefs were detrimental to the development of nuclear families that should make up the composition of the churches; in Kate McBeth's words, bands "supplanted the family."[13]

Despite attempts by the missionaries to eradicate bands, the dynamics of band organization followed the Nez Perces into the church.[14] When one Nez Perce churchman observed that "Christian Indians didn't have any bands. They just belonged to a church," he failed to recognize that the choice of church was usually based on band affiliation.[15] Indeed, most conversions in the 1870s among the Nez Perces were by band or village, prompting one anthropologist to speak in terms of the establishment of "church-village complexes."[16] These complexes were rooted in pre-Christian villages so that by 1887 in Idaho Territory there were churches serving the largest village groupings of Kamiah, Lapwai, North Fork (Ahsahka), and Meadow Creek.[17] The Treaty of 1863 had effectively severed a few bands entirely from the church's influence when it drastically reduced the reservation, favoring the northern bands in the Kamiah and Lapwai area.[18]

Although in time Christian Nez Perces identified more closely with their churches than bands, the churches continued to represent various band divisions that often proved problematic for church organization.[19] For example, the first church established among the Nez Perces was at Kamiah, one of the largest village groupings. Members of several bands were incorporated into the new church, including the band led by the Lawyers. In 1890 Archie Lawyer, by that time one of eight Nez Perce pastors, frustrated with Robert Williams's pastoral hold on the Kamiah Church, gained permission of the presbytery to organize the Second Presbyterian Church of Kamiah.[20] He was joined by his own village members as well as several others opposed to the Williams family, splitting the church nearly in half.[21] This rupture in the "mother church"—due largely to rivalry between bands—was especially grievous to missionaries who feared the destruction of the church. Few left the Presbyterian Church, however; they simply rearranged themselves according to band loyalties.[22]

More critical for the church was Eddie J. Conner's departure from the Lapwai (Spalding) Church in 1909. He was apparently disgruntled because he believed his year of formal seminary training made him better fit to lead the congregation than the older, locally trained Mark Arthur.[23] Like Lawyer, Conner left the church, taking with him several related families totaling nearly seventy-five persons, about a third of the membership.[24] Unlike Lawyer, however, he did

not receive the support of the presbytery to found a seventh Presbyterian church among the Nez Perces. Eventually, the band organized a new church under the Southern Methodists that reflected
much of the same structure as the Presbyterians.[25] Band association
could prove effective not only in building up a congregation but in
dismembering it as well.

The symbiosis among bands and churches was equally pronounced
among the Dakotas. The Dakota missionaries actually used band
divisions in service to the church and thus perpetuated their existence.[26] They discovered during the period of incarceration that the
new Christians "naturally fell into classes according to their former
clans or villages."[27] The missionaries utilized these divisions to organize the work of Christian education and nurture.[28] Among those
imprisoned at Mankato, Minnesota, the "hunkayapi," or church elders, were chosen from each band to be instructed by the missionaries so these could, in turn, instruct and take responsibility for their
own relatives. This enabled the small group of missionaries to
respond to the unprecedented number of new converts in the
prison. It also encouraged whole families to turn to Christianity
together. Artemas Ehnamani, one of the hunkayapi, reported joyfully of the conversion of his entire band: "The doctor [Dr. Thomas
Williamson] told me, 'Preach to your people earnestly.' Thus, all of
my people are now good young men. Accordingly God extended
His mercy to their children and their wives and all their relatives."[29]
By appointing "Ruling Elders in nearly all the separate bands" and
a "female helper from each band" in the family camps to help oversee Christian instruction, the prison church benefited from the
social structure in place before Christianity was established.[30]

After the prisoners were freed, Christian churches continued to
provide one of the best means of preserving the Dakota bands. Following incarceration, the Dakotas endured three disastrous years
on the Crow Creek Reservation in Dakota Territory. These experiences nearly decimated the Dakotas and undermined the band
structure. The bands did live on, however, in the churches.[31] When
former prisoners of the Dakota war reunited with their families
and organized the Pilgrim Church in 1866, it numbered nearly four

hundred members.[32] The church continued the prison practice of assigning members to smaller groups for instruction by breaking down the large congregation into "ten different classes according to the bands to which they belonged, as, the Yellow Medicine Class, the Leaf Shooters' Class, the Prairie Dwellers' Class, etc."[33] Each band chose hunkayapi for church elders. As the Dakotas began to spread out over the reservations to which they were assigned, they organized new churches. These, too, tended to revolve around former band divisions and their leaders.[34]

Despite their social base, Nez Perce and Dakota churches did not, however, become just bands with another name nor traditional tribal organizations in disguise. Not all members of a band or reservation became Christian. In some contexts, Native ministers led their congregations in disassociating themselves from the practices, celebrations, and even people of their tribes that the ministers and missionaries perceived as detrimental to the Christian faith. The earliest converts were the most zealous in their renunciation of what they believed were unchristian practices. Pastor Ehnamani claimed late in life that for thirty-eight years "[t]he old ways I have put by."[35] A missionary noted of the Nez Perce ministers that they were "fearless folks and not a bit afraid to attack the sin of old heathenism wherever they find it."[36]

Many converts explicitly conceived of their new lives in terms of a separation from their non-Christian tribal members. When they converted to Christianity, they left their villages, as Paul Mazakutemani reported: "We formed ourselves into a separate community."[37] Converts did not, however, have to move away physically from home to experience the sense of being set apart by their conversion. James Dickson described his membership in the Kamiah church in terms of "separating myself from many of my heathen friends, even my father."[38] Dakota and Nez Perce missionaries and church leaders encouraged their Indian congregations to separate themselves both culturally and physically from their surroundings if they would save their souls.

When American Indians talked or wrote of beginning new ways as Christians, they often sounded like the missionaries who taught

them.[39] Many identified their former ways of life as "heathen,"
"degrading," and "evil."[40] Believing Dakota culture was detrimental
in some ways to Christian living, Ehnamani claimed that "the old
ways are the ways of death out of [which] we barely escaped—we
sh[ou]ld not of ourselves seek [to] put ourselves in again."[41] He dis-
tinguished Native Christians as those not "drawn in" by the "drum
beat," nor "the Devil's customs."[42] John Renville spelled out those
customs in his condemnation of his cousin, Gabriel Renville, for
"such *Heathenish* things as having three wives and encouraging the
wild dance of the Indians, [Gabriel] says their must be a stop put to
all marriages."[43] A committee of four Dakota ministers and elders
recommended to the members of their presbytery that the Grass
Wisp Dance be avoided because it was "equal to the custom of Gambling" in that it "works evil in the care of the Flesh" by encouraging
people to give away clothing, food, horses, and wives and "Makes
the Soul Dirty" by drawing church members away.[44] He and other
Native pastors exacerbated certain distinctions between the Christian way and tribal ways. In so doing, they often widened the gulf
between Christian and non-Christian Indians. Like the missionaries who had schooled them, it appeared that many did not believe
in a middle way.

In practice, however, Nez Perce pastors such as James Hayes, who
called their people to "come out to Christ,"[45] recommended giving
over any practice that would hinder one from receiving the power
promised those who trusted only in Jesus the Christ. Hayes expected
the people to leave behind any practice that was "not good of Christians but hath of unbelief."[46] Mark Arthur preached against the
"prevailing sins, war-dances, medicine dances, gambling . . . and the
evils he knew were connected with them," claiming "these things
will kill your [C]hristianity, will kill your church and send your souls
to hell."[47] Enoch Pond chastised the Spokans for "dancing with
superstitious and with enchantments."[48] He told them it was not
good to "sing with evil spirits but of Christians is good sing with
Gospel."[49] He entreated the Spokans to forsake the feasts for the
dead along with their other dances and "banqueting" associated
with tribal customs.[50] He further charged them with practicing

"witchcraft," because it would stand in the way of receiving any help from the Christian God.[51] Traditional celebrations ceased to be a part of the Christian converts' activities, as much for their association with activities believed to hinder spiritual power as for the close association with non-Christians, who might persuade them to leave the Christian faith.

Perhaps fear of falling back into the old ways and off their chosen path caused Native Christians to separate themselves from certain indigenous celebrations and cultural practices as well as from the participants in those activities. Ridicule and derision of non-Christian tribal members was likely a factor warranting separation. Struggles for limited social and political power also promoted boundary-setting between Christian and non-Christian parties. Most likely, there were a variety of reasons for disassociation from non-Christians; and the missionaries' approval would have encouraged such a move. Physical separation from the non-Christian community with its hindrances to living "holy lives" was behind the Christian Dakotas' formation of Dakota communities, such as the Hazelwood Republic of 1856 and Bend of the River, or Flandreau, begun in 1869.[52] Both communities sought to build Christian strongholds in the midst of non-Christian bands. Missionaries hoped that the Hazelwood Republic, in which Paul Mazakutemani served as the first president, would provide for the "mutual protection and higher progress" of the Christian Dakotas.[53] Mazakutemani himself simply said, "The Agent was well pleased with our onward movement, and said, 'It would be well if all the Dakotas would do so.' It was well."[54]

After the Dakota war a group of twenty-five Christian families settled off the reservation at Flandreau. They had "concluded it was beneficial for traditional people to own land because this was the only way they could quickly become self-sufficient" and get out from under the rule of only nominally Christian Indian agents.[55] When the government seemed reluctant to let the Dakotas try this experiment in homesteading, missionary John Williamson defended them for doing what the government had been trying to get them to do all along.[56] Although Hazelwood did not survive the antagonism and intimidation of Dakotas opposed to the experiment,

according to historians, Flandreau remained the "most successful
and most securely based of the various fragments into which the
Santee Sioux had been dispersed since 1862."[57]

The Nez Perce Christians also sought physical separation from
non-Christian Indians. The annual observation of the summer sol-
stice and food gathering became a source of conflict that left the
Nez Perces no possibility of choosing a middle ground. By the
mid-nineteenth century, influenced by both British and American
fur traders, this largely tribal celebration had evolved into a two-
week Fourth of July party of gaming and entertainment attended by
Nez Perces as well as non–Nez Perces.[58] It became the scene of a
"traditional feast with traditional clothing, gambling, horseracing,
and (an added element) drinking."[59] According to the missionaries
and most of the Native church leaders, however, the "drinking, gambling, horse-racing and changing of wives" it fostered was contrary
to the church's moral standards.[60] One Native church elder despaired
of its effect on the Christian community and confessed to the missionary, "I now see the door is open back to heathenism."[61]

As early as 1874, the Nez Perce Presbyterians began to hold their
own Fourth of July ceremonies centered on the traditional camas
and kouse root gathering and church meetings led by the Native
pastors and elders.[62] With the return of Chief Joseph's nontreaty
Nez Perces from Oklahoma in 1885, however, the non-Presbyterian
celebration gained popularity and appealed even to many of the
Presbyterians, who now had relatives and friends in the other camp.
The Nez Perce government agent tried to encourage a unified celebration in 1887, but it soon became a "pivotal point of conflict"
between the Christian and non-Christian Nez Perces until the camps
were separated once again in 1891.[63] By 1897 the Native Presbyterian ministers, backed by the presbytery, threatened to excommunicate any who crossed over from one camp to the other.[64] That year,
in a dramatic encounter, the non-Christian encampment mounted
a procession and tried to ride through the Presbyterian camp. Seven
Nez Perce church elders and ministers drew their horses in a line
across the road to stop them.[65] The separation was complete.

Lapwai (Spalding) Presbyterian Church, site of one of the early Nez Perce annual campmeetings before settling at Talmaks in 1910. Photo by E. Jane Gay, circa 1890, courtesy of the Idaho State Historical Society, Boise. Photo number 63-221.259/B.

The Nez Perce Presbyterians worked toward deepening the division. They rotated their annual July camp meetings between churches for several years. They solidified the program of the two-week event to include daily worship services, singing, games, activities for the youth, and a campwide feast on the Fourth following a pageant and oration commemorating the day's significance.[66] In 1910 the six churches chose a camp meeting board that, in turn, chose an area of over six hundred acres of pine-covered hills several miles from the reservation at a place called Talmaks for a permanent campground.[67] It had enough acreage to pasture their four or five hundred horses, along with their tents, all of which they secured behind wire fences.[68] It had the added advantage of being far enough away from the non-Christian celebrations and celebrants to preserve its Christian identity, even though the non-Christian celebrations had virtually disbanded by this time.[69]

The cultivation and preservation of a Native Christian identity was, perhaps, the greatest motivating factor in American Indian attempts to remove themselves from Native cultural and physical surroundings. It was not so much a rejection of traditional ways as a redefinition of them in the profound cultural upheaval of the era. Native Christians sought a place where they could make sense of their world and find power to negotiate within it. In their tie to the missionaries and the larger Presbyterian Church, they hoped to live lives of meaning and purpose in ways that allowed them to maintain Native agency within a dominant culture. The creation of Native congregations and religious practices within a Presbyterian structure produced distinct American Indian churches while providing Indians with new tools for cultural transformation and survival. A better understanding of the dynamics involved in this process is gained by studying how Indian Christians actually organized and ran their churches.

Although American Indian Presbyterian churches reflected tribal differences, they shared some common features. As among the Choctaw churches studied by Clara Sue Kidwell, Nez Perce and Dakota Presbyterian churches provided a focal point for socializing and fellowship.[70] They formed, in the words of one Nez Perce missionary, "the centre of interest in each community" as well as of worship.[71] They served as community social centers, forums for discussion of the important issues of the day, and places to mourn and to celebrate the benchmarks of Native existence. Above all else, however, they were sacred houses dedicated to the rituals and relationships that succored the believers' new lives.

Influenced by the shape of Presbyterianism nationwide, American Indian churches adhered to regular meetings, a prescribed order of worship, and leadership roles defined by the church. Within these imposed forms of Presbyterian worship, however, Indian Presbyterianism showed a strong tendency to follow its own path. Both Nez Perces and Dakotas extended almost any church affair into protracted, sometimes emotionally charged meetings. Mary Crawford marveled at the untiring Nez Perces, who were known "to stay up, preaching, praying, and singing, until three or four in the morning."[72] The spirited and often moving services of the Nez Perces reminded Kate McBeth of the "kind of experience meeting" more associated with the Methodists than the Presbyterians.[73] It was the fervency and sincerity of worshipping Dakotas imprisoned at Mankato that convinced the missionaries of the propriety of baptizing more than three hundred in the winter of 1863. The Native leadership led the converts in hymn singing and prayer, and, according to John Williamson, they were "filled with the Spirit and prophesied."[74]

The appeal of public singing and ceremony was embedded in precontact Nez Perce and Dakota societies. Famed Indian photographer Edward Curtis called songs the "essentials of religion" among the Plateau peoples, and ethnographer Herbert Spinden noted that they were performed with a "freedom from ceremonial restraint."[75] Missionary Riggs wrote that among the pre-Christian Dakotas the "whole ritual of their worship is chanted, whether engaged in by the single devotee or the sacred assembly."[76] Whether for thanksgiving, supplication, memorializing acts of bravery or kindness, or identifying one's source of guardian power, music was central to most Native celebrations.[77] Presbyterian Indians made it central to Christian worship as well.

Both Nez Perce and Dakota missionaries commented that the Indians loved to sing, "at the Mission . . . in their homes and in their churches," but missionaries clearly believed that Indians needed to be taught to do it properly.[78] Thomas Williamson despaired of Robert Hopkins's musical ability at Mankato, even though he appreciated the elder's spiritual leadership. Williamson wrote Riggs, that "We much need a better singer than Caske [Hopkins]. He sings as well as he can and by practice has improved . . . but many of the hymns he is unable to sing."[79] They most often criticized the Native style of worship songs, referring to them as "heathen mystic chants," or "loud, wild notes." One missionary claimed such songs "were doubtless animating to their spirits and pleasing to their ears, but not to mine."[80] Missionaries tried to replace the "weird chant in a minor key" which they found so objectionable with the "melody of some world-known tune like Silver Street, Ortonville, Martyn, [or] Olivet" and the translated words of popular hymns.[81] The Nez Perce missionaries believed that Indians benefited by learning "good music" as well as by having "the Gospel fairly sung into them."[82]

It was evident, however, that the newer tunes did not completely replace the old. Musicologist Frances Densmore wrote of the Sioux that song and dance were so integral to their way of life that they were the "last element of native culture remaining in favor" among them following contact.[83] She observed a growing number of American Indians in the early 1900s making recordings of their "social songs," as they had become known, since the "use of songs for ceremony, war, societies, and the hunt [had] passed away."[84] Densmore was pleased with the "readiness to adapt the means of civilization to an end which is purely native."[85] Christian Indians, however, also adapted hymns to Native ends. Recent studies have shown that in a number of tribes where Native-led Christian churches evolved, the use of hymn singing brought the community together in celebrating victories, mourning losses, and reinforcing Native virtues such as generosity and self-sacrifice.[86] Hymn singing, though championed by the missionaries, became a means of expressing Native cultural ideals, language, and even tunes.

Indian pastors, often using the new forms available to them, maintained the prominent role of music in the life of the congregation, despite attempts to change their tunes. Many Native pastors and elders led their congregations in both worship and song by learning to play the melodeons, pump organs, and other instruments brought by the missionaries. Traditional Indian instruments such as pipe and drum were frowned on for their association with non-Christian worship and not usually allowed in the church. Sue McBeth commended two of her students for their musical ability, writing that "Mark [brother of Robert Williams] is a sweet singer and a good player on the cabinet-organ. Archie, too, sings well."[87] Kate McBeth came to rely on the Nez Perces to provide the music for services and noted in her diary one evening that she "was disappointed that neither Mark [n]or James was here [in church] to play. My playing is so limited."[88] Dakota pastor John Eastman was a noted organ player.[89] Using the means of making music available to them, Native leaders were able to retain some control of this important aspect of their worship.

Native pastors also translated and composed hymns, which allowed even greater influence in shaping their spiritual lives. Robert Williams, James Hayes, and elder Jonas Levi collaborated on producing the first Nez Perce hymnal entitled "Gospel Hymns in the Nez Perce Language."[90] It was dedicated to Williams, who died in 1896 as the book was going to press. John Renville became a noted hymn writer and translator, following the example of his father, Joseph Renville. The senior Renville had helped the early missionaries produce the first "Dakota Odowan," or Dakota hymnbook, using many French tunes.[91] The church compiled a second, expanded edition with notes following the Dakota war to assist the large numbers now in church. In a fifth revision and expansion of the hymnal in 1879, John Williamson and Alfred Riggs noted that the new version, compiled of many hymns composed by the Dakotas themselves, had expanded with and was testimony to the growth and development of the Dakota churches.[92] The Native language hymnals produced by and still in use in both Dakota and Nez Perce churches indicate the important position they gained in American Indian worship.

Densmore lamented that "coming under the restrictions of civilization" translated into "less freedom in musical expression" for the Dakotas.[93] While the churches transformed the music of the Nez

Perces and Dakotas, Native elements definitely remained. Riggs
noted that the Dakotas sang "in heartiness, power, and worshipful-
ness" both gospel hymns and "their own irregular but impressive
native airs."[94] Joseph Renville's "Dakota Odowan 141," like others
of his translated hymns, put Christian lyrics to a Dakota tune:

> Many and great, O God, are Thy things,
>   Maker of earth and sky;
> Thy hands have set the heavens with stars,
>   Thy fingers spread the mountains and plains.
> Lo, at thy word the waters were formed;
>   Deep seas obey Thy voice.
> Grant unto us communion with Thee,
>   Thou star-abiding One,
> Come unto us and dwell with us:
>   With Thee are found the gifts of life.
> Bless us with life that has no end,
>   Eternal life with Thee.[95]

The focus of the hymn on images of nature and the beautifully
crafted "star-abiding One" for God reflect Dakota symbols and concerns. While in no way offending the missionaries' orthodoxy, the
hymn would readily resonate with Dakota ears. According to one
Dakota story, this hymn was sung by thirty-eight Indian prisoners,
nearly all of whom had been baptized, as they went to the gallows
at Mankato following the Dakota war. Its Dakota words and Dakota
melody led bystanders to believe the prisoners were singing a traditional death chant. They were, according to one Dakota account,
singing a "hymn of praise to God."[96]

Even some of the Nez Perces, despite the constant missionary
attempt to "teach them to learn to sing and play new hymn tunes,"
showed signs of a desire to hold on to older music.[97] Archie Lawyer
fell out of Sue McBeth's good graces when he attempted to print a
Nez Perce hymnbook without submitting it to her for revision. She
feared his work would be too close in message and tune to older
worship songs since he, as she claimed, "knows nothing of the rules
of musical notation" and his theology was suspect.[98] McBeth wielded
a great deal of influence on the kind of music that was sung by the

Nez Perces, but it was remarked that songs sung in Nez Perce had a "weirdness and beauty" enhanced by the fact they were sung a cappella.[99] Densmore appreciated that music continued to be a valued part of Native society. It remained so among Christian Indians primarily because Native Presbyterians insisted on its preeminence in worship services.

Like the structure of the worship services, the structure of church leadership was based on Presbyterian forms. The process of choosing leaders and governing the church, however, was just as susceptible to American Indian adaptation, despite missionary attempts to control or guide the conditions and proceedings. According to Presbyterian polity, the minister of the church was "called" or chosen to serve by vote of the congregation. The church was actually run, however, by the session, made up of elders and the minister, who was a nonvoting member. Elders were elected from among the parishioners for life terms, serving actively for three years at a time. Both men and women were usually eligible to vote for their leaders, although only males could serve in the elected positions.[100] This democratic framework was loose enough to accommodate the consensus-style leadership typical of both the Nez Perces and the Dakotas. Because leaders were usually chosen by the people rather than appointed from outside the congregation, it also allowed the Indians to put their stamp on Presbyterian polity.

Indian women, like non-Indian women, in the Presbyterian Church found their voices channeled rather than stifled. Women's voices mingled with the men's voices in singing and in prayer at Presbyterian church services.[101] Kate McBeth noted that in the Nez Perce churches, "there was no such thing as a woman refusing to pray."[102] Women, however, did not preach. Nineteenth-century gender relations in the church, as in society at large, were often expressed in terms of gender-specific behavior that carried political overtures of authority and submission.[103] As one missionary journal reminded all Presbyterian women, "[W]oman's work in the church still obeys the law of Paradise . . . she is helper of man, not his rival nor antagonist."[104] Admittedly more culturally egalitarian or complementary, especially on the Plateau, Native society nevertheless was marked by

distinct gender roles.[105] Native women in the church tended to function in the less prominent roles typically assigned to women, for
which there was some precedent in Native society. Although denied
access to the pastorate or the session until well into the twentieth
century, Indian women found ways to be heard, much as they had
in precontact days when prohibited from serving as Nez Perce or
Dakota chiefs or on councils.[106]

Presbyterian women had ample opportunity through women's
benevolent societies to be involved in the life of the church.[107] Mod-
eled after those organizations of non-Native women, the missionaries encouraged wives of Native pastors to take the lead in setting
up and running committees to benefit the church. In a letter printed
in a Presbyterian journal, Dakota pastor Pierre La Pointe lamented
his wife's recent death but ended with this tribute to her: "And the
women work very hard in their society which meets every Wednes-
day. They work sewing all day to earn some money for the church.
So I am glad and remember how my wife worked to start the society."[108] Mary Jane Eastman, wife of the Dakota pastor John Eastman
at Flandreau, wrote in the *Iapi Oaye* about "how our ladies aid[e]
are working for the lord."[109] She reported that in the one year they
had been meeting (1879), they had raised "$47.20 and from there,
$25.00 went to help with the National Mission and $5.95 went to
help repair our church. They bought on[e] nice carpet. In the
future they will sew one day to raise funds."[110] Led by Mary Renville,
wife of Dakota pastor John Renville, the women of the Ascension
Church on the Sisseton Reservation in South Dakota began a sewing
circle in 1874 that they called "Iyopta," or the Advance Society. In
the first six years they earned $504.95, which they donated to help
purchase church seats, plaster the church, support the Dakota newspaper the *Iapi Oaye,* buy an organ for the Good Will Church (also
on the Sisseton Reservation), and support "a Native Missionary sent
from the Ascension [Church] or whosoever in the Providence of
God may be chosen."[111] They also donated $12 in clothing to their
chosen missionary pastor, Isaac Renville, another grandson of
Joseph Renville, Sr., and nephew of John Renville.

The Lapwai Indian Women's Missionary Society, the first missionary society in Idaho, with Kate McBeth. Photo by E. Jane Gay, courtesy of the Idaho State Historical Society, Boise. Photo number 63-221.246.

Benevolent organizations offered churchwomen a way to contribute to the work of the church. They also allowed the practice of Native crafts in an approved setting. The Lapwai Indian Women's Missionary Society in fourteen years contributed to the Home and Foreign Mission Boards of the Presbyterian Church, bought new seats for the church, put money toward the purchase of a bell for the steeple, and "did many other things to make the dear church look beautiful."[112] They accomplished all this by sewing moccasins, doing beadwork, and weaving baskets for white churchwomen in the East. Dakota women "brought in beautiful moccasins, and fancy work of various kinds," including "crazy patchwork" to sell for the Native missionary society.[113] Sewing societies allowed American Indian women to pursue skills that were being quickly eroded by their conversion to Christianity and its attendant "civilization." Kate McBeth missed the irony when she observed that the churchwomen's "work is not so very nice, for the wilder the woman, the better bead and fancy work she makes."[114]

Women also benefited from what could be called a "committee virus." The proliferation of committees provided the best means to include everyone in the work.[115] Dismayed that their women's groups could have only one president at a time according to parliamentary rules, the Dakotas decided to have "plenty of officers, and thus all matters were amicably adjusted."[116] This also provided churches an opportunity to honor the elderly and the deserving by awarding them the top offices. Anthropologist Deward Walker noted that by the mid-twentieth century one Nez Perce church alone had sixty-two offices, and many members held multiple offices or committee chairs.[117] In the nineteenth and early twentieth centuries, women had few opportunities outside of the church for leadership.

The primary responsibility for the oversight and maintenance of the church fell to the session. Composed of the elected elders and the church minister, its duty was the "discipline of the congregation in the areas of morals, of participation in worship, and of Christian knowledge."[118] The Book of Order of the Presbyterian Church outlined the election process of church elders. Qualifications for office reflected biblical standards of conduct as well as Victorian interpretation of those standards. Based on the Christian scriptures, elders and deacons (those chosen to serve as the compassionate arm of the leadership) were admonished to be "blameless, the husband of one wife, vigilant, sober, of good behaviour, given to hospitality, apt to teach; not given to wine, no striker, not greedy of filthy lucre; but patient, not a brawler, not covetous; one that ruleth well his own house."[119] The Presbyterian Church interpreted that to mean that leadership should be refused to anyone with multiple wives, a drinking problem, or known to gamble, dance, or hold to any practices associated with "heathenism." For the most part, Christian Indians who had placed high value on moral rectitude in pre-Christian society accepted these requirements.

In practice, Dakota and even Nez Perce church elders and deacons were often selected or rejected because of their family connections. For example, when the Lapwai (Spalding) Church reorganized in 1879, it "decided to elect three elders—one to represent the North Fork people, one the Cottonwood people, and one the Lapwai people."[120] In contrast, when the Hill (Pahata) Church on the Yankton Reservation in Dakota Territory asked Dakota elder Adam Pazi to become its licensed pastor, the presbytery found among a minority strong objections that "arose from the fact that he was not one of their people." The presbytery, however, found that reason wanting and "gave the Church some counsel as to what they considered the proper course to pursue."[121] It nearly became a moot point when Pazi failed the licensing exam. He eventually passed, but his tenure at Hill Church was a brief two years. Although a factor in choosing Native elders, kinship was not the only consideration. Churches tended to select those who, as in pre-Christian times, proved their ability to perform the job to the satisfaction of the community.

Selection of the first elders and preachers was heavily influenced by the missionaries, who looked to those who had been educated in mission schools or were early converts. Many were from prominent families. When Spalding began preaching among other tribes after his return to the Nez Perces in the early 1870s, he chose Chief Lawyer to help, along with Timothy and Jonathan (Billy)

Williams, from among the first converts. The Dakota missionaries turned to such leaders as Simon Anawangmani and Paul Mazakute-mani, educated in the mission school at Lac qui Parle and brother of Cloudman, a Wahpeton headman. Once churches were for-mally organized, however, selection became the work of the church membership.

As a part of organizing a new church, the congregation was called upon to put forth names for the election of the elders and deacons. Where no previous church existed, the congregation often chose elders from among former tribal leaders. For example, when the Spokans organized the Deep Creek Church in 1880, they chose as their elder William, their tribal headman, who was, according to the missionary, "in many respects . . . a wonderful man for the light he has had."[122] A band of Dakotas fled to Manitoba, Canada, during the Dakota war, led by Henok Appearing Cloud. When a kinsman and Dakota pastor, Solomon Tunkansaiciye, organized Middle Hill Church (Pahacokamya) near Fort Ellice in the Northwest Territory among them in 1878, the congregation chose Henok as elder.[123]

When churches split off from previously existing churches, con-gregations usually chose former elders or church leaders as the new elders. At Fort Snelling, Minnesota, where about sixteen hundred of the "less dangerous" prisoners of the Dakota war were held, the church organized by John Williamson chose four former elders: Simon Anawangmani; Paul Mazakutemani and Antoine Renville (son of Joseph Renville and father of Isaac Renville), both formerly of the Hazelwood Church in Minnesota; and Joseph Napesni, for-merly of the Zoar Church, also in Minnesota.[124] The new commu-nity of Flandreau organized its church in 1869. Of the forty-nine members who made up the roll of the Wakpaipaksan or Bend of the River Church (or River Bend, later called Flandreau First Church), forty-four had been members of the Ohnihde or Pilgrim Church before coming to Flandreau. The three elders chosen had all been elders in their previous church, and the missionary noted that two of them had "acted as preachers since last spring and seem to have given satisfaction."[125] One of them, Joseph Iron Old Man, had also been a hunkayapi in the prison, and thus was being re-elected a third time, but he died of exposure during a snowstorm before he could finish his term of office.[126] As in pre-Christian days, the Dakotas and Nez Perces looked for proven leadership when the choice was theirs, creatively using the Presbyterian offices to perpetuate older leadership positions.

Indian innovations were most visible in the work of the church session. Used to arbitrate disputes, to discipline the membership and to maintain social order, the session tried, not always successfully, to fulfill the role of the pre-Christian Native council to monitor social behavior. In precontact times, tribal elders, shamans, and leaders served informally to curb deviant behavior, administer disciplinary measures when necessary, and keep younger ones in line. They used ridicule, shaming, and at times even corporal punishment.[127] With the erosion of traditional leadership patterns, the church became a means of social cohesiveness that incorporated Native elements but invested leaders with even greater power than held previously.[128]

Elders had the power to decide who could join the church, who could stay, and who could—and under what terms—return if severed from church fellowship. Both Nez Perce and Dakota elders took their responsibilities of "preaching, teaching, worship, and discipline" seriously and turned a rather mundane office into a coveted social position with formidable powers.[129] With few other leadership options open, the session was the one place to wield legitimate social and political power. Because much of Native life revolved around the church, the ability to decide who could and who could not join the church effectively determined who could and could not participate in the life of the community. Membership in the organization was extended to any of those who "profession their faith to their Saviour Jesus Christ."[130] Those wishing to unite with the church "were examined as to their religious experience" by the session and, if conversion seemed sincere, "received to the sealing ordinances of Baptism and the Lord Supper."[131]

As a member of the church, a new convert became subject to the authority of session in matters both sacred and temporal. Church discipline focused on acceptable Christian conduct and was rigorously

Tipiwakan Wakpaipaksan, River Bend meeting house (First Presbyterian Church, Flandreau), built in 1871 and sold to government for day school in 1873. Photo circa 1910, courtesy of the William L. Beane Private Collection, Flandreau.

enforced in a manner similar to other Presbyterian churches of the day. "Sins" of the congregational members, however, were broader in scope than they were in most white churches.[132] Church elders controlled the morality of the community by condemning offenses such as Sabbath breaking, adultery, drunkenness, gambling, practicing or appealing to shamanism, and avoiding church fellowship.

The minutes kept of church session meetings reveal the scope of the session's power. For example, on July 6, 1885 Nez Perce pastor Silas Whitman and the elders of the Lapwai (Spalding) Church opened their session meeting with prayer and proceeded to meet with "a great number of members [who] presented themselves for religious conversation and advice[.] [T]hey were patiently heard in all their troubles and instructed as to their work and duty in the future."[133] In the course of the meeting the session barred one woman from Communion for her confession to working on the Sabbath; barred one man "present by citation" for refusing to marry the woman he was living with; barred two of their own elders for skinning a deer on the Sabbath; restored one woman to church privileges who had been suspended the previous winter upon her confession of sorrow and a "strong desire to live a Christian life"; exonerated one man who confessed "some trouble he had had"; and examined three persons wishing to be baptized, after deciding that one would have to be re-baptized having been first baptized in the Catholic Church.[134] A Communion service was held at the end of the session meeting, with a sermon by Rev. Archie Lawyer, followed by the three baptisms.[135]

The confessional nature of the session meetings, where elders and ministers attempted to regulate behavior both in church and out, was one factor in the church elders' inordinate power. Church members appeared before the session of their own volition or by request of the elders to answer to charges of moral or behavioral lapses. Kate McBeth noted, "[W]hat a disgrace to be Sessioned by this people."[136] Failure to respond to a summons by the session could mean excommunication from the church, although an acknowledgment of wrongdoing could also lead to excommunication. In most cases, punishment came in the form of exclusion from the

Communion services for a period of time. If the wrongdoer displayed repentance and remorse, he or she was welcomed back into fellowship. For example, when a woman of the Wellpinit or Spokane River Church in Washington Territory was called before session for attending war dances, "[s]he admitted that she had done so, professed sorrow and promised to try to avoid such things in the future. Elder Samuel gave her admonition and kindly encouragement."[137]

Perhaps it was the attention to rituals of purification in pre-Christian days surrounding the sweat bath that made the Plateau peoples particularly given to the idea of public confession for cleansing the soul. Even the Catholic missionaries noted that the Nez Perces were "excellent fasters and gave extremely detailed confessions of their sins."[138] So confessional did some sessions become that one white minister at Wellpinit took the church to task for allegedly misusing that body. He wrote into the church minutes, "Many people, who still regard the meetings of session as a 'Confessional' appeared with their troubles. All of them were reprimanded for the idea and told to go daily in prayer to God, the hearer of prayers, who can and will forgive for Christ's sake."[139] Regardless of the background of the practice, Presbyterian Nez Perces, in particular, used the power of the session to monitor and modify both public and private behavior and provided an element of social control in an era of upheaval.

Matters of discipline that came before the session could result in policy decisions that would govern the entire congregation. The Dakota church in prison had twelve elders who were confronted with the issue of members who appealed to medicine men in the absence of agency medical doctors. Although the missionaries had made known their views, they left it to the session to rule in the matter, guided by "their knowledge of the teachings of the Bible, and the requirements of Christ's religion."[140] In unusual openness to the role of Native culture in the life of the people, the missionaries told the session: "[T]he gospel of Christ moulded the customs and habits of every people by whom it was received. There might be some wrong things in a national custom which could be eliminated, and the custom substantially retained; or the custom might be so radically absurd and wrong that it could not be redeemed. In that case,

Christianity required its abandonment."[141] The policy set forth by the session would be adopted. In a vote of ten to two, the session decided against the practice of consulting medicine men for any reason, claiming that they no longer believed that sickness was the cause of spirits but that "conjuring brings men into contact with the spirits of evil, and tends to lead them away from Christ."[142] This policy decision was not unlike that of the Wellpinit session among the Spokans, which decided that on the "subject of gambling & drinking & the Medicine dance . . . a second offence in either of these evils will be followed by excommunication."[143] The session's power was far-reaching and often authoritarian.

The church session, however, was not without checks upon its power. Elders were held to the same rules of behavior as were parishioners. When two elders from the North Fork Church confessed to "skinning and dressing a deer on a Sabbath morning recently" and promised not to do so again, they were "for sake of the example . . . requested not to commune" at the next Communion service by other members of the session.[144] Upon the complaints of the congregation of the Lapwai (Spalding) Church, an elder was reprimanded by the session "for assuming and exercising too much authority and meddling with matters out of an elder's provinence," for which he was "kindly rebuked and exhorted to be more cautious in his official work and investigation in regard to private matters of the members."[145] When he failed to heed the advice and "used certain language which is not proper for an elder to use and was unkind both in his action and language," his fellow elders and their minister, Archie Lawyer, voted him out of office.[146] A Dakota pastor, "losing ground and being aware of it act[ed] crabbed and unevenly."[147] He refused to marry a couple, bawled out his congregation for refusing his salary, and then threatened to "go off to the Gentiles."[148] The congregation responded by leaving the church and joining the Episcopalians.

Likewise, an elder of the Wellpinit Church among the Spokans was voted out of office for "having the sorcerer to practice in his family during the illness of his wife" and for having "loaned his horse to be run on the race-track."[149] Despite his objection that it was Chief

Lot that had ordered the sorcerer, and that Chief Lot and the Indian agent had assured him that using his horse for a race would not jeopardize his eldership, the "session required that he be dismissed from the eldership."[150] The session asserted its authority in church matters, irrespective of the power of chiefs or their agents, and often to spite them.[151] Although the session held extreme powers to control the social behavior of church members, abuse of its powers would not be tolerated; and when elders overstepped their authority, they were disciplined by the very body of which they were a part.

For the most part, however, congregations chose elders because they were proven and respected leaders. Regardless of education or training, many served the church faithfully and well. In the first forty years of the Dakota church, it ordained twenty-five men to the ministry and two or three times that number as elders. Many fit the profile of Joseph Hillers, elder of the Flandreau First Church, appointed to attend the Presbyterian General Assembly in 1889. John Williamson explained:

> Joseph Hillers is a good average representative of Indian eldership, of whom we have 41 in Dakota Presbytery. He was a wild heathen Indian at the time of the Minnesota Massacre in 1862, and for connection with it was put in jail, where he was converted in the great revival. He was too old to go to school and learn English, but learned to read his own language, studied the Bible, and grew to be one of the pillars [of] the church, as our elders are.[152]

Much responsibility was placed on the elders, as born out in church records and missionary papers. John Williamson noted the concern of some of the Dakota elders who particularly felt the burden of seeing "that God[']s worship is properly conducted."[153] Expected to preach, teach, attend meetings of the church's governing bodies, and fulfill the functions of ministers in the absence of ordained clergy, they often formed the pool from which Native ministers were drawn, particularly among the Dakotas.[154]

As in other Presbyterian churches across the nation, on Sunday morning Nez Perce and Dakota Indians often gathered in steepled clapboard edifices for worship services of hymn singing, prayer, and a sermon given by the minister or, in his absence, a church elder. Following the church service, Sunday school classes focused on a biblical lesson, children and adults usually in their own classes. People visited together after the class. Prayer meetings later in the day or the week focused on "witness-bearing," or confession and prayer. Christian Endeavor classes for the young, Temperance Societies, and Women's Missionary Societies played an important role in the life of the congregation. Officers were elected, committees formed and governed by parliamentary procedure, and funds raised by socials, sales, and bazaars for special projects or gatherings.

Differences persisted, however. Nez Perce and Dakota churches were less concerned to begin and end at a certain hour. They began when everyone got there and ended when they felt they were done with worship. Hymns, prayers, and conversation were usually in the Native tongue. There was a proliferation of church committees to carry on the work of the church. Session meetings often became confessionals, and the elders' power over the congregants' lives was extensive. Indian leadership gave a definite stamp to Indian congregations.

Kate McBeth came to the conclusion that the Nez Perces "want their own churches, with their own Native pastors and elders."[155] She was astute enough to recognize that "[t]his is well for them spiritually" and that "they certainly know how to manage their own churches better than any white."[156] Indian congregations reflected Indian values, support systems, and leadership. These communities of faith continued to serve both as perpetuators and innovators of Native culture within the Presbyterian Church.

CHAPTER 5

Indians and Missionaries

I will say that Miss Floyd is a good help mate for me. She minds to her own business.

PERRY IDES

American Indian Presbyterian churches differed from most other Presbyterian churches in one major way: they came with missionaries. Not only did missionaries take part in beginning churches, they often continued on in some role within the Native church years after the church was established. Seeking to root the church firmly in Christian faith and doctrine, the missionaries frequently lent helpful advice and encouragement to young churches. Their long tenure, however, also tended to complicate matters for the inchoate Native leadership. Even when relationships were mutually satisfying, negotiating and renegotiating boundaries between Indian and missionary often distracted from the work of the church. Eventually, however, American Indian churches with Indian pastors prevailed because Indian people wanted them.

The prevailing missionary strategy that governed the Presbyterian Church had been established by the ABCFM missionary statesman Rufus Anderson in the first half of the nineteenth century.

Along with mission strategist Henry Venn of Great Britain, Anderson believed that the "grand object of missions is to plant and multiply churches, composed of Native converts; each church complete in itself, with presbyters of the same race, left to determine their ecclesiastical relations for themselves, with the aid of judicious advice from their missionary fathers."[1] He hastened to add that once missionaries had planted a church with Native leadership, they were to leave the rest of the work to the Holy Spirit and go on to another field.[2] The Presbyterians endorsed this method of doing mission work, but in reality, many missionaries found it difficult to move on. The missionaries to the Nez Perces and the Dakotas were ones who stayed on, encouraging Native leadership to find creative ways of governing their churches and sustaining a working relationship with the missionaries.

The mission to the Nez Perces was, perhaps, most unique among American Indian missionary ventures. Between 1874 and 1932 the nearly exclusive training of pastors and elders was in the hands of three women in succession: Sue McBeth, her younger sister Kate McBeth, and their niece Mary Crawford. None of these women was seminary trained or ordained in the church; and yet, through their agency, eighteen men became ordained Presbyterian ministers filling pulpits among the Nez Perces, the Spokans, the Umatillas, and the Makahs, among others. These strong women, at times revered and at times reviled, were both a blessing and a curse to the very leadership they were trying to raise up.

For both the women and the Indian men they taught, avenues for achieving positions of authority in the church were limited. Too often, they found themselves competing for that authority. It was definitely to the Nez Perces' advantage that the women could not share the pulpit with them, but that did not prevent the women from trying to wield what power they had. Both Native pastors and missionaries turned to constructs of race, class, and gender in order to support claims to authority.[3]

Nez Perce efforts to establish an identity as Native pastors coincided with what historian Peggy Pascoe has termed the "female search for moral authority."[4] As she has noted, women reformers and missionaries working in the American West had had moral influence throughout the Victorian era but not social power. What they hoped to do was "to turn their influence into authority" in order to remedy society's ills.[5] Most believed they were called of God to enter into mission work and empowered by God to complete it.[6] Typical of these women was Sue McBeth's claim that she did not work "for any benefit or any Board, but for *my Master*, who is 'with me alway.'"[7]

The mission, however, was one of the few places in the last century that allowed women such as McBeth the fulfillment of a career outside the home. As Michael Harkin has noted in his study of the missionaries to the Heiltsuks (a Native people on the coast of British Columbia also known as the Bella Bellas), these were "the first professional career women . . . independent souls who ventured out to make their way in the world."[8] They also organized and supported their own mission projects and boards and sent out their own missionaries even as they remained within "women's sphere" by doing what began as "women's work for women."[9] Perhaps, as R. Pierce Beaver suggests, had women been given "a real share in home-base activities and field ministry," they would not have had to go in search of their own avenues and authority to effect change.[10]

Churchwide movements also affected the mission to the Nez Perces. By the end of the Civil War, "women's work for women" was well established in most denominations. Although the term applied originally to the women and children of the foreign fields who were secluded and thus inaccessible to male missionaries, it had come to include American Indian men of the home or domestic missions. This understanding allowed the McBeths and Crawford to take over the education of Spalding's group of male church assistants. It also contributed to a tendency among the missionaries to infantilize male students. Sue McBeth made frequent reference to "my boys," who in turn called her "Pika," the "little mother."[11] As endearing as those references may have been, such an attitude at times failed to prepare the women to accept Native men as adults and peers. Believing their students to be as tractable as children, the women associated with the Nez Perce mission never seemed quite at ease when challenged by Nez Perce men who disagreed with them.

These women, who seemed unwilling to grant equality to American Indian men they considered subordinate to them, were simultaneously challenged by white men who thought the women had become too independent. The growing visibility of women in church leadership provoked a national reaction among Presbyterian men that ended shortly after the turn of the century in the consolidation of women's mission boards under male leadership.[12] Its more immediate effect on the women of the Nez Perce mission was evidence of a heightened insecurity in their position as teachers of theology—a job most mission boards believed outside the realm of women's work.[13] Only after Sue McBeth successfully prepared several students to pass presbytery approval for licensure did the mission board stop badgering her to quit teaching theology. The necessity of having to prove herself often caused her to be overly sensitive to questions of her authority and rendered her intolerant to criticism from any source.

These local and national trends contributed to a siege mentality among the missionary teachers of the Nez Perce mission. The battle for authority meant that the position of the Native pastors was forged, at times, in the midst of bitter recriminations and controversy. The particular constellations of power, however, allowed Nez Perce pastors unusual freedom to increase their autonomy and a sense of their own identity, since the power of white women ultimately posed far less of a threat to ordained ministers of the church than did the power of white churchmen. Not all these relationships descended into acrimony. Native men and missionary women also made many strong and lasting friendships, even though these were often tried by fire.

Archie Lawyer, one of Sue McBeth's first students, illustrates the complexity of these gendered and racialized conflicts over authority in the church. Lawyer was the son of the former Chief Lawyer, who was appointed by American government personnel as head chief in 1848 and led the Nez Perces through the turmoil of the treaty years, carefully trying to negotiate a path of peace with the whites. One of the early converts to Christianity, Chief Lawyer perhaps hoped, as one early missionary suggested, to "increase [his] influence and sustain [his] dignity among the people."[14] It was an accusation McBeth would use against his son some years later.

When Chief Lawyer died in 1876, the tribal chieftainship as it had originally been instituted was being replaced, as mandated by government decree. The Nez Perces began electing their leaders by democratic process under the direction of the Lapwai Indian Agency. Chief Lawyer's oldest son James (Jimmy) served as chief for two years. By 1881 the federal government had disposed of the office of chief altogether and replaced it with agency-appointed Indian police and courts. To the missionaries, however, it seemed that "the chiefs were [not] all dead—for they were standing around thick, in Kamiah."[15] An aura of nobility clung to the Lawyer line; and Chief Lawyer's sons, both James and Archie, continued to use their former status to try to influence the tribe.

James and Archie Lawyer attended Sue McBeth's school when she took it over in 1874 following the death of Spalding. Robert and Mark Williams, two sons of Kamiah Church elder Billy Williams (one of the first converts), also attended, along with James Hines, an older convert and cousin to the Lawyers.[16] As late as 1878, McBeth claimed her students were "from the 'pick' of the tribe," and Archie Lawyer, along with Robert Williams, became the "principal preachers—and good preachers."[17] From the beginning, however, the Lawyer brothers challenged her. Already respected for their ancestry, they were also quick-witted, fun loving, and not reluctant to torment their humorless teacher. They let it be known early on that they were not accustomed to taking orders from a woman.[18] Their spotty attendance in school following the 1877 flight of Chief Joseph did not endear them to McBeth.

Faced with the graver challenge of having to convince the mission board that she was capable of teaching theology, McBeth chose to downplay her trouble with the Lawyers.[19] In 1879, however, the government allocated funds to send three Christian Nez Perces to minister to Chief Joseph's people exiled in Indian Territory. She was relieved that Archie Lawyer, although licensed but not yet ordained, was eager to go and Robert Williams chose to remain.[20] Mark Williams and James Reuben, son of Chief Reuben (who succeeded Chief Lawyer in 1876), accompanied Lawyer. They made a few converts, but Lawyer and Williams soon returned due to ill health while Reuben stayed on to teach. It was upon their return to Kamiah that trouble began to escalate between McBeth and Lawyer.

Lawyer's willingness to go to Joseph's people, as he had gone earlier on preaching trips among the Crows, reflected his dissatisfaction with affairs at home, where he was still only a licentiate and Robert Williams held the pulpit in Kamiah. It also revealed his affinity with the band that had defied the U.S. cavalry and, as in former days, showed the warrior prowess of the Nez Perces. On his return from Indian Territory, he brought back pictures of Sitting Bull and regaled his family and friends with stories of the "good old days," before the coming of the now-dominant society. Much to McBeth's chagrin, Lawyer used the church picnic to gather his "long haired band from Lapwai" and give his "dissertation on the glories of their heathen-warrior days with their Crow allies."[21] His antics did not fail to rile his teacher. Whenever possible, he seemed determined to challenge her preference for Williams and to stir up Nez Perce Christians.

Feeling, perhaps, a little more secure in her position with the mission board, but not as secure in her relationships in the church community (where the Lawyers had a significant following among the people), McBeth revealed her dissatisfaction with Lawyer. She did so by questioning the influence of his class and race on his Christian commitment. According to McBeth, "[S]ending him [Archie Lawyer] to Joseph has been a very bad thing for him—I am afraid reviving his taste for the heathenism in which his eminance and power—and that of his crafty elder brother—had its roots, and in which he was a full grown man when the gospel reached him.[22] She deplored their "grand manner," was incensed by their popular following, and accused them of intriguing to return the reservation to its "heathen tribal relations" ruled by "an absolute Monarch [Archie] . . . [and] fettered by customs and superstitions" contrary to "civilization and progress."[23] McBeth accused Lawyer of trying to set up an "*ideal Church*" in Indian Territory, with himself as head and a hand-selected session of the elite members of the tribe, including

Chiefs Joseph and Yellow Bull.[24] When he returned to Kamiah, she accused him of similar machinations on the churches in that area. She wrote to the board, "[I] *like* him—but *trust* him *not*."[25] She recommended he be kept from assuming his own pulpit.

McBeth claimed that Lawyer's heritage was to blame. "I sometimes wonder that Jimmy and Archie are even as 'decent' men as they are knowing their inheritance of blood and training—their mother, too, was a big 'tewat'—or conjurer," she wrote in 1880.[25] She wished to discredit him by virtue of his behavior and his upbringing; the former could be changed, the latter could not.

Lawyer challenged his teacher by showing an independence of spirit that kept him beyond her control. The more she tried to circumscribe his activities, the more he defied her. She refused to endorse him for ordination.[27] Her sister, Kate McBeth, already recognizing "these Lawyers, how they do trouble people . . . so much intriguing & plotting for power," still believed her sister responsible for the rift between the two.[28] Kate McBeth attributed the difficulties to Sue McBeth's "jealousies & maneuvering to enthrone & establish Robert even at the expense of Archie."[29] While acknowledging that Sue McBeth had some justification for her assessment of the Lawyers, Kate wrote in her diary of Sue McBeth, "Was there ever an other human so ambitious to rule[?]"[30]

While McBeth maligned Lawyer by condemning his class and race, Lawyer tried to use McBeth's gender against her. He appealed to the male leadership of the church and sought solidarity among their numbers. To the mission board he wrote, "We heard something from Miss McBeth or Miss Kate I not know who was wrote to you about me. Dear brother before God I know myself I am alright and brother Mr. Deffenbaugh he knows me very well . . . I always pray to God and preached with the Gospel of our Lord Jesus Christ."[31]

As a fellow minister of the gospel, Lawyer turned to "brother Mr. Deffenbaugh," under whose care the entire mission had been from 1878 to 1888, to speak on his behalf. Deffenbaugh blamed McBeth for causing the rivalry because of "her prejudice [against the Lawyers] more than anything else."[32] Although he acknowledged Lawyer's penchant for display, slackness in sermon preparation, and domineering spirit, Deffenbaugh supported the erstwhile minister for his "standing fairly and squarely in the faith as it is revealed in God's Word."[33] He defended Lawyer's Christian commitment and his 1881 ordination, which made Lawyer a member of that fraternity of Presbyterian pastors to which McBeth could never belong.

It was Sue McBeth's undisguised preference for Robert Williams, whose status in the community came only from his role as minister and had no root in pre-Christian history, that most served to alienate Lawyer. To discredit Williams, Lawyer conspired with the agency police to have Robert Williams hauled into court on charges of adultery. The matter went before the all-male Walla Walla Presbytery and Williams, despite McBeth's pleas for his innocence, was charged with "imprudence" and forced to take a six-month leave of absence. He was reinstated five months later.

The presbytery, concerned over the evidence of strong factions within the Nez Perce community, endorsed Deffenbaugh's idea of splitting the Kamiah congregation in 1889 to allow Lawyer to establish the Second Presbyterian Church of Kamiah across the river from the first. Before Deffenbaugh could formally separate the congregation, Lawyer had taken half of the 280 members of the original Kamiah Presbyterian Church, built them a new church on land donated by one of the group, and "organized as they thought" their own church.[34] According to one study, the new church leadership "consisted of a disgruntled Native preacher who had not been assigned a church, a shamanness, the head of the agency police, two ex-subchiefs, and some relatives of leaders killed in the War of 1877."[35] Furthermore, this study noted that although the presbytery promptly recognized the new church organization, and it continued Presbyterian, the new church showed "a greater tendency to reassume aboriginal beliefs and practices traditionally classed as pagan by Presbyterians."[36] As a respected leader among his own people and an ordained minister, Lawyer ultimately had the upper hand over McBeth. Even then, McBeth tried to discredit the new church in the eyes of the board by pointing to its rather unorthodox beginnings to prevent Lawyer's hold on it, but to no avail.[37]

First Presbyterian Church of Kamiah, organized December 25, 1871, the oldest Protestant church in Idaho still in use. Photo by E. Jane Gay, circa 1890, courtesy of the Idaho State Historical Society, Boise. Photo number 63-221.258.

The split between Lawyer and McBeth, and ultimately, between the First and Second Kamiah churches, might have been avoided had McBeth been Rev. S. L. McBeth, as she had begged the mission board to consider her, if only "for an hour."[38] The distrust and recriminations may have sprung from legitimate concerns on both sides, but the inability to come to an amiable decision was exacerbated by the struggle for authority. In the end, Lawyer's ministerial status left him in a better bargaining position than McBeth. While she tried to frame the argument in terms of class or race, the issue became one of gender. Being "Miss McBeth" kept her from participating in the fray with Lawyer as an ecclesiastical equal so as to advance her own ends. Being Rev. Lawyer helped enable Lawyer to achieve his goal, however: a Native Presbyterian church perhaps more tolerant of Native ways.

The experiences of James Hayes and Helen Clark, friend of the McBeths and missionary to the Makahs at Neah Bay, Washington, paralleled those of Lawyer and McBeth. The two became locked in a double battle for authority that again encompassed issues of both race and gender. Although Hayes bent to the immediate desire of the missionary, his authority as a minister and his perseverance ultimately gained his objective of establishing a Presbyterian church of a more inclusive nature among the Makahs.

In the judgment of most missionaries, Hayes was a model Christian Indian. His teacher, Sue McBeth, claimed that "from the time of his conversion, until now, he has lived an exemplary life—And he has a great deal of good sense and judgment—though 'full of fun' as any boy. I have not a more promising pupil than James, nor any— save Robert, whom I trust more."[39] She even pegged him as her successor.[40] Her frequent praise of her "shaggy headed, broad shouldered six foot, youngest 'boy'" left little doubt of her anticipation of his potential as a preacher.[41] He did not disappoint her. Hayes became a shining light in the eyes of most missionaries. Amelia Frost, missionary among the Shoshones, regarded him as instrumental in building up the Native church. She wrote, "If you could have heard brother Hayes['s] Christ like counsel and advise you would realize what a help he was to me and to my Indian brothers & sisters in the church."[42] She welcomed his visits and he numbered her among his good friends. Hayes received rave reviews from the missionaries among the Shivwits, a Southern Paiute band in southern Utah. Following an evangelistic trip to their mission, Shivwit missionary H. M. Foster wrote, "My! Our Indians are anxious for him to come . . . they ask nearly every day how long till 'Jim Hay he be comin.' His work is still growing."[43] The white minister in the area, Charles Kilpatrick, was so impressed with Hayes's "cheery and genial ways" and the results of Hayes's ministry that they became friends and met together whenever Hayes was in the area. Kilpatrick joined Hayes on at least one of his preaching missions, and Hayes delighted in being with his "old friend" with whom he could talk and laugh.[44]

Missionary journals also touted the Nez Perce pastor. At the fiftieth anniversary commemorating the organization of the First Presbyterian Church at the Whitman mission in Oregon, Hayes apologized for the deaths of the missionaries. "As I stood at the graves of the mission, my heart wept. I was sorry that it was the red people who caused those graves to be made. But they have changed now and want to do better. Love us. Love Jesus."[45] The Christian press hailed him as "a St. John, [who] gave the most convincing proof that the blood of these martyrs had been the seed of the church . . . an object for those to whom seeing is believing."[46] Hayes was an exemplary Christian Indian who delighted missionary personnel, made good copy for missionary publications, and furthered the cause of Presbyterian missions. It was, thus, surprising to find him at odds with missionary Helen Clark.

Clark was a veteran missionary before she reached the Makahs in 1899. She had served first among the Iroquois in the East for a year or two and then among the Spokans in eastern Washington for six years. She rounded out her missionary career with just over twenty years among the Makahs.[47] A single woman, Clark had found meaning and significance through her work among American Indians.[48] She was a respected missionary and had earned high praise from the Spokan agent for her "handling" of the irascible Chief Lot. She was told that should she return to the Spokans she "might have the run of the school and the whole Res[ervation]."[49]

By the time Clark arrived at Neah Bay, her views of Indians were fairly well established. She had come to the conclusion that "the Indian needs oversight."[50] To her way of thinking, even the Indian pastor of an Indian church needed "backing and someone to engineer for him."[51] Like the missionary women of Pascoe's study, her gendered assumptions were that Presbyterian Indian women were "pure, pious Christian women" at heart, but American Indian men—even Christian ones—were suspect.[52]

On the strength of the reports she had heard about the success of Hayes's evangelistic trips among various tribes, Clark invited Hayes to visit the Makahs in 1905. Her expectations of James Hayes were spelled out in a letter to Kate McBeth, who had become teacher at the McBeth mission following the death of Sue McBeth, in 1893. Clark indicated that she was praying that "the Spirit may be poured out and his services blessed in the salvation of many souls."[53] But she also expressed her "hope [that] he will not push to baptize any one but those I think fit."[54] Neah Bay had become her domain and she had strong notions how best to run it.

Upon his first visit to Neah Bay in 1905, Clark received Hayes cordially; housed him and his co-worker, Nez Perce minister Mark Arthur; and even doctored them with cough medicine when they became ill. Hayes, who initially took the medicine with gratitude, eventually concluded that "hot water is better then every medicine."[55] The evangelistic meetings were apparently quite successful. Hayes baptized eleven Makahs and made plans to return the next year. He expressed concern, however, over setting up a church. He wrote, "I don't know yet what I do I organize the Church or not. But Lord knows what I do. And I don't say any thing about these Indians, because I don't know yet."[56] He gave no reasons for his hesitation. He and Mark Arthur had the authority, as ordained ministers, to petition the Seattle Presbytery for a church to be organized, and they had sufficient numbers to fill it.

Apparently, though, the Nez Perces received no encouragement from Clark, whose recommendation as resident missionary would have carried weight and increased the possibility of presbytery approval. Perhaps all agreed that the Makahs were not yet ready because they planned for Hayes to return the next year. Clark appeared to look forward to Hayes's second coming. She expressed some concern, however, at a lack of judgment on his part. Just before his arrival in 1906 she observed that "some he baptized last year have hardly darkened the church since."[57]

If they did not come out for services during the year, the Makahs came out in force during Hayes's visit. Hayes reported to McBeth, "we have very good service since I came here. So many Indians come out to our service and listen the Gospel of Christ."[58] He seemed to be on good terms with Clark who, he wrote, was going to buy some whale meat for him to sample.[59] He told of his conferring with Clark over the desire of two young men to attend McBeth's school, though the father of one of them was a leader of the Shakers. There was no indication that trouble was brewing between him and the missionary, unless the preface of his letter to McBeth, "to let you know about my work in this dark land," held multiple meanings.[60]

Despite the large crowds attending his services, however, Hayes baptized only four men and did not organize a church.[61] The record of the baptisms, kept by Clark, did not mention the name of the minister. Penciled in by another hand, however, were the words, "John Hanks [one of the baptized in 1905] says Rev. James Hayes was the minister."[62] And then, despite his work, Hayes's name fails to appear anywhere in the brief "Beginnings of Presbyterian Work at Neah Bay," sent in by Clark in 1924 as an introduction to the *Session Book of the Neah Bay Presbyterian Church.*[63]

It is difficult to discern from this distance what transpired between Hayes and Clark or why nearly twenty years intervened before his next visit to that part of Washington state. Clark gives some clues in her letter to her friend, Kate McBeth: "Your loan [of James Hayes] was much appreciated but I was sorry he went away disappointed and very much dissatisfied with me. His heart was set on forming a church but I could have told him before he came he could not do it. . . . Just now they are in the height of Shakerism and the others are wanted at the Indian dance in Seattle and in Portland and say they will be Christian when that is over."[64] While disagreement over establishing a church was the reason she gave, there are indications from her letter that her disagreements with Hayes went beyond this.

Clark and Hayes clashed over their acceptance of those who wanted to maintain a foot in both the Shaker church and the Presbyterian. Clark "objected to taking them into church fellowship unless they were willing to give up the Shakers."[65] Their devotion to Shakerism, she believed, could have been overcome: "If we had had a true revival as I hoped and prayed for . . . it would have shaken Shakerism to the foundation."[66] She apparently held Hayes somewhat responsible for not fostering a full-fledged revival to stamp out the Indian Shakers and for failing to assist her in keeping the Shakers out of the Presbyterian fold.

Hayes was more flexible in his view of the matter. Recognizing the interest of the Shakers in the Presbyterian meetings, he even suggested evening services to accommodate those who "have . . . dance about the same time when we have service in afternoon."[67] Although he gave little indication of his thoughts regarding Shakerism, he was willing to allow the opportunity for those in the Shaker church to join in the Presbyterian meetings. The limited number of baptisms he performed, however, shows that he was not as sanguine about church membership as Clark made him out to be. Clark, however, apparently objected to Shakers even attending the church meetings: "He wants me to have service in the evening but it is impossible. Some of the wild young people will not go home after it and the mission gets the name of leading them astray."[68]

Ultimately, Clark refused entry of the Shakers into the church meetings unless they were willing to forsake all association with the Shaker church. As she had written earlier, "[M]y call is 'come out from among them, be ye separate.'"[69] She noted that "when their fury is past they will be ready for a true church."[70] Despite Shaker claims of religious compatibility, their worship and ritual smacked too closely of traditional Native religious practices, and their claims to orthodoxy were too loosely defined for acceptance by the missionary. Her intolerance of the expression of cultural differences in worship, combined with her devotion to a strict orthodoxy, set her at odds with the Nez Perce minister.[71]

While Hayes also seemed to object to Shakerism as less than the true faith, he found it more compatible with Christian ideals than did Clark. He therefore seemed less offended by it and more willing to embrace those who practiced it, no doubt believing their exposure to Presbyterianism would, in time, win them over. In fact, many Shakers who claimed conversion to Presbyterianism entered the church when Clark's tenure was past and, in part, through the ministrations of the visiting Nez Perce pastors.[72]

It seems, however, beyond tactical differences, that Clark also felt personally rebuffed by the visiting minister. She accused Hayes of not appreciating her hospitality. She wrote McBeth that although Hayes "boarded with me [he] went out among the Indians whenever asked. He seemed much more grateful for anything they did for him then what I did."[73] She elaborated in another letter:

> James is fond of something good to eat with out doubt. He seldom got up before eleven for breakfast, dinner about four and his third meal when he came from church. I would not cook at that hour and gave him cold meat and fried eggs. He did not like fried potatoes told me his wife always fed them to the hens and cooked new ones. I told him I thought likely she did not pay $2.00 a sack for them.[74]

Clark seemed to have had the most difficulty with Hayes's gender. Although he was "a good man," she indicated her trouble with him by claiming that "unfortunately [he] does not know everything."[75] Her superior knowledge, however, was no match for his superior status in the church. Helen Clark's struggle "to turn [her] moral influence into authority" meant setting the terms of Makah church membership.[76] Hayes threatened her tenuous position because he had the power—available only to men as ordained ministers—to force her to submit to his version of church membership.

To protect her standards for church organization and to prevent loss of her authority in Neah Bay, Clark did not invite James Hayes back. Although she had claimed earlier that "all are pleased with James even the Shakers," and that the large number of Makahs that attended his services indicated their pleasure, she justified her position by writing to McBeth after his second visit that "the Indians have never asked for him again so I never asked his return," and concluded he was, in her estimation, "not suited to these Coast Indians as well as the interior ones."[77]

Further, Clark implied that Hayes's interest in the church was for personal aggrandizement and not for the care of souls. She attributed his liberal terms of church membership to a concern with making a good impression on his fellow ministers by trying to baptize large numbers. She did not see his position as a different view of the spiritual condition necessary to new members. Like all the white men in the church, she complained, he simply "wants to have 'a showing at Presbytery.'"[78]

Clark was not alone in her assessment of the men in the church. Her benefactor, Mrs. Caroline Ladd, president of the Women's Northern Pacific Presbyterian Board of Missions in Portland, on whose largesse Clark depended in order to remain in Neah Bay, reportedly did "not desire [the mission] to go into the hands of the men."[79] Confident of Ladd's support and apparently sharing her thinking, Clark confided in McBeth that "with all their boasts of consecrated men today it does not appear the church is over supplied yet. Would gladly get one in here but do not know where to turn for one who would not pander to the whites and forget his real mission."[80] She included Hayes with the rest of the churchmen for whom she had little use. Not only did he fail to see things her way, but also as an ordained minister, white or American Indian, he could have insisted on doing things his way. It was best to keep James Hayes at a distance, and she succeeded during her tenure in doing so. She also managed to keep out a formal church organization until her retirement in 1921, although she is credited with the founding of the church.[81]

While Helen Clark commended Kate McBeth's work in training Indian pastors, noting that she had "the real apostolic succession on the Nez Perce Res[ervation]," Clark would not allow the Native pastors to interfere with either her understanding of Presbyterian doctrine or her realm of influence at Neah Bay.[82] Although she decried James Hayes's suggestions, style of leadership, diet, and expectations of her, her main concern was with his potential to upset

her plans for a church established on her terms. Her insecurity on
this point was apparent by the agitation she expressed at not knowing just what Hayes was thinking, and, thus, what recourse he might
try to take. She complained of his silence to McBeth: "Tell me what
he has to say and I can explain. He talked very little."[83]

While it is clear that Clark won the immediate battle with Hayes,
it is not so clear that she won the war. Whatever Hayes thought of
her, he did not write it down. Nor did he return to Neah Bay until
after she left. He had plenty of other invitations to attend to without having to deal with a recalcitrant missionary. In 1924 the new
Neah Bay Presbyterian Church invited him for a visit. Hayes's return
to the Makahs was a warm one. As one church member remembered
it, they enjoyed Hayes's "jolly" nature, his love of singing and of sto-
rytelling. Many years later, this parishioner still recalled one story
Hayes told with great enthusiasm about a proud moose who was
humbled by a wren who took up residence in his nose. Hayes not
only enjoyed sharing his own stories but wanted to hear the Makahs'
stories and learn of their ways, even to their particular way of preparing and cooking salmon.[84] While at Neah Bay, Hayes also adminis-
tered the Lord's Supper, performed a baptism, accepted several into
church membership, moderated the session, and befriended many
Makahs.[84] His influence, it would appear, extended beyond his visit.
At the next session meeting, a leading Shaker, Lans Kalapa, and several others joined the church.[86] And the next year the Neah Bay
church called its first minister: Perry Ides, a Makah graduate of the
McBeth school.

The battle between James Hayes and Helen Clark for authority
cannot be understood outside the categories of race and gender.
Clark struggled with a cultural system that allowed her to achieve
positions of power because of her race but limited her authority on
account of her gender by denying her the access to church office
that males of both races possessed. In other words, as a white
woman, she could wield authority over Indian church members but
not over Indian ministers. Hayes, schooled by Sue McBeth, had
learned to respect the authority and power of women missionaries,
even as he learned to maintain boundaries around his own author-

ity. McBeth, recognizing his cooperative spirit, had also learned of his intransigence when "'bossed' by a woman." He would not tolerate losing respect among his peers, and she warned her sister, Kate McBeth, to avoid testing him. As she put it, "[H]e is a *man* and feels his manhood."[87]

This double struggle often led to frustration and conflict, and sabotaged constructive relationships between the missionary and the very persons most necessary to the success of her mission. Hayes found that, despite the status associated with his ministerial office within the church and the benefit of being male in Victorian America, it was not enough to guarantee the authority his ministry was supposed to give him. He was, perhaps, simply unwilling to put himself in the line of the missionary's fire. In the end, the mutual goal of establishing a Presbyterian church among the Makahs was hindered by their inability to work together.

The acrimony between Clark and Hayes was the extreme. The missionary women and Native men of the McBeth mission, despite clashes of will and personality, were able to achieve working relationships that ultimately resulted in the establishment of six Nez Perce churches with Nez Perce pastors. When Kate McBeth died in 1915 the mission board asked James Hayes if the Nez Perces would prefer a male missionary. He responded,

> If Miss Sue and Kate McBeth had been men, they might have had this land from here to the river fenced with hog tight wire, and the ground from here back to the hills covered with chicken houses, but they wouldn't have cared for our souls. But Miss Sue and Kate were women who cared not for land or money, but loved our souls, and that is the reason we, today, have the Bible, churches and have been redeemed from our sins. I've "finished my mind" and would rather have the women missionaries.[88]

The relationships between the Dakota pastors and their missionaries carried a different dynamic. The missionaries that took up the reins following the Dakota war of 1862 were neither female nor novices. They were the sons of the original missionaries, had grown

Nez Perce ministers with James Hayes, *third from right,* and missionary
Kate McBeth, *far left.* Photo courtesy of the Department of Interior,
National Park Service, Nez Perce National Historical Park, Spalding,
Idaho. Photo number NEPE-Hi-3305.

up among the Dakotas, spoke their language, and were ordained ministers. John Williamson was the son of Dr. Thomas and Margaret Williamson; he was eventually joined on the mission field by Alfred Riggs, son of Stephen and Mary Riggs. While some of the missionary assumptions of superiority and paternalism were evident in their relationships with the Dakotas, struggles for power and authority did not seem to be an issue. In fact, the very real possibility of Williamson and Riggs keeping Dakotas as Native helpers under their authority did not materialize. It appears that from the beginning the missionaries looked on their Dakota bothers as partners in mission and the effect was to encourage greater expansion of the Dakota churches and Dakota ministry.

The relationship between John Eastman and John Williamson was in marked contrast to that of Sue McBeth and Archie Lawyer. The record appears to be one of mutual friendship and trust. Although the one had trained the other, once ordained, Eastman was encouraged to run his church and lead his community at Flandreau while Williamson went on to a new mission field at the Yankton agency in Dakota Territory. Williamson did, in fact, follow Rufus Anderson's advice; while he stayed connected to the Dakota pastors, he worked alongside them, not over them, in the effort to take the gospel to new tribes.

John Eastman converted to Christianity with his father, Jacob Eastman, while incarcerated following the Dakota war of 1862. They both took the family name of Eastman from John's deceased mother, Mary Nancy Eastman, daughter of American painter Seth Eastman and his Dakota wife, Stands Like a Spirit. He began schooling in his late teens with missionary John Williamson at Bazile Creek in Nebraska, where the Dakotas were settled after incarceration. Of his first day at school with Williamson, Eastman wrote, "He knew me, although I had not seen him for over two years, and said, 'You are Manylightnings' son.' At that time I wore a blanket and lived according to the custom for Indian young men, but from that time on I began to go to school, and since then I have always been near to Mr. Williamson."[89] Although miles would separate them, the two would continue to be close, Eastman eventually becoming a teacher in the school.

Dakota minister John Eastman, *seated left*, and family. Photo courtesy of the William L. Beane Private Collection, Flandreau.

In 1869 he immigrated with his father to Bend of the River, later called Flandreau. It was there that the Eastmans and about twenty-five Santee families began their experimental Christian community.[90] According to a Dakota historian, these families "made the decision to take control of their lives, to leave the uncertainty of life on the reservation."[91] It was a reservation ruled by non-Christian Dakotas and subject to frequent and unsettling removals by the government. To stay meant "to fall in under the old chiefs," supported by Indian agents and "the old tribal arrangements and customs" they had rejected while in prison.[92] The Christian Dakotas left the reservation hoping to make new lives for themselves as free men and women.

According to Eastman's account of the founding of Flandreau, written up in an 1890 issue of the *Iapi Oaye*, the Christian Dakotas sought justice. They desired to live under the "kind of justice" of the white people, in which persons were treated as individuals and not made to suffer as a group for the crimes of one individual.[93] He implied that the community was weary of being judged by the misconduct of a few. Forfeiting tribal connections, therefore, they homesteaded according to the Homestead Act of 1862, the first Indians to try to do so.[94] One descendant claims that it was the Dakotas' "first positive step back to self-reliance."[95] They succeeded in establishing a flourishing community, despite difficulties with farming, drought, and a federal government that insisted on imposing an Indian agent over them.

Eastman's relationship with John Williamson strengthened as Williamson championed the community's goals of independence. Williamson succeeded at first in preventing an Indian agent from being installed when he agreed to be a special agent to the Flandreau Dakotas. Refusing to accept any pay, Williamson noted that his "dealings with the Indians were conducted on altogether a different plan from the common agency regime which is founded on the idea of their being paupers or wards. I treated them as men and citizens. . . . I encouraged them to do everything for themselves and on their own judgment. They felt themselves free citizens and rejoiced in their liberty."[96] Unfortunately, the government eventually insisted that

Flandreau be treated like any other American Indian community and placed an Indian agent over them in 1878.

Eastman's relationship with Williamson continued and eventually led to Eastman's decision to become a minister. He was ordained to the Presbyterian Church in 1876 and installed as pastor of the River Bend (Wakpaipaksan) Church of Flandreau (known as Flandreau First Church after 1879), where he served for thirty years.[97] He was also given oversight of the government school; joined his brother, Dr. Charles Eastman, in petitioning the federal government for promised annuities; and pastored at Good Will Church on the Sisseton Reservation for nine years. In the last few years of his life he served as general missionary to the Dakotas. In the way of his teacher, he worked for the church among American Indians and prepared others to do the same. He wrote to the mission board,

> You want to know about my work for our Savior Jesus. I am Pastor of Flandreau Church (Indian) since I am ordain to preach, that eleven years this fall. I have not large church *but church is growing in Spirilioul* I have *two young man candadete to preach* the Gospel of Jesus and Last five years some of my church member going out west and teach the Indians and *I am incouraged* by my work here.[98]

This letter was, in fact, a plea for the board to provide the means to support a new church that Eastman and the Native Missionary Society had helped to organize earlier at White River in Dakota Territory among the Lower Brules. Since the nascent church, however, could not afford to pay a "man to stay there and preach to them" regularly, Eastman requested support of a full-time preacher and a schoolhouse.[99] He ended his letter with "I hope you would come to see our Mission meeting and know more about our work among our own people. Your Brother in Christ Jesus, John Eastman."[100] Like his friend and teacher Williamson, Eastman had become a minister and a missionary, starting up new churches, training and ordaining ministers for them, and seeking means for their support, even as he continued to minister within his own church.

Dakota minister John Eastman, *center front with clasped hands*, and members of Good Will Church, Sisseton, South Dakota. Photo courtesy of the William L. Beane Private Collection, Flandreau.

Eastman and Williamson served together for years as fellow ministers and members of the Dakota Presbytery. This relationship allowed them to work with each other but also independently of each other. At his death in 1917, Eastman eulogized the missionary by noting that though he gave Williamson the respect due an older man, calling him "my father," he thought of him as his older brother. Eastman claimed that Brother Williamson "had compassion on the Dakota people . . . carrying his pack as they did theirs, oftentimes hungry and thirsty and tired, but he remained with them because he wanted to tell them the Good News."[101] Indeed, by the time Eastman gave this tribute to Williamson, nearly forty Dakotas had been ordained to the Presbyterian ministry, all within the missionary's tenure.

The relationships between the American Indian ministers and the missionaries to the Dakotas and the Nez Perces were enduring, often endearing, and not without tensions. Cultural, personal, and gender differences could and did sabotage both the friendships and the development of the churches, especially in the Northwest. The perseverance of the Native pastors did prevail, though, as they sought working relationships with the missionaries in their midst. The wise missionaries were the ones like Kate McBeth who recognized that the "Nez Perces want their own churches, with their own Native pastors and elders. This is well for them spiritually."[102] To the credit of both missions, Presbyterian Indian churches headed by ordained American Indian ministers were established. Clearly, Presbyterian Indians wanted their own churches and were willing and able to lead them.

CHAPTER 6

Indians in the Presbyterian Church

If they don't want me to preach I can get out, I'm a pretty good farmer yet.

JOSEPH COOK

In 1932 Nez Perce pastor Joseph Cook was serving the Fort Hall Presbyterian Church among the Shoshone and Bannock tribes in southern Idaho, where he and his family had been for four years. He was chairman of the Foreign Missions Committee of the local presbytery and getting ready to be sent as one of their representatives to General Assembly.[1] That same year Nez Perce minister James Dickson was at the Owyhee Presbyterian Church among the Shoshones of the Duck Valley Reservation in northern Nevada, where he and his family had been for the last three years. Nez Perce ministers were also serving the Nez Perce churches: Robert Parsons was at Meadow Creek, Mark Arthur was at North Fork and Stites, Harry Moffett was at the First and Second Kamiah Churches. Spokan minister Daniel Scott served the Lapwai (Spalding) Church, and Makah minister Perry Ides was over his home church of Neah Bay. All were members of their local presbyteries and served regularly on committees of presbytery and synod. Most had even attended General Assembly. All were graduates of the McBeth mission school, where

Mary Crawford was still teaching a Bible class of eight students when she received word that the mission school was being closed. She heard about it because John Frank, elder of the First Kamiah Church, was serving on the presbytery committee that, in effect, gave the school its death-knell.

Membership in the Presbyterian Church required participation at three levels beyond the congregational level. Each church belonged to a local presbytery and sent representatives from among the elected elders to oversee the working relationships and activities of its several congregations. All ministers were considered members of the presbytery and not of the churches they were called to serve. Committee membership was rotated among the ministers and representative elders and held responsibility for inspecting church session minutes and financial records, mediating disputes within and between congregations, deciding policies affecting the member churches, and ordaining new ministers. Several presbyteries composed the synod, which was charged with their oversight. Finally, the General Assembly, meeting annually, was composed of representatives of all church levels and congregations, and directed denominational doctrine and policy. All of these governing bodies were representative in nature with a paid executive over each.[2]

American Indian elders and ministers, despite the challenges of language and travel, took part in all levels of the Presbyterian Church, as well as maintaining relationships with the church mission board under which their missionaries served. Participation in these bodies, however, was never easy. Language difficulties, lingering paternalism, and discrimination plagued relationships within the church. Only with persistence, patience, and creativity, and sometimes with the help of missionary personnel, did the Native clergy begin to carve out a place for themselves in the larger church.

Dakota and Nez Perce ministers and elders served on standing committees at both the presbytery and synod levels, and regularly attended annual meetings of the General Assembly held in various places throughout the United States. In 1880 Dakota pastor Artemas Ehnamani was commissioned by the Dakota Presbytery to attend the General Assembly, replacing a white missionary for the first time.

John Eastman attended in 1882, and from then on Dakotas served regularly as commissioners.[3] The Nez Perce also began attending this annual gathering of American Presbyterians, although less frequently. When in 1892 General Assembly met in Portland, Oregon, Robert Williams, James Hayes, and Robert Parsons attended, with a number of others accompanying them.[4] James Hayes went on to become a commissioner at several other meetings.

Participation at the synod and presbytery levels was more common and even included opportunities to host these meetings.[5] Synod and presbytery meetings offered Dakotas and Nez Perces opportunities to see "the great world beyond" the reservation, as well as to gather with family and friends, so these events often took on a festive air.[6] In 1925 the Nez Perce were especially proud to entertain the entire Synod of Washington, 150 men and a few women, for a week at Talmaks.[7] Missionary Mary Crawford boasted to the Board of Indian Commissioners in 1924 that the "Nez Perce ministers take their places in the presbytery beside the white ministers, are made responsible for the work of their own churches and report direct to presbytery."[8]

Full participation was difficult, particularly for the Nez Perces, who did not have their own all-Indian presbytery. As late as 1927 Crawford admitted in a letter to a friend, "Because they are as yet limited in the use of the [E]nglish language, they have not held the important offices [of the presbytery] but we are hoping that some time they will be able even for that, but they now vote and take part in the meetings and serve on committees."[9] By 1932 Crawford was pleased to report that Nez Perce elder John Frank had been made the vice moderator of the Synod of Idaho.[10] It had taken fifty years, but the Nez Perces seemed to be taking their place in the larger Presbyterian Church.

If Native leadership in the larger church was slow in coming, at least members of the synod and presbytery had encouraged participation from the beginning. To the Nez Perces, membership in the Walla Walla Presbytery had been, in fact, quite advantageous. The presbytery proved a useful ally to the Nez Perces when it backed the ministers who sought to prevent church members from

joining the "heathen" camp during the July Fourth activities, effectively ending those celebrations in the late 1890s. The presbytery
had also helped in the formation of the Second Kamiah Church
by endorsing its establishment when the Lawyer faction was ready
to leave the church in 1891.[11] The presbytery also supported Meadow Creek pastor Enoch Pond when two disgruntled elders locked
him out of his church in an attempt to evict him from his pulpit in
1892. They demanded the elders unlock the church doors or face
excommunication.[12]

Dissatisfied members of a congregation could find recourse
through an appeal to the presbytery. The Lapwai (Spalding) Church
turned to the Walla Walla Presbytery over the issue of the appointment of a pastor. A church without a minister could be assigned one
by the presbytery "after consultation with the session."[13] The "stated
supply," as he was called, served only a year at a time and moderated the session meetings, if asked to do so by the session.[14] As stated
supply of the Lapwai (Spalding) Church, Peter Lindsley apparently
decided to trim the church rolls, even attempting to remove an elder
or two.[15] A wary church turned to the Walla Walla Presbytery and was
reminded that the elders on the session retained control of the
church and not the minister.[16] The presbytery also indicated that it
"did not approve of Rev. Lindsley being made Pastor," and he should,
therefore, no longer receive the funding provided by the mission
board.[17] Disapproval "with [Lindsley's] way of doing things," led to
his censure.[18] When the session moved to renew Lindsley's call as
stated supply despite the opprobrium of presbytery and mission
board, Lindsley, apparently put out over the whole thing, declined.[19]

Relationships with members of the larger church made through
involvement with the governing bodies of the Presbyterian Church
could also prove beneficial to both Native and non-Native churches.
Kate McBeth noted that members of the Walla Walla Presbytery usually attended the annual Talmaks campmeeting. She commented
that the "white brethren" were as much a "help and encouragement" to the Nez Perces as they were helped themselves by "sitting
among our devoted worshipping people" and seeing the "zeal and
earnestness" of the Christian Nez Perces.[20] At a synod meeting in

Walla Walla Presbytery meeting at Kendrick, Washington, circa 1903. Photo courtesy of the Idaho State Historical Society, Boise. Photo number 2808.

1896, a delighted McBeth reported that both Nez Perce and white members took part in the devotional exercises and "Christians looked into each other's faces, sat together at His [the Lord's] table, and felt that we were all children of the same Father, travelling towards the same home."[21] Meetings of the presbytery and synod offered opportunities for Native and non-Native clergy to get to know one another and so strengthen their Christian ties. Mary Crawford noted in 1916 that when the usual crowd of Nez Perces in attendance at the fall synod meeting was not there, they were noticeably missed by their white brethren.[22]

The advantages of being a part of the presbytery were at times, however, outweighed by the disadvantages. Since ministers were members of the presbytery and not of the churches, they had to submit to the discipline of the presbytery, as in Robert Williams's case. When suspended for "imprudence" in 1890, Silas Whitman was assigned as pulpit supply. When Whitman was taken to task by the presbytery for trying to dictate sessions' actions and excommunicate Williams, he chose simply to walk out. Rebuked by the presbytery for acting too independently of the church session, Whitman took such offense that he "resigned at once, [and] took to the mountains for a hunt."[23] The presbytery was acting at the request of the congregation, but the offended minister remained disaffected except for a short stint as minister among the Spokans.

The Nez Perces were further disadvantaged by the fact that Native voices, muted by language differences, were easily lost in the deliberations of presbytery or synod. Furthermore, the power of these bodies over ministerial relations, access to church records that were inspected annually (required of all member churches in the presbytery), and judicial authority over the churches at times seemed intrusive to Nez Perce pastors. To guard against unsolicited intervention of presbytery and missionaries, the Nez Perces resorted to the formation of an innovative and unique Presbyterian body: the Joint Session.

The Joint Session began in the 1890s as an informal gathering of the ministers and elders of the Nez Perce churches. Unlike any other body within the Presbyterian Church and without legal standing, it nevertheless evolved into a vital organization to strengthen and protect the authority of the six Nez Perce churches in the larger Presbyterian Church.[24] The Joint Session coordinated the various affairs of the churches, including the annual weeklong evangelistic meetings held at each church during the winter months, evangelistic trips among other tribes, and even allocation of funds for Nez Perce activities. In time the Joint Session began to represent the voice of the Nez Perces. For example, by 1927 ministerial students had come under the jurisdiction of not just their own session but of the Joint Session, which oversaw their schooling and presented them to the presbytery for examination.[25] In 1916 the Joint Session received a request for evangelistic services from the Nespelems in north-central Washington. After they "talked and prayed over the call," the Joint Session decided to send "two of their number, a minister and elder to look over the field and report on the situation."[26] When the mission board closed the Fort Hall mission near Pocatello, Idaho, in 1931 the Joint Session voiced its disapproval as a body.[27] When in 1938 the mission board wanted to place a "young girl, untrained for religious work and inexperienced, among our people as our missionary," the Joint Session sent a letter of protest to the board, though it went unheeded.[28]

Mary Crawford noted that though the Joint Session had no legal standing in the church, its usefulness to the Nez Perces was its work as a "counseling body." She wrote that, with its "complete understanding of their own work, it has often been able to solve many of their problems in a wise way."[29] She should know. By the time of her tenure as missionary it was also serving as a disciplinary body. Apparently she was about to be called on the carpet for holding a youth meeting during a church prayer meeting. She defended herself by confessing that she thought she had permission and was, after all, simply working with the church to provide activities to keep the youth in the church. She went on further, to remind the Joint Session that, though willing to meet with the Joint Session, she was not under their jurisdiction as she was a member of the Presbyterian Board of National Missions.[30] It was, no doubt, a fact of which the Joint Session was all too well aware.

The Joint Session was a thoroughly indigenous body formed to meet the special needs of the Nez Perce community, where divisiveness could mean losing control over churches, already unduly susceptible to the power of outsiders.[31] In time, the power of the Joint Session over the churches caused one observer to call it "an expression of the tribal nature of Nez Perce Presbyterianism." He claimed that in practice, the Joint Session lessened the "significance of actual Presbytery membership for the Indians."[32] While the deliberations and decisions of the Joint Session affected all of the churches, and while it held the separate churches accountable to one another, the Joint Session also gave Native church leadership greater clout and authority in the larger Presbyterian Church because it resonated with the timbre of Nez Perce voices.

The Dakotas' situation was similar to that of the Nez Perces. The white ministers, who clearly outnumbered the American Indian ministers of the Dakota Presbytery, were intent on reaching the growing numbers of white settlers. This was not the Dakotas' concern. In John Williamson's words, the Dakotas were being "overlooked, and their claims crowded out."[33] The Dakota churches, however, resorted to another tactic to protect their authority and autonomy in the larger church. In 1867 Williamson petitioned the presbytery for a separate all-Indian presbytery for the Dakota ministers and their three churches. The petition was granted, and in 1868 the Dakota Presbytery was split into two. The one retaining the name was all-Indian; the other, renamed Mankato Presbytery, was made up of all-white churches.[34] The new Dakota Presbytery, encompassing the growing number of Dakota Indian churches, eventually spanned eight reservations in three states.[35] It became one of the few nongeographical presbyteries in the Presbyterian Church.[36] The Dakota Presbytery provided a place for the Native churches to grow, for Native pastors to thrive, and for a Native identity to be retained within the Presbyterian Church.[37]

Non-Native forms and structures were imposed on the Dakotas, but "[e]ven as the Dakotas accepted White programs they adjusted them."[38] The establishment of the Dakota Presbytery—which was able to establish new churches, mediate differences between them,

Members of Dakota Presbytery in 1886: *front row, left to right,* Rev. John P. Williamson, Rev. Louis Mazawakinyanna, Rev. John Eastman, Elder Adam Wakanna, Rev. George Wood, Jr., Rev. John Flute; *back row, left to right,* Rev. Daniel Renville, Rev. Isaac Renville, Rev. Charles Crawford, Elder Grey Buffalo (who may also have been known as J. Taniyawaste or Jacob Sunkawaste), Elder Samuel Hopkins (later ordained), Rev. David Greycloud (or Pierre La Pointe). Photo courtesy of the William L. Beane Private Collection, Flandreau.

and ordain pastors—gave Dakota churches greater power than the Nez Perces churches, whose Joint Session carried no legal weight.

The Dakota Presbytery also gave the Dakotas greater opportunity to preserve their values and do things their own way. As the senior ordained pastor of the new all-Indian Dakota Presbytery, John Renville took his turn as moderator of that body.[39] He helped to create an institution that, on the surface, differed little from the non-Native presbyteries that surrounded it. According to the minutes, members examined candidates for the ministry, formed committees to govern and decide important issues, and discussed matters brought before them for response. However, closer scrutiny shows some subtle differences. For one, the meetings were usually held in Dakota, although missionary John Williamson as stated clerk of the Dakota Presbytery from 1867 until 1915 usually took down the minutes of each meeting in English for synod's approval.[40]

With the power to decide the direction of their churches, the Dakotas at times surprised missionaries and other churchmen with their initiative.[41] For example, at a meeting of the presbytery in which only Indian ministers happened to be present, the members discussed "the best mode of the evangelism of the masses."[42] They decided that it should be the responsibility of each of the churches to send out elders for "Sabbath appointments in destitute neighborhoods and on these tours to take with them one of the brethren who were not officers."[43] This concern for others of their tribe eventually flowered in the suggestion of Native pastor David Greycloud that the Dakotas support their own missionary efforts, apart from the Presbyterian Board.[44] To that end, in 1876 the Dakotas organized the Wotanin Washte (Native Missionary Society), chose a three-member board (which included missionary John Williamson as treasurer), and collected $240 to send Greycloud as missionary to the Standing Rock Agency.[45]

Enthusiasm for the Native Missionary Society remained strong. Williamson called it the "crowning glory of the Dakota Mission" and claimed it was fully supported by all the Dakota churches and especially the women's societies. By 1886 the churches were raising $1,100 annually, more than a dollar per church member from people who had little or nothing extra to give.[46] By 1917 the Dakota churches were sending out as many as seven missionaries at a time and raising $3,000 a year to support them.[47] New churches were added to the presbytery through these efforts, including the Wood Lake (Mdecan) Church and the Pahacokama Church among the Canadian Sioux in Manitoba.[48]

Perhaps the most telling evidence of an American Indian stamp to this presbytery, though, is not immediately visible in the written record. Two or three generations after its founding one missionary witnessed distinctive patterns of ministry: "non-vocal presbytery meetings (where the long silences waiting for the second to a motion would make a White man itch), feasts, wakes, kinship loyalties, a ministry trained by experience, unconcern for money and book-keeping, etc."[49] There are only hints at these practices in the minutes. For example, a general lack of enthusiasm for the Presbyterian emphasis on written documentation of all meetings can be seen in an entry for early adjournment because "statistical reports had not all arrived."[50] It is also found in frequent entries stipulating that churches without "suitable books for Records, having their only records in small memorandum books or slips of paper," were encouraged to put their books in order.[51]

Other practices, such as preference for a ministry trained by experience, however, surface only in a study of those licensed or ordained. Generally, candidates were licensed to preach (the first step toward ordination) upon satisfactory completion of an oral examination and the preaching of a sermon before the presbytery.[52] Seldom were candidates required to take an approved course of instruction. In 1889, however, that began to change, as the minutes reveal that a candidate was not approved "on account of his limited education, having never had any training in any but the Dakota language."[53] It was also noted that a "large minority of Presbytery favored his being received as a candidate."[54]

By 1891 the Dakota Presbytery records indicate that three of the five candidates had attended Pierre University and add that the "Presbytery is diligently working to advance the standard of its native ministers."[55] It is also clear, however, that the presbytery continued to ordain ministers without a college education, and that the bottom line was whether or not they had proven themselves good ministers. As a churchman at Flandreau put it, the church always "help[s] the ones who belong"; and it became the experience of the Dakota churches that their survival depended on belonging to their own presbytery.[56]

The Dakotas and the Nez Perces found that more than English proficiency and having their own organizational bodies was needed to assure an American Indian presence on equal footing with their non-Indian peers in the larger church. By the 1920s they also needed a formal seminary education. In 1891 the General Assembly of the Presbyterian Church, concerned with the proliferation of new churches in the West, instructed the presbyteries to recommend a college degree and at least two years of theological training "under some approved divine or professor of theology."[57] If a college degree was not possible, the church recommended three full years of theological training. By action of the General Assembly in 1922 an examination in the English Bible was also required.[58] By the 1930s the Presbyterian Church was moving toward requiring all candidates for ministry to complete a college degree and two years in a "recognized Presbyterian theological seminary" or "an educational equivalent, judged satisfactory by the presbytery."[59]

The standards of the Presbyterian Church no longer allowed Native pastors to receive theological education while performing ministry. This hurt the Nez Perces more than the Dakotas, who were already pushing their ministerial candidates toward college and seminary training. As early as 1899, Dakota Alfred Coe was ordained with degrees from Pierre University and Omaha Seminary.[60] The Dakotas were thus better situated than the Nez Perces to meet the requirements of the larger church as it standardized its ordination requirements. The McBeth mission school, however, failed to meet even the minimal requirements for educating Native pastors.

Perhaps because they themselves were not seminary trained, the women of the McBeth school were less inclined to encourage their students to pursue a more formal education than the one they provided. When in the 1920s overtures were made by presbytery and synod that the McBeth school was no longer adequate for training Indian ministers, Mary Crawford took umbrage. While Crawford acknowledged that the Nez Perce pastors did not have "the broad education a white man has," she pointed out that they passed the same presbytery exams as all other pastors, although still exempted from the Greek and Hebrew requirements. They also made "splendid pastors and have the advantage of knowing Indians and knowing how to deal with them as a white man never can."[61]

Crawford further defended the work of the McBeth school when it was suggested that it might be better to move the students to the Presbyterian college, Whitworth, in Spokane, Washington, several hours from the reservation. She raised the question, "What would one hour of Bible study each week be to these men? Here they get twenty hours of actual work, not counting their study hours."[62] She was not completely opposed to a college and seminary education; but as the college separated them from the support of the Nez Perce community, students who had attempted a Whitworth education had not succeeded in completing one.[63] As did her aunts before her, Crawford believed that most of what the ministers needed to know they could learn in her classroom and in the pulpit.

The changes in the Presbyterian Church as it entered the twentieth century were magnified by both political and economic events that had a tremendous impact on American Indians. The appointment of John Collier as commissioner of Indian affairs in 1933 heralded nearly a complete reversal of the government's American Indian policy, with goals of Indian self-government and religious freedom replacing an emphasis on cultural assimilation. Coinciding as it did with the economic downturn of the Great Depression, the Indian New Deal struck a double blow to Native Presbyterians. Taken together with the new ordination requirements, Native ministers had to wonder if the Church and the government were conspiring against them.

The Wheeler-Howard bill, or Indian New Deal, was not well received by most Christian Indians or missionaries. By seeking to return to the tribes the right of self-determination, the government hoped to reverse the deleterious effects of wardship and restore an element of self-respect while preserving a vestige of Indian culture. The Dakotas were split in their response to the bill, some communities such as Sisseton rejecting it and others, such as Flandreau, passing it.[64] To the Christian Nez Perces, however, it was a step backward: an attempt to return them to "heathen" influence and chieftain rule.[65] They responded with a petition to repeal the act and remove John Collier from office. They believed that the bill would bring back "the old religious ceremonial with it's immorality" and "destroy every church, break up evey home and desbauch every Indian boy and girl." It would, in effect, "close the mouth of every minister, missionary and Christian worker if they were not allowed to denounce SIN."[66] Furthermore, they believed that they would lose their rights as American citizens if returned to self-rule and the resurrection of tribal chiefs. Enough non-Christian Nez Perces agreed that the Nez Perces succeeded in rejecting the Indian Reorganization Act that would have placed them under the regulations of the bill.[67]

Even a visit from John Collier to the reservation failed to move the Christian community. Arguing that Dr. Somerndike of the Presbyterian Board of National Missions was in favor of the bill, Collier tried to pressure the reluctant churchmen. Native pastor Harry Moffett responded that at the last meeting of General Assembly in Cleveland, Ohio, Moffett had had an opportunity to talk with Somerndike and change his opinion about the bill. The Nez Perce churches were, however, chagrined when several disgruntled church members came out for the bill, and Somerndike reverted to his former opinion and endorsed the bill.[68]

While the American government was seeking to redefine its relationship with American Indians, the Presbyterian Church was similarly reorienting itself. The decision to close the McBeth mission school could be viewed as an attempt to bestow greater freedom and autonomy on Indian ministerial candidates by allowing them to train on par with non-Native candidates. To the Nez Perces loyal to the McBeth School, however, it came as a blow. "What are they trying to do to us? Do they want us to worship like the white man?" asked one Nez Perce.[69] When Sam Watters failed to pass the presbytery's examination for licensure in 1929, Dr. Leland C. McEwan, a member of the committee and pastor of the Lewiston Presbyterian church in Lewiston, Idaho, took the matter up with the synod in Seattle, suggesting that the "McBeth School had outlived its usefulness."[70] Although the aging missionary Crawford and graduates of the school disagreed, the Nez Perce pastors were not able to fend off the church's decision and the school was closed.

Speculating on the many reasons why the Presbyterian Board of National Missions, the presbytery, and the synod would want to close down the school, Mary Crawford wrote,

> I hear many surmises as to why the mission has been closed. Some say the Board does not want a fundamentally trained leadership among the Nez Perces, a thorough gospel training, others that the Board does not want missionaries with minds of their own who will have something to say about how the work is conducted on the field. Some say and a goodly number, that Dr. Matthews [on the Synod of Washington National Missions Committee] and Dr. Thomson [Synod of Washington Executive] are responsible for its closing, and still others say that we women are under MAN RULE and that we will lose out in the end. The Nez Perces say that the Board is putting an English education above the study of the Word of God.[71]

While all of these may have played a part in the decision, what most outraged Crawford was that the decision was made without consulting her or the Nez Perces "who are most vitally interested and who have an official relation to presbytery."[72] Either the larger Presbyterian Church still considered their American Indian brothers in the faith unable to make wise decisions, or they saw them as far more capable and wanted to free them of a backward education. The former would seem to be the case according to their treatment of Perry Ides, of the Makah Reservation in Neah Bay, Washington, and a graduate of the McBeth school.

In 1925 Perry Ides became the first, and only, Makah minister of the Neah Bay Presbyterian Church. The retirement of missionary Helen Clark allowed Ides, one of the first converts and a trusted translator for Clark, to settle into his role as pastor with relative ease.

His teacher, Mary Crawford, commended him over a white minister at Neah Bay for she believed him "far more capable of handling
the situation and taking charge of the work at Neah Bay . . . [and]
he knows the language of his own people, is related to the Quilleutes
[another West Coast tribe] and understands them."[73] At his ordination in 1925 he was lauded for "passing a very creditable examination and making a fine impression on Presbytery."[74] Despite his
many qualifications for leading the church at Neah Bay, though, it
remained a mission church, and Ides had to deal with women missionaries throughout his ten years as minister.

With Clark's departure and Ides's promotion to pastor, the
dynamics at Neah Bay had changed. Ides was inclined to take command of a situation. When examined by the Seattle Presbytery, he
asked permission to stand for his oral exams, explaining that, "if I
sat down I would get nervous, and knew I would not if I see all the
earnest faces."[75] After successfully completing his examinations, missionary Ruth Lee, who expected him to plunge right into the job,
found he had a mind of his own.[76] As Ides wrote to Crawford, "I kind
of disappointed them when I told them I wasn't ready to take up
active work right at present, and Miss Lee's face change for a while,
and I told them of the trip we are planning to take."[77] He was not
going to let the missionary's expectations interfere with his own
plans. He assured Lee, however, "I am ready to help in every way,"
which seemed to mollify her.[78]

Ides preferred the relationship he had with Lee's successor, missionary Lulu Ruth Floyd, who he wrote to Crawford "is a good help
mate for me. She minds to her own business."[79] Ides was not adverse
to the support of the larger church and the missionaries who were
sent to Neah Bay, but he preferred it when they left him to be the
minister of the church while they worked in the community. He did
not believe he needed their oversight to run his church and was fortunate that all were women who did not stay more than a few years
and so could not secure a hold on the community, as Clark had.

Ides led the church at Neah Bay for ten years, two-thirds of his
support coming from the Olympia Presbytery. The church's membership of about thirty climbed to nearly one hundred by 1935.

That fall the church dedicated a new church building, and a month later, according to the church records, the Board of National Missions appointed a new missionary to oversee the work: Rev. William S. Thorndike. The Presbyterian Church was not convinced that Ides could manage without help.[80] As the first male missionary to the mission, Thorndike also came as the first ordained minister. It must have soon become clear that the church was not large enough for two ministers. Ides was encouraged by the mission board to take disability due to blindness in one eye and to go into retirement.[81] Ides had no means to fend off the intrusion of one from the dominant society, however well meaning the intruder.[82]

For two years Ides dropped out of any official capacity in the church, according to the church session minutes. He did not, however, drop out of the church. In April 1937 he was listed as the superintendent of the primary Sunday school classes.[83] In December 1939 Ides approached the session with a bill for fifty dollars, "which he said was due him for salary at the time of his retirement as pastor," and he continued to preach on occasion.[84] He remained on the Christmas committee for a number of years, with the elders and their wives, and the missionary in charge.[85] He did not simply fade away. He remained a staunch member of the Makah community, serving on the school board and in other avenues of leadership. Perry Ides outlasted three subsequent white ministers and continued as a member of the church until his death in 1958, revered by both Indians and whites for his Christian faith.[86]

Forced into retirement herself by the board three years earlier, Mary Crawford rose to the defense of her former pupil. In a series of letters to friends, board members, presbyteries, and synods, she addressed the injustices being dealt American Indian pastors in the Northwest by the Presbyterian Church. Her poignant letters, written even before the closing of the school in 1932 and her death in 1946, summarize some of the difficulties the Native pastors faced as a part of the larger church. Although pensioned, she remained at her home in Lapwai on friendly terms with the Christian Nez Perces and was eventually buried among them. Admitting to her own hurt at being forced into retirement by the church, her major diatribes concern the thinning ranks of Indian ministers and the inability of the Presbyterian Church to work with the remaining pastors to address the loss. Crawford's criticisms were aimed primarily at the failure of the church to appreciate the legacy of sixty years of mission work among the Nez Perces, who for forty years had been supplying their own churches with pastors while providing pastoral care for over half a dozen other Indian churches as well.[87]

Crawford's overarching theme is that the church had discriminated against the Native ministers for years by refusing to treat them like other members of the clergy. She pointed out that their salaries had never equaled that of their peers. In 1937 Nez Perce pastors' salaries were raised from $360 to $500 annually for overseeing two churches, still less than half the national average.[88] She was painfully aware that younger men could not be asked to live on such meager salaries. Mark Arthur's son told his father, "We can't all be preachers or we could not live. Daddy, you do the preaching and I'll make the living."[89] Crawford also alleged that the needs of the Native ministers had always taken a backseat to the needs and wants of white ministers.[90] She was especially alarmed at the number of white ministers by 1938 who were being placed in Indian pulpits: Ides had been replaced at Neah Bay; James Dickson had been replaced at Owyhee on the Duck Valley Reservation; Daniel Scott, a Spokan, had never been allowed to supply his own churches and then had been removed from the mission station at Taholah, Washington, all to make way for the "white man."[91] She cited the discouragement of younger potential ministers who asked, "What is the use of us taking up the ministry, when they give our churches to white men?"[92]

The closure of the McBeth ministerial training school, according to Crawford, was the ultimate insult to the Nez Perces, who were not even consulted in the decision. Not only did it cut out the possibility of immediate training for replacement of aging ministers, but furthermore, current ministers trained at the McBeth school would be scorned for having received an inferior education.[93] Despite the successes of the Native ministry under the Nez Perces, it seemed to Crawford that they were still not considered full members of the Presbyterian Church.

Ministers and students of the McBeth mission school, circa 1924: *front row, left to right*, Rev. Joseph Cook (Nez Perce), Tom Peterson (Nez Perce), Rev. Daniel Scott (Spokan); *back row, left to right*, Rev. Harry Moffett (Nez Perce), Rev. Perry Ides (Makah). Photo courtesy of the Northwest Museum of Arts and Culture/Eastern Washington State Historical Society, Spokane. Ms. 17, Box 6:26.

Unfortunately, little record remains of the pastors' responses except as expressed by Crawford. When a disheartened Joseph Cook told Crawford that since the church seemed to have little appreciation for Native pastors perhaps he should return to farming, he spoke as one of a waning number of McBeth trained ministers. By 1935 Mark Arthur, James Dickson, and Perry Ides were retired or nearly so. Only Harry Moffett and Daniel Scott were left to serve the six Nez Perce churches while Cook remained at the Fort Hall mission church. Less than half a dozen Nez Perces would be ordained in the next seventy years.

The Presbyterian Church has always guarded against entrusting ordination to "weak and ignorant men" or those "insufficient" or "unprepared" to assume the "sacred office."[94] Once American Indians had received training and been ordained, they were considered sufficiently qualified and thereby were required to take their place among the clergy at all levels of the church. The Nez Perces participated in the work of both presbyteries and synods through service on selected committees, hosting some meetings, and occasionally attending General Assembly. The Dakotas, in contrast, carried on nearly the entire work of the Dakota Presbytery as only a few non-Natives were ever members at one time.[95] In the hands of Native pastors the Dakota Presbytery became a presbytery of, by, and for the Dakotas, with nearly constant representation at both synod and General Assembly levels. The number of ministers eventually ordained, seventy to date, over that of the Nez Perces' twenty-two, indicates the effectiveness of having an all-Indian presbytery.[96] However, numbers alone fail to tell the whole story. While both Nez Perces and Dakotas often showed resourceful and creative ways of being part of the larger church, they could not always be assured of a welcome. In the end, it was the faithfulness and persistence of the Native pastors, regardless of their reception, that kept them in the Presbyterian Church.

CHAPTER 7

Native and Christian

I am glad when they dressed like Dakota people again. But I did not like how they behaved.

JOHN EASTMAN

When James Hayes preached in English to the white people of an eastern church in 1927, his audience did not question his authority on things Nez Perce. Despite his western-style suit and short hair, his halting English and swarthy complexion testified to them of his past as "a wild heathen boy" of the White Bird band of the Nez Perces.[1] But he also spoke as an ordained Presbyterian minister. When he claimed that "Jesus Have power to save to every creature," even the Nez Perces, they accepted his authority by virtue of his being an ordained minister in the Presbyterian Church.[2]

Hayes addressed his audience as Dr. James Hayes, having received an honorary doctorate of divinity degree from Whitworth College the previous year. He was an educated, multilingual, Presbyterian Indian pastor. In an era of general confusion over boundaries of race, culture, and even nationality, Hayes and the other Native pastors often defied easy categorization.[3] They generally found this fluidity an advantage in negotiating their identity within social, political, and religious communities. Bureaucratic institutions, however, were less sanguine about such flexibility and tended to define and defend boundaries of race, gender, and culture. For that reason, despite their best efforts, Native ministers frequently found themselves trying to convince church officials that being Nez Perce or Dakota did not compromise their being Presbyterian, and in fact enriched the larger church even as the faith enriched Native lives. They chose various ways, however, of being both Native and Christian.

Nineteenth-century understandings of race and culture were held hostage to ethnocentric and racialist interpretations during the lifetime of James Hayes.[4] The westward movement earlier in the century had heightened awareness of and exposure to non-European peoples and cultures living within the boundaries of the United States. In an effort to quantify and classify the emerging diversity of peoples and cultures, scientists, anthropologists, and social scientists often conflated biological and cultural markers to distinguish differences.[5] They identified race as a trait that determined "character as well as physiognomy."[6] Culture and behavior were believed to be products of race that could be used to identify race.[7] In the wake of Charles Darwin's work, this confusion of the biological and the cultural was exacerbated by the common evolutionary belief that human societies progressed from the savage to the barbaric to the civilized. In essence, the "wild heathen Indian" was at the bottom of a ladder that ascended to the Christian Euro-American, whose cultural achievements evidenced the superiority of Western civilization.[8]

The assimilationist thinking that drove much of American Indian policy throughout this era was based on the assumption that a person was or was not Indian. Although an individual could move from one position on the evolutionary ladder to another (either up or down), one could not keep a foot in two camps. What Hayes and other Native pastors illustrated, however, were identities that refused to be essentialized. In trying to convince both political and religious institutions that one could, in fact, be both an American Indian and an American citizen, both Native and Christian, they chose different ways of maintaining those identities, although it was never easy.

John Renville, an older contemporary of James Hayes, testified

Mark and Mary Arthur, *left*, James and Fannie Hayes, *right*, and children at home. Photo by E. Jane Gay, courtesy of the Idaho State Historical Society, Boise. Photo number 63.221.308.

to the complex issues often involved in negotiating one's identity, and thus one's relationships, within the Presbyterian Church. His correspondence with the American Board indicates a growing identification with the Dakotas even as he also identified more and more strongly with the Presbyterian Church. Two conflicts emerged in the course of this movement: one with the mission board over his claim to being both a missionary to the Dakotas and a Dakota; the second with the government over his claim of being both a Dakota and an American citizen. In both cases, his battle was to convince others that the categories of missionary and Dakota, American citizen and Dakota, were not mutually exclusive. The tendency of both the Presbyterian Church and the government to racialize these categories and bind him to one or the other, however, made it difficult for Renville to convince either of them of who he was.

Renville's early life clearly reflected his ease within several cultures. Having welcomed the missionaries from the ABCFM in 1835, Joseph Renville, with his Dakota wife, raised John and his siblings in a bicultural Christian community.[9] Of mixed-blood, John married a white woman, Mary A. Butler, and was engaged as a government teacher for the Dakota mission when the Dakota war broke out.[10] Held captive by Little Crow's people, along with other mixed-bloods and whites, upon his release he served with a number of his relatives as scouts for the federal government. His job was to bring in other American Indians still at war. Renville also served as an itinerant preacher, licensed by the Presbyterian Church, until he was ordained in 1865 as an evangelist who proved to be "eloquent and mighty in the scriptures."[11]

It seemed obvious to the warriors of Little Crow's band that Renville was part of the dominant society. And yet, in letters to the missionaries, he stressed his identification with the Dakotas. That identification became stronger during his years as their pastor. Prior to his ordination, his wife Mary noted his desire to "spend his life among the Dakotas."[12] Shortly after his ordination, she wrote of his suitability to serve as their spiritual guide because of his "perfect knowledge of the customs [and] languages of the Dakotas and their entire confidence in his integrity."[13] Renville's own letters reflect a growing identification with those he served. His early letters, written while living in the largely white communities of St. Anthony and Beaver Creek, Minnesota, speak of meetings held, baptisms performed, and visitation "among the Dakotas."[14] After spending a summer on the reservation, he wrote, "I intend Providence permitting to [go] to my people again soon and in fact see a great necessity of my living constantly among them . . . for are not this people my people[?]"[15]

Renville's identification with the Dakotas was at once sincere, flexible, and strategic. It expressed his loyalty to a people among whom he had been raised and from whom he was descended. His identity as a Dakota also legitimized any requests he made of white churches, governments, and mission boards to ameliorate the needs of "his people." Who knew their needs better than one who lived among them and spoke their language? Yet when it was necessary, he could as easily claim identification with the dominant society. When he pleaded with the mission board to intervene on behalf of Christian Indians over the selection of an Indian agent, he wrote both as a Dakota, whose grasp of the situation could not be questioned by those far away, and as a Christian missionary, for whom Indians were another people. In a Dakota voice he wrote, "Could I speak English like you I would say to the men of your nation rise up [ac]quit you like men. . . . If necessary I would go to Washington with you, though you know I am not bold but for my Master. I think he could strengthen me in the inner man and you could be tongue for me."[16] At the same time he wrote that because of this situation, he was "being cut off" from "all Treaty stipulations" because he was an American citizen, and "at the mercy of the Indians [who] were they so disposed they could drive me off the Reserve any time."[17]

Renville's ability to identify with others melded with Paul's admonition to the Christians to be all things to all people that by all means some may be saved.[18] This attitude, however, placed Renville in a precarious position. To the mission board he decried the leadership of both the Indian agent assigned to the Sioux, "an honest man but he is not a keeper of the Sabbath," and Gabriel Renville, the "Ruling Chief (my own cousin) a man of mixed blood although its understood at Washington that he is of a full blood Dakotah."[19] Renville described his cousin as "a man opposed to all religious movements and [who] adheres to heathen practices[.] I don[']t mean by this that he has Medicine dances but that he has three wives. . . . I don't think such a man should be the leader of a Nation unless he leaves off those things."[20] Renville showed himself clearly in the Presbyterian camp by his condemnation of the activities of his cousin as well as the agent who failed to keep the Sabbath. He also indicated his disdain for the behavior of his cousin who, because of his upbringing, like Renville's own, should know better than to continue in a lifestyle the church considered irreverent and the dominant society saw as objectionable.

Renville's challenge stemmed from the ambiguities that plagued cultural intermediaries: as one with a foot in two worlds, he at times could find a home in neither.[21] He looked to the Presbyterian Church to secure his position within its fold and lessen the strain. With some anxiety, he wrote to the board, "[H]ow can I stand my ground cut off from the Dakotah tribes entirely still should I desire it I cannot I am told become a member of the American Board[?] I don't understand this[.] If you have any small document that could be sent by mail will you be so kind as to forward it if it contains the qualifications necessary or instructtions matter as to what is necessary to become a member of the American Board."[22] He could not have been happy with the reply from the American Board's secretary, Selah Treat: "When you speak of becoming a *member* of the Am. Board, I presume you mean, 'Become a *missy* of the Am. Board' like Mr. Riggs. We do not appoint any *missionaries* from the people among whom they labor."[23] Although the board expected Native pastors to do the evangelistic work that defined a missionary, and often gave some financial support, only non-Natives could actually be members of the ABCFM. In essence, Treat found the roles of ABCFM missionary and American Indian mutually exclusive.

Renville's predicament was heightened by the conflict over his citizenship. He was not only a Christian pastor among a "pagan people," but he was also a Dakota who had taken a homestead, renounced tribal affiliation, and become an American citizen.[24] While Renville had no difficulty with being both Dakota and an American citizen, the Indian agent wanted him to be one or the other. Renville's mixed-blood status contributed to the apparent confusion of the agent, who seemed anxious to use Renville as an example of a "civilized" and industrious Indian even as he deprived Renville of treaty benefits.[25]

Renville's dilemma was not in deciding who he was, a Dakota Christian minister, missionary, and American citizen, but in having to convince others of it. He seemed able to move back and forth among the Dakotas and the white society with the ease of a practiced cultural broker. Others, however, tried to confine Renville to one society or the other. His cousin Gabriel Renville, the ruling chief, although also of mixed-blood, was allowed to settle in the domain of his choosing. He dressed as Renville did, had been educated as he had been, and yet chose to adhere to certain Indian customs and claim an Indian identity, which Washington, D.C., was willing to allow him. Because Gabriel Renville chose to identify with the Dakota culture, religion, and community in which he also had strong biological ties, white society more readily accepted his choice. John Renville, by claiming to be Presbyterian, missionary, Dakota, and American citizen, blurred the constructed categories and met resistance.

Renville, in the end, maintained his mixed identities. Two years after petitioning the board to become a missionary, and still complaining about his cousin's practices as ruling chief, Renville wrote, "Can Government think that we as a Nation can or will submit and be content long under such a Chief[?]"[26] Without relinquishing his American citizenship, Renville lived on the reservation, gratified that the new agent, Moses Adams, was a Presbyterian minister and former missionary who "accepted the invitation to join with us at Communion . . . the first Agent to join in worshipping God and that in our language."[27] Renville's identity as a Dakota and a minister allowed him friendship with and access to Agent Adams.

When pushed to define himself, it seems Renville became more Dakota. But on closer scrutiny, this was not simply a matter of being forced into one camp because of rejection from another. Renville, even as he moved toward greater acceptance by the white community in becoming a Presbyterian minister, continued to move toward greater identification with the people he had chosen to serve. He went from occasional preaching trips, to summers among the Dakotas, to finally settling among them permanently. His letter of 1873 was written from Ascension, on the Sisseton Reservation where he pastored the Native church, with 145 members. Fortunately for the Dakotas and the Presbyterian Church, Renville continued to defy pigeonholing. He continued to serve as a minister active in both the local and the larger church, and a missionary among his own people until his death in 1903. In so doing, he not only strengthened the faith of the Christian Dakotas and kept them in the Presbyterian Church, but did so as one of them.

Another Dakota, John Eastman, followed Renville's example in providing stable and capable leadership to the Native Presbyterian community. But while Renville moved from the margin of Dakota society closer to its interior, Eastman moved from its interior to the margin to embrace both Native and Christian identities. He held on to what he saw as Dakota virtues by encompassing elements of white culture that would allow him to preserve and protect those virtues. Limited by the reservation's boundaries, Eastman sought escape by assuming enough of the dominant society's identity to gain the privileges and freedoms it offered those who were not American Indian. He believed that the more elements of white society the Dakotas adopted, the less different they would appear to the larger society, and the more they would be free to live their own lives. Insofar as Indians could adapt to the prevailing order and be at peace with it, they could avoid the excesses of both cultures and the interference of either society. For this reason he would claim, "It is good to live in the manner of the white man, however difficult it may be."[28]

Eastman's identity with the Native Christian community was formed in the aftermath of the Dakota war of 1862. When he and his father converted to Christianity while in the prison camp, Eastman was fourteen years old. He took his maternal grandfather's name, but it was his grandmother's name, Stands Like a Spirit, or Stands Sacred, that most defined his life. His quest of the holy, and the influence of the missionary John Williamson at that impressionable age, led him to become a Presbyterian minister. When he and his father joined the Christian Dakotas who immigrated to Flandreau, he was seeking the freedom to be himself. Eastman did not want to be held captive to the tribal identity of the reservation.

Dakota ministers: *front row, left to right,* John B. Renville, Charles Crawford, John Eastman; *back row, left to right,* unidentified, missionary John Williamson, Daniel Renville. Photo courtesy of the William L. Beane Private Collection, Flandreau.

He wanted a chance to stand on his own and be respected for who he was.

If the move from the reservation was a step away from his tribal identity, John Eastman went even further once in Flandreau. Granted U.S. citizenship when he homesteaded in 1869, he became a Republican. As he told an eastern newspaper, "We pay taxes just as our white neighbors do. We go to the caucuses and conventions and affiliate with the political parties of our preference . . . We vote, and we don't sell our votes any oftener than white people do theirs, while we don't buy votes so often as the white men do; so I guess we average up with them on the point of civic virtue."[29]

Eastman used his political identity to appeal to the Indian Rights Association for their support on the basis of his voting Republican. Having finally succeeded in acquiring a new federally funded Indian boarding school in Flandreau, it appeared that Eastman's influence over it (he was appointed "disciplinarian" by the superintendent, who Eastman claimed was a "moral and Christian gentleman") was in jeopardy.[30] Citing his concern that "some of the Catholic Democrats in this county . . . are trying to remove us when there is a change in the administration," Eastman pleaded with Herbert Welsh, president of the organization, to intervene in Congress on behalf of the Flandreau Indians.[31] He reminded Welsh that "of course, the Indians here are all Republicans since they became citizens for the last twenty four years."[32] Eastman used his party affiliation to gain support for his cause, even as he had done with his pastoral association when he approached the mission board to finance a Native missionary to Devil's Lake.

Eastman's identity as a Presbyterian and a Republican was based on his choice to worship with the one and to vote with the other. His decision to adopt certain cultural practices identified as white, however, did not translate into Eastman's becoming any less an American Indian. Nor did he intend that it should. He judged Indians in terms of their good or bad behavior, not their racial or cultural identity. He disapproved of behavior that alienated Indians from whites or was unbecoming to Indians. The former must be avoided for Indians to live peaceably with their more numerous neighbors, the latter was unthinkable because it would reflect on all Native peoples. When Eastman visited some Dakotas from Flandreau who were living in St. Paul, Minnesota, he wrote in the *Iapi Oaye*, "I am glad when they dressed like Dakota people again. But I did not like how they behaved."[33] His criticisms were twofold: that they were consumed with making money, and that they encouraged the young to dance. In the same way he criticized the Ghost Dancers, whose adherence to "the Dakota way of doing things . . . causes people to act as if they were crazy."[34] As he saw it, "in their conduct toward the white man, they bring dishonor to their name."[35] These actions, Eastman believed, did not contribute to American Indian virtues, nor enhance Indian-white relations.

John Eastman's identity could not be conceived of apart from his relationship to other Indian people. A descendant of chiefs, he identified himself as a "traditional man."[36] To be able to be who he was, however, entailed being independent enough of both his heritage and his present associations to make his own decisions. This meant living in a society where individuals could be self-sufficient even as they lived together in community. John Eastman, however, never sought to become white. His sense of who he was remained Dakota, and his purpose was to allow his people to live Dakota and Christian lives according to their own understanding. "We traditional men," he wrote to his countrymen, "are indeed of the human race."[37] It was therefore imperative that they "live together as fellow human beings," at peace with all peoples.[38] It was what both his Dakota upbringing and his Christian religion taught and it was what his experience confirmed. Harmonious relations with those in the dominant society, in whose institutions he also participated, were necessary in order to practice those virtues he most valued.

Confusing as this might be to an outsider, Eastman had no difficulty adjusting to elements he valued in both cultures. When asked in a 1903 newspaper interview if there was a race problem in Flandreau, which by 1900 had a large white population, he replied, "No. . . . Perhaps that fact is largely responsible for the progress our people have made."[39] He then noted that the Dakotas of Flandreau lived in houses like white people, farmed nearly as well as they did, paid taxes just as they did, and voted in elections as did their white neighbors. As he told the reporter, "Nobody ever thinks of raising the race line in schools or in politics. The white people accept us, apparently, as entitled to the benefits we pay for."[40] Although this could appear too rosy a picture, it reflected Eastman's understanding of the community. He believed that the acceptance of their neighbors allowed the Dakotas to seek self-sufficiency and not be subject to others.[41] Eastman was active in the Presbyterian church and the Dakota Presbytery and a civic leader of Flandreau who pursued funds and favors of the federal government for the community. He remained a staunch advocate for the benefits of Christianity, American citizenship, and membership in the Republican party insofar as they gave comfort and independence to his people. His identity, forged of all these elements, made him the multifaceted person he was. He saw no conflict between being a good Christian and a good Dakota.

Just as Renville and Eastman seemed at home with both Dakota and Christian identities, Dr. James Hayes appeared at ease as a Christian Nez Perce. As he addressed his eastern audience in 1927, his dress, demeanor, and message spoke eloquently of his decision to become a Presbyterian. He claimed that "I don't think you need any thing in your Home but we need Jesus every one of us," and, furthermore, this "Jesus [h]ave power to save to every creature."[42] Hayes, like those to whom he preached, believed that there was power in the one they followed, and that that power was for any who claimed it. By virtue of his heritage, however, to those in attendance Hayes was also unquestionably Nez Perce, and his words to them held unmistakable pride in that identity. Speaking of the virtuous reception of Lewis and Clark and the desire for God's word, Hayes showed strong resolve to remain a part of that community. He was a good Christian but also a good Nez Perce.

Renville, Eastman, and Hayes refused to allow Indian Christians to be essentialized. They actively participated in carving out meaningful lives that embraced multiple ways of being both Native and Christian. If their identities were "mixed, relational, and inventive"—as, according to James Clifford, historian and cultural anthropologist, all identities are—they still respected certain boundaries.

Rev. John Eastman, *left,* and Nicholas E. Hale, *right,* of Culbertson, Montana. Photo courtesy of the William L. Beane Private Collection, Flandreau.

Their definition of Christian did not transgress those boundaries. Hayes suggested that a good Christian was also a good Nez Perce, and Albert Moore went further by claiming that a good Nez Perce *was* a good Christian. In fact, as a minister in training, he went as far as to say that the Nez Perces were Christians before the missionaries came to tell them about Christ.

Moore put Christian faith to the test. He dissolved all distinctions between the Dreamer religion of which he had been a part (known as "ipnu' tsililpt)" and Christianity. Recognizing some similarities, although loath to take advantage of them to encourage Christian conversion, the Presbyterian Church drew the line at suggesting that all religions were equally beneficial. In his attempt to blur the boundaries between the Christians and the Dreamers, Moore placed himself outside the bounds of the church.

Moore came in to the Presbyterian Church from the Dreamer religion as a young man. A mix of Christian and older Nez Perce beliefs, the Dreamer religion evolved from Smohalla's visions during the 1850s.[43] The Dreamer religion had gained adherents during the uncertainties and privations of the treaty era. Like other revitalization movements, it called for a rejection of non-Indian dress and culture and a return to life as it had been lived prior to the arrival of white people. Relying on dreams, rituals, and ceremonies influenced by Catholic worship forms and older practices, Dreamers hoped to rid the land of the white man. For Moore, its eclectic nature opened him to exploring the Christian faith, although it does not appear that the Dreamer religion typically served as a bridge from indigenous religions to Christianity.

For Moore, the teaching of the Presbyterian Church paralleled what he had learned among the Dreamers: "We were told to believe in 'good place in heaven.' When you die you go up there if you live right in this world, keep your friendships with your enemies and love everybody. . . . A real Indian is true and faithful; he never lies to you. He does not lie, does not steal, does not love another man's wife . . . same kind of teaching."[44]

Moore equated the two religions because they preached what appeared to be the same morality. He discerned no clear difference between them because both "real Indians" and Christians did not lie or steal, and both rewarded good behavior on earth with the promise of heaven. His confusion was understandable but also problematic. When he made this statement, Moore had studied Christian theology for several years and concluded that there were more similarities between the two religions than differences.

Moore had not only joined the church but also spent three years at a Bible college in southern California in the 1910s preparing to become a minister. When he pointed out to Mary Crawford that Christianity was "[j]ust like old 'ipnu' tsililpt,'" he learned one significant distinction: it was not as tolerant of differences.[45] She offended the minister in training by calling the Dreamer religion "savage," to which he responded by "stepping out" of the Presbyterian Church and the ministry.[46]

Hayes and Moore both found in Christianity parallels to previously held social mores as well as to certain conceptual beliefs. They valued the qualities of kindness, goodness, and honesty. They believed in heaven as the place where good people go after death. They recognized that the Nez Perces were a people worthy of God's attention and acceptance. Hayes and Moore separated, however, at this point. Moore maintained, in light of their similarities, that the Nez Perces "were Christians before the White man came," and, therefore, Christianity brought nothing new. Hayes, in contrast, claimed that although the Nez Perces acted like Christians, they were not. One could not, he claimed, "go to Heaven without the gospel of Christ and without atonement of Jesus Christ."[47] Despite the similarities, there were definite differences; and to deny such would make conversion unnecessary and Christ insignificant. Neither Hayes nor the church was willing to do that.

While the debate over what it means to be a Christian is better taken up by the theologians it is clear that Hayes and the Native pastors held to the view that Christianity encompassed both ways of living and ways of believing. And although there was some latitude in expressions of faith, there were boundaries that Native pastors held to as rigidly as non-Natives. These beliefs also informed their identity and kept them faithful to a church in which they were not always graciously received. Native Christian ministers, by virtue of their theology, made it clear that being Nez Perce or Dakota did not compromise their being Presbyterian. And, indeed, they could share a common bond with white brothers and sisters whose belief in Christ empowered, comforted, and enabled them to meet the vicissitudes of life.

Christian Indians have been called, "heretical, inauthentic, assimilated, and uncommitted."[48] The conclusions of older studies still seem to hold sway over public opinion: "[t]o convert the Indians of America was to replace their Native characters with European personae, to transmogrify their behavior by substituting predictable European modes of thinking and feeling for unpredictable native modes."[49] However, an estimated 10 to 25 percent of American Indians today still claim Christian identity and face the difficulty of asserting that "'Christian Indian' is not an oxymoron."[50] A growing number of Native Christians themselves are beginning to speak out and address these issues. There is strong evidence from nineteenth- and twentieth-century, as well as contemporary, Native Christianity that Indian Christians continue "drawing strength from living traditions and [are] actively constructing their own meaningful, viable religious identities" as Christian Indians.[51]

Although, as Native Christian James Treat admits, Native Christianity is "both historically and culturally problematic," attempts to classify and draw boundaries between the Christian and the Indian may be misguided.[52] Cultural change is much more complex. Conversion was not simply a matter of exchanging one lifestyle or worldview for another. Much of Native life lived on in Christian Indian communities creating new forms of worship, new ecclesiastical structures, and new relationships. Many Christian Nez Perces and Dakotas established meaningful and congruent lives in the midst of conflict and change. Largely through the agency of Native pastors and their congregations, Native Christianity today is a vital source of Indian spirituality.

The letters, sermons, and records left by Native pastors and their churches, as well as the missionary records and testimony of Native Christians, help to explain how Indian communities, institutions,

and cultures have changed and endured. Native leadership, traditional values of friendship, and kinship relationships were all instrumental in building Christian congregations. By maintaining their
identification as Indians, receiving ministerial training in the Nez
Perce or Dakota languages in their home communities where leadership was validated, and with the authority granted by ordination,
a Native clergy emerged that was capable of providing strong leadership for those congregations. Together with the missionaries,
Native pastors actively shaped and directed Indian Presbyterianism
among the Dakotas and the Nez Perces.

Indian leaders stressed what compatibilities existed between
Native and Christian cultures and constructed a church upon these
perceived similarities. The Nez Perces and Dakotas valued generosity, hospitality, and care of kinship ties before they were Christians.
As Christians they continued to teach and practice those virtues.
When James Hayes needed a coat to attend McBeth's school, Robert
Williams gave him his best one—the one intended for presbytery
meetings. Williams quoted the scriptural admonition of giving to
those in need, but his parents and grandparents had taught him
that a good Nez Perce was generous. When Hayes needed a home,
Williams took him in. Hospitality was both a Christian duty and a
Nez Perce tradition.

Not only did Indian Presbyterianism reflect and build on Native
cultural forms, but perhaps more important, it also created new
ones. Native ministers and their congregations developed unique
blends of Presbyterianism and Indian ways. John Renville, Archie
Lawyer, and many others took the Dakota and Nez Perce love of
music into their churches. They wrote Christian lyrics to Native
tunes and put Indian languages to Presbyterian hymns. They turned
prayer meetings into extended song services and evangelistic meetings into community gatherings. They used church offices to recognize and honor the deserving. They even created new structures
neither Presbyterian nor Indian, such as the Nez Perce Joint Session
and the proliferation of church committees.

Native Presbyterianism was most successful when it entered Nez
Perce and Dakota worlds through Nez Perce or Dakota means.
James Hayes came to Christianity through the preaching of another

Nez Perce, Robert Williams, and James Dickson through the preaching of James Hayes. Mark Arthur came into the Presbyterian church because of a spiritual visitation such as he had experienced on a vision quest. Fish Hawk also had a vision that propelled him toward the church. He came to understand and express his conversion in terms of a shamanistic healing ceremony. The most important skills of Native ministers were their ability to speak to Native concerns, to interpret Native existence in terms of Indian and Christian concepts, and to provide for their people continuity, meaning, and hope in changing circumstances. They served to indigenize the church and make it their own.

Native Presbyterian ministers came from varied and diverse backgrounds, but they shared the flexibility of seasoned cultural brokers. Pastors forged their individual identities as they worked among Native and non-Native, Christian and non-Christian, mission personnel and people not associated with the mission. Each minister had to define his identity in the context of shifting social circumstances and larger church bodies that were often expressed in racialized and gendered relationships. They also defined themselves and their Christianity in very personal ways that evolved over time. John Renville, of Dakota and French heritage, chose to identify more strongly with his Dakota parishioners as his ministry developed among them. John Eastman, as a founder and minister to the community of Flandreau, chose at the same time to identify with white neighbors in order to live as a good Dakota. James Hayes and Archie Lawyer, in working with the women missionaries in their midst, identified themselves in gendered terms and with other Presbyterian ministers as they worked to maintain authority among their people. These Native pastors grappled with and negotiated their identities, but they did not seem confused by the struggle. That nearly all served as ministers their entire lives and built vital and enduring congregations is testimony to the fact that they found congruence in being both Indian and Christian leaders.

Between the ordination of the first Dakota as a Presbyterian minister in 1865 and the end of the McBeth mission nearly seventy years later, almost sixty Nez Perces and Dakotas were ordained. Trained in the midst of their culture and the communities that nurtured and legitimized their leadership, and ordained as ministers to meet the spiritual and material needs of their congregations, they brought many others into the church and began new church organizations. The James Hayes Presbyterian Church among the Shivwits of southern Utah, named for the Nez Perce pastor that fostered its growth, is but one testimony of the efficacy of ordained Native ministers even when they operated beyond the boundaries of their own people.

Another seventy years have passed since the closing of the missionary era. The 1930s heralded significant changes for Native ministry in the Presbyterian Church. While the Collier years expanded opportunities for Indians to engage in alternate forms of leadership and wage earning, the depression narrowed the possibilities for service in the churches due to shrinking funds and the constriction of pulpits. In a concern for standardizing the requirements for ordination, the Presbyterian Church made seminary mandatory for all clergy. This policy further restricted access to the ministry for many American Indians. Since the 1930s only half a dozen Nez Perces have become Presbyterian ministers, and less than thirty Dakotas have been ordained.

This crisis in the church has prompted the organization of another churchwide study. The Presbyterian General Assembly Special Task Force on Native American Ministries has been directed to determine the causes of the paucity of pastors and to suggest possible remedies.[53] Undoubtedly there are lessons to be learned from the history of American Indian clergy and their congregations that should not be ignored by the church or by historians. The long and vibrant history of Indian Christianity has much to add to our understanding of cultural change and vitality and confirms the crucial role of indigenous leadership in shaping and affirming Native Christian identity. Missionary John Williamson recognized this when he praised his colleague in ministry: "Rev. John Eastman the present pastor is one of our most talented Indian preachers, and has done an excellent work for the church. There are more young men in this church capable of taking hold of Christian work than in any other, and it is principally due to his influence. And so it happens that not only we, but the Congregationalists and Episcopalians come here for the most of their helpers."[54] Eastman's words were simply an invitation that still remains: "I hope you would come to see our Mission meeting and know more about our work among our own people."[55]

Presbyterian Native Pastors Trained at the McBeth School, Ordained from 1879 to 1927, and Churches Served

NEZ PERCE PASTORS

Robert Williams (1879)

1879–96	Kamiah First

Archie Lawyer (1881)

1885–86	Tutuilla
1887	Lapwai/Spalding
1888	Deep Creek
1889–90	Spokane River/Deep Creek
1891–93	Kamiah Second

William Wheeler (1883)

1883–84	Tutuilla
1885–86	Wellpinit
1887–1900	North Fork
1901	WC*
1902	North Fork
1903	North Fork, Stites
1904–1908	Stites
1909	Kamiah Second
1910–12	Stites

| 1915 | North Fork |
| 1918 | Tutuilla |

Silas Whitman (1883)

1883–84	Tutuilla
1885–86	Lapwai
1887	WC
1888–91	Wellpinit
1892–94	WC
1895	Wellpinit, Spokane River
1896–1905	WC

James Hayes (1884)

1884–86	WC
1887–94	Tutuilla
1895–96	WC
1897–27	Kamiah First

James Hines (1884)

1885–86	North Fork
1887	Deep Creek
1888–97	WC
1898	Lapwai
1899–1909	WC

Peter Lindsley (1884)

1885–86	Deep Creek
1888–93	Lapwai
1894–96	WC
1897	Lapwai
1898–1900	WC
1901	North Fork
1902–1907	WC
1908–12	North Fork
1913–15	Meadow Creek

Enoch Pond (1885)

1887	Wellpinit
1888–92	Meadow Creek
1893–1903	WC
1904–1906	North Fork

Moses Monteith (1893)

1894–1907	Kamiah Second
1908–1909	WC
1910–16	Kamiah Second

Robert Parsons (1894)

1893–1909	Meadow Creek
1910	WC
1911–13	Stites
1914–15	WC
1916–17	Stites
1918–20	Kamiah Second
1921–24	North Fork
1925	Lapwai
1926–27	Meadow Creek
1928–30	Stites
1931–32	Meadow Creek

Mark Arthur (1899)

1900–20	Lapwai
1921–25	Kamiah Second
1926	WC
1927	North Fork, Stites
1928	WC
1929	Meadow Creek
1930	North Fork
1931–33	North Fork, Stites
1934	Stites
1935–36	Meadow Creek, Stites

Eddie J. Conner (1908)

1908–1909	Tutuilla
1910–11	Meadow Creek
1912–18	not listed (Methodist)
1919–22	Tutuilla

James Dickson (1908)

1910–14	Tutuilla
1915–16	WC
1917	North Fork
1918	Stites
1919	North Fork, Stites
1920–25	Stites
1926–28	Tutuilla
1929–33	Owyhee
1934–35	WC
1936	North Fork
1937	North Fork, Lapwai
1938	WC
1939–40	Kamiah First, Stites

Elias Pond (1914)

1914–15	Stites
1916–25	Meadow Creek
1926–29	Lapwai

Harry Moffett (1925)

1925	North Fork
1926–30	Kamiah Second
1931–34	Kamiah Second, Kamiah First
1935–38	Kamiah Second
1938–41	Kamiah Second, Meadow Creek
1942–52	Kamiah First, Kamiah Second, Meadow Creek, Stites
1953	Kamiah First, Kamiah Second

Joseph Cook (1927)

1928–43   Fort Hall

NON–NEZ PERCE NATIVE PASTORS

Perry Ides (Makah, 1925)

1925–35   Neah Bay

Daniel Scott (Spokan, 1925)

1931	Lapwai
1933	Lapwai, Stites, Meadow Creek
1934	Lapwai, Stites, North Fork
1935	Lapwai, North Fork
1936	Wellpinit
1937	Meadow Creek, Stites
1938	Meadow Creek, North Fork
1939–50	North Fork, Lapwai

SOURCE: *Minutes of the General Assembly of the Presbyterian Church in the U.S.A.* Philadelphia: Presbyterian Board of Publication, 1865–1869, 1884–1955; New York: Presbyterian Board of Publication, 1870–83.

*WC indicates "without church."

Presbyterian Dakota Pastors Ordained from 1865 to 1930, and Churches Served

John B. Renville (1865)

1867	Scouts Camp
1870	Lac qui Parle
1871–77	Ascension
1878–79	Ascension, Good Will
1880–99	Ascension
1900–1903	WC*

Artemas Ehnamani (1867)

| 1867–82 | Pilgrim/Ohnihde |
| 1883– | Pilgrim (Congregational) |

Titus Ichaduze (1867)

1867–75	Pilgrim
1876	River Bend/Flandreau
1877	WC
1878	Hill
1879–82	WC

Solomon Tankansaiciye (1868)

| 1870 | Long Hollow, Kettle Lakes, Drywood Lakes/Good Will, Ascension |

1871–77	Long Hollow
1878–89	Pahacokamya/Middle Hill
1890–97	Buffalo Lakes
1898–1908	Pajutazee (Pajutazizi)
1909	WC

Daniel Renville (1870)

1871–76	Good Will
1877–88	Brown Earth
1889–95	Crow Creek
1896	Wood Lake/Mdecan (Bdecan)
1897–1900	Crow Creek
1901–1903	Wood Lake, Raven Hill/Kangipaha
1904–1905	Crow Creek
1906	WC
1907	Crow Creek
1908–1909	WC

Louis Mazawakinyanna (1870)

1871–72	Kettle Lakes, River Bend
1872	Kettle Lakes
1873–75	Mayasan
1876–77	Kettle Lakes, Buffalo Lakes
1878–84	Buffalo Lakes
1885–88	Buffalo Lakes, Long Hollow
1889–95	WC
1896–1905	Lake Traverse

William[son] O. Rogers (1871)

1872	River Bend, Buffalo Lakes
1873	River Bend, Buffalo Lakes, Kettle Lakes
1874–75	River Bend
1876–77	WC
1878–83	not listed (Episcopal)
1884	Wood Lake
1885	Wood Lake, Hill
1886	Wood Lake, Long Hollow

1887–93	Wood Lake
1894–1902	WC
1903	Buffalo Lakes
1904	Wood Lake
1905–18	WC

David Greycloud (1873)

1874–75	Kettle Lakes, Buffalo Lakes
1876–89	Mayasan
1885–87	Mountain Head

John Eastman (1876)

1877–79	River Bend/Flandreau
1880–1906	Flandreau
1907–14	Good Will
1915–21	WC

Joseph Irondoor (Tiyopamaza) (1879)

1879–84	Long Hollow

Isaac Renville (1879)

1879–86	WC
1887–1918	Long Hollow

Henry Tawa Selwyn (1879)

1880–87	Yankton
1888–94	Yankton, Hill, Cedar
1894	Yankton, Hill, Cedar, Greenwood, Heyata
1895–1912	Yankton

Charles Crawford (1881)

1880–81	Good Will
1882–83	Good Will, Hill
1884–1905	Good Will
1906–19	WC

194
APPENDIX B

John Flute (1888)

1889–97	Mountain Head
1898–1900	Wounded Knee/Johnson Memorial
1901–1902	Ascension
1903–11	Mayasan
1912–13	Pajutazee
1914	Kangipaha/Raven Hill
1915–19	Kangipaha, Mdecan
1920–21	Mdecan
1922–23	Kangipaha, Mdecan
1924	Flandreau, Pajutazee
1925	Flandreau, Conkicakse, Cedar
1926	Flandreau, Conkicakse

Joseph Rogers (1888)

1888–98	White River/Mniska (Miniska)
1899–1900	White River, Red Hills
1901–1902	Crow Creek
1903	Crow Creek, Conkicakse
1904–1910	Buffalo Lakes
1911	WC
1912–13	Cansutaipa/Oswego
1914–19	Upsijawakpa/Redeagle Memorial
1920	Flandreau
1921–28	Upsijawakpa

Samuel Hopkins (1889)

1890–91	Raven Hill/Kangipaha, Mayasan, Brown Earth
1892–97	Raven Hill
1898–1905	Mountain Head
1906–18	Ascension
1919–20	WC
1921–25	Matowakpa, Paha Waste, Eagle Nest, Canumsapa

James Lynd (1892)

1892	Mayasan, Red Hills
1893	Mayasan, Red Hills, Wounded Knee

1894–1902   Mayasan
1903–1905   Ascension

Pierre La Pointe (1893)

1894   Red Hills
1895–99   Hill
1900–1906   Cedar
1907   Heyata
1908   Mniska, Pahasha
1909   Mniska
1910–11   Mniska, Pahasha
1912   Hill
1913   Hill, Wolf Point
1914   Yankton
1915   Crow Creek

Louis De Coteau (1897)

1897   Mountain Head
1898   WC
1899   Porcupine
1900   Ascension
1901–1908   WC
1909   Flandreau
1910–13   WC
1914–16   Hill, Cedar, Heyata

Alfred N. Coe (1899)

1898–99   Raven Hill, Wood Lake, Hohay
1900   Crow Creek, Porcupine, White Clay
1901   Crow Creek, Conkicakse
1903–1904   White Clay
1905–1907   WC
1908–1909   not listed
1910   Heyata, Hill, Cedar
1911–12   Heyata, Cedar
1913   WC
1914–16   Mniska
1917–21   WC

1922–23	not listed
1924	Conkicaske, Crow Creek
1925	Mniska, Pahasha
1926	not listed
1927	Cedar, Wounded Knee, Hill
1928–29	Heyata, Cedar, Hill

Robert Clarkson (1901)

1901–1903	White River
1904–1909	Hill
1910–11	Crow Creek, Conkicakse
1912	Mniska, Pahasha
1913–16	WC
1917–20	Cedar
1921	WC
1922–26	Heyata, Hill
1927–33	Mniska, Pahasha

Moses Makey (1902)

1903–1905	Makaicu
1906–14	Mountain Head
1915–16	Yankton
1917	Yankton, Heyata
1918	Yankton
1919–22	Mountain Head
1923–24	Mountain Head, Ascension
1925	Mountain Head, Buffalo Lakes
1926	Mountain Head, Mayasan
1927	Mountain Head, Kangipaha, Mdecan
1928	Mountain Head, Mayasan, Good Will
1929	Mountain Head, Mayasan, Long Hollow, Lake Traverse
1930–31	Mountain Head, Mayasan, Long Hollow
1932	Mountain Head, Mayasan
1933–36	Mountain Head

George Firecloud (1906)

| 1907–1908 | Lake Traverse |
| 1909–11 | WC |

1912–19	Wakpacika
1920	Kangipaha
1921	WC

Samuel K. Weston (1907)

1908–1909	Porcupine
1910–14	Flandreau
1915–24	Porcupine
1925	Makasan
1926	Mniska, Pahasha
1927	Canumsapa
1928–29	Canumsapa, Matowakpa, Paha Waste
1930–34	Matowakpa, Paha Waste

Jacob Goodbird (1908)

1908–11	Mdecan, Kangipaha
1912	Kangipaha, Wood Lake
1913–25	Mayasan

Basil Reddoor (1911)

1911–12	Makaicu
1913	Kangipaha, Mdecan
1914	Makaicu
1915–16	WC
1917	Mnisda, Makaicu
1918	Mnisda
1919	Crow Creek, Conkicakse, Mniska, Pahasha
1920	WC
1921–22	Mnisda
1923–24	Cansutaipa
1925	Canipa
1926	Makaicu
1927	Makaicu, Mnisda
1928	Mnisda
1929–30	WC
1931–32	Upsijawakpa
1933–35	Wakpacika

George Head (1911)

1911–17	Lake Traverse
1918–19	Good Will
1920–22	Yankton
1923–24	Buffalo Lakes, Good Will
1925	Lake Traverse, Pajutazee, Ascension
1926	WC
1927	Pajutazee, Good Will
1928	Kangipaha, Mdecan

Titus Icadusmani (1911)

1911–14	Buffalo Lakes
1915–16	WC
1917–21	Buffalo Lakes
1922	Lake Traverse, Long Hollow
1923	Lake Traverse
1924–25	Mnisda
1926	Pajutazee
1927	Mayasan

John Wakeman (1917)

1917–19	Pajutazee

Hugh M. Jones (1918)

1918–19	Hill
1920–22	Pahasha, Mniska, Conkicakse, Crow Creek
1923	Conkicakse, Crow Creek
1924	Yankton
1925	Inyanhewita, Wakpacika
1926	Inyanhewita

Amos Oneroad (1919)

1920–22	Good Will
1923–24	WC
1925	Good Will
1926	Good Will, Lake Traverse
1927–28	WC

1929–30	Yankton
1931–33	Yankton, Cedar
1934	Flandreau, Pajutazee
1935–37	Yankton, Cedar

Samuel Renville (1921)

1921–22	Ascension
1923–25	Long Hollow
1926–28	Long Hollow, Buffalo Lakes
1929–31	Buffalo Lakes, Good Will
1932	Lake Traverse, Buffalo Lakes, Long Hollow
1933	Buffalo Lakes, Long Hollow
1934	Long Hollow

George Titus (1923)

1923–24	Wakpacika
1925	Kangipaha, Mdecan
1926	WC
1927–28	Cansutaipa
1929	Ascension

Samuel Benjamin (1924)

1922	Wakpacika
1923–24	Makaicu
1925	not listed
1926	Kangipaha, Mdecan

Albert Hemminger (1928)

1928	Pajutazee, Ascension
1929–33	Pajutazee, Flandreau
1934–37	Buffalo Lakes, Ascension
1937–40	Buffalo Lakes, Ascension, Good Will
1941	Buffalo Lakes, Ascension, Long Hollow
1942–43	Buffalo Lakes, Ascension
1944–49	Ascension

Peter Thompson (1928)

1927	Canipa
1928–29	Makaicu
1930–32	Kangipaha, Mdecan
1933	Lake Traverse, Ascension, Good Will
1934–37	Lake Traverse, Good Will, Mayasan

Chester Arthur (1929)

1928–29	Inyanhewita
1930–31	Cansutaipa
1932	Cansutaipa, Canipa
1933–38	Kangipaha, Mdecan

Homer Redlightning (1929)

1929	Upsijawakpa
1930–31	Lake Traverse, Ascension
1932	Ascension, Good Will
1933–38	Upsijawakpa
1939–41	Upsijawakpa, Kangipaha
1942	Upsijawakpa
1943–44	Upsijawakpa, Makaicu

Joseph Eaglehawk (1930)

1929–38	Tasunkekokiapi

SOURCE: *Minutes of the General Assembly of the Presbyterian Church in the U.S.A.* Philadelphia: Presbyterian Board of Publication, 1865–1869, 1884–1955; New York: Presbyterian Board of Publication, 1870–83.

*WC indicates "without church."

Notes

PREFACE

1. J. P. Williamson to J. C. Lowrie, December 15, 1873, *American Indian Correspondence: The Presbyterian Historical Society Collection of Missionaries' Letters, 1833–1893*, 31 (N)/28 (hereafter cited as AIC).

2. While most early accounts tended to make heroes and martyrs of the missionaries, these accounts judged the mission effort a failure. See, for example, Cannon, *Waiilatpu.* Later ethnologists and historians have tended to see both missionaries and mission as having failed: McWhorter, *Hear Me, My Chiefs!* Josephy, *Nez Perce Indians.* More contemporary historians have sought understanding of the complex nature of the missionaries and their mission but still point to the lack of Native converts as proof that the mission was a failure: Jeffrey, *Converting the West;* McCoy, "Sanctifying the Self and Saving the Savage."

3. Although many have written on the Whitman mission, Clifford M. Drury's works remain some of the more useful for their gathering of primary sources. See, for example, *Marcus Whitman, M.D.; First White Women,* vols. 1–3, recently republished; *Marcus and Narcissa Whitman,* vols. 1 and 2. Other sources include Ruby and Brown, *Cayuse Indians;* Webster, "Oregon Mission."

4. Drury, *Marcus Whitman, M.D.,* 406. This was Five Crows, who according to Drury was not a party to the Whitman murders.

5. Elements of Christianity such as worship of a single creator God, belief in an afterlife based on morality of actions in this life, and observance of a Sabbath day of rest were noted by premissionary contacts and attributed to the influence of Hudson's Bay Company and early mountain men. See, for example, Curtis, *North American Indian,* 8:7; D. E. Walker, *Conflict and Schism,* 33–39; and Josephy, *Nez Perce Indians,* 107, 109, 110.

6. Statistics taken from Beaver, *Native American Christian Community,* 13–26. These statistics were culled from several atlases published between 1901 and 1925. The total number of ordained Protestant pastors never exceeded 268, the number recorded for 1923. In that year alone, 31 percent were Presbyterians.

7. Ibid., 13, 14, 32. Beaver also indicates that Protestant church membership climbed from 5 to 10 percent of the Native American population between 1900 and 1925 but plateaued there for most of the rest of the century.

8. The bulk of this correspondence is in the McBeth-Crawford Collection of the Idaho State Historical Society Library and Archives, Boise (hereafter cited as McB-C). Two other archival boxes are in the Kate C. McBeth Letters and Papers of the San Francisco Theological Seminary (SFTS) Library, San Anselmo, Calif. The entire collection was gathered by Clifford Drury, formerly professor of church history at SFTS. Other correspondence by the Nez Perce pastors was subsequently found in the Clifford M. Drury Papers at the Eastern Washington State Historical Society, Spokane, (hereafter cited as Drury Papers, EWSHS) and the microfilmed *American Indian Correspondence: The Presbyterian Historical Society Collection of Missionaries' Letters, 1833–1893.*

9. The most extensive use of the collection appears in Drury's works and in Morrill and Morrill, *Out of the Blanket.* Of course, the correspondence appears in books published by both missionaries to whom many of the letters were addressed: McBeth, *Nez Perces,* and Crawford, *Nez Perces.*

10. Most of the correspondence of the Dakota pastors was found among the Thomas S. Williamson Papers, the Stephen R. Riggs Papers, the Grace Lee Nute Papers, and the American Board of Commissioners for Foreign Missions (ABCFM) Papers, all collections of the Minnesota Historical Society, St. Paul. While about a dozen letters were in English, nearly fifty others were in Dakota, of which a few have been translated. Some two hundred letters written by other Dakotas incarcerated during the Dakota war of 1862 remain to be translated, although work on the Dakota Letters Project began in 1999 by members of the community of Flandreau, S.Dak., with grant moneys from the federal government. The Dakota Letters Project continues to seek funding to finish the job while there are still Native speakers available. Letters and articles were also found in the *Iapi Oaye,* a Dakota-language paper, and the companion English-language version, the *Word Carrier.*

11. Drury, *Presbyterian Panorama.*

12. Fisher, *Contact and Conflict,* xiv.

13. On the emergence of ethnohistory as a discipline and its impact on historians see Axtell, "Ethnohistory," in Axtell, *The European and the Indian*; Edmunds, "Native Americans."

14. Ronda and Axtell, *Indian Missions*, 5.

15. Ronda, "'We Are Well As We Are,'" 82.

16. Fisher, *Contact and Conflict*, 125.

17. Axtell, *The European and the Indian*, 43. See also Axtell's extension of this theme in *The Invasion Within*.

18. Berkhofer, *Salvation and the Savage*, 158, 159.

19. Kidwell, *Choctaws and Missionaries*, 183, 201.

20. Bosch, *Transforming Mission*, 447.

21. A few of the studies that look seriously at the role of Indian ministers are D. E. Walker, *Conflict and Schism*; McLoughlin, *Champions of the Cherokees*; Ronda, "Generations of Faith"; Patterson, "Native Missionaries."

22. J. Hayes to K. C. McBeth, undated, McB-C, box 3.

23. Treat, *Native and Christian*, 13.

24. Weaver, *Native American Religious Identity*, xii.

25. Kidwell, Noley, and Tinker, *Native American Theology*, x.

26. For discussions of the Nez Perces, who have always contested that name, see Josephy, *Nez Perce Indians*, xiv; Spinden, "Nez Perce Indians," 171, 172; Curtis, *North American Indian*, 8:4, 5; see also Ives Goddard's discussion in D. E. Walker, "Nez Perce," 437. For information on the Sioux see Meyer, *History of the Santee Sioux*, 5; J. R. Walker, *Lakota Society*, 14. See also Douglas Parks's explanation in DeMallie, "Sioux until 1850," 749: "*Sioux* never meant 'snake'" but is a "misrepresentation based on the alternate meaning of the word for "Northern Iroquoian." Like the Nez Perce designation, however, the misrepresentation remains the most commonly held understanding of the word.

27. DeMallie, "Sioux until 1850," 718.

28. Phillips, *Protestant America*, 1–12.

29. Hutchison, *Errand to the World*, 7, 43–61.

INTRODUCTION

The epigraph source is J. Hayes to K. C. McBeth, June 13, 1904, McB-C, box 2. Hayes was quoting Chief Tiyawashat of the Spokans in response to Hayes's preaching to the Nespelems on the Colville Reservation earlier that day.

1. J. Hayes, sermon in letter to M. M. Crawford, February 4, 1927, McB-C, box 5.

2. Spellings and translations are taken from Josephy, *Nez Perce Indians*, 88, 89.

3. Josephy, *Nez Perce Indians*, 85–94; McBeth, *Nez Perces*, 27–35.

4. See, for example, Pond, *Dakota*, 85–113. Although writing derogatorily of Dakota religion, Pond's observations of early beliefs and practices shed light on the pervasive spirituality of the Dakotas in the early nineteenth century. See also Irwin, *Dream Seekers*, 64–71; Martin, *The Land Looks After Us*, 5–29; DeMallie, "Lakota Belief and Ritual," in DeMallie and Parks, *Sioux Indian Religion*, 27–43; Josephy, *Nez Perce Indians*, 22–24; D. E. Walker, *Conflict and Schism*, 18–30.

5. The term "black robes" usually referred to Catholic missionaries. Anglican missionaries in the Red River Valley, however, had been labeled "black robes" to distinguish them from the "long robes" of the French Catholic priests across the river. Spokan Garry, schooled at the Anglican Mission School in the Red River Valley, brought back that term, leading to later confusion over whether or not the St. Louis delegation wanted Catholic or Protestant missionaries. See Josephy, *Nez Perce Indians*, 78. For various treatments of this delegation, see Miller, *Prophetic Worlds*, 51–62; Josephy, *Nez Perce Indians*, 85–95; Drury, *Marcus and Narcissa Whitman*, 1:28–50.

6. Statistics are difficult to come by for the early years, but the most reliable resource to compile this data is found in Beaver, *Native American Christian Community*, 14, 22–26. According to his statistics, the total number of ordained Protestant ministers in 1911 (the first statistics that separated the ordained from the nonordained) was 158, of which 34 were Presbyterian, U.S.A., (there were also 8 in the southern branch of the church) and 27 of those were Presbyterian Nez Perces and Dakotas alone (see appendixes A and B for lists of pastors). Baptists reported 37, northern Methodists had 10 with 32 in the southern church, the Episcopal Church reported 30, while the rest of the churches reported a total of 4 ordained clergy.

7. Bowden, "Native American Presbyterians," 238. Bowden, citing Beaver's *Native American Christian Community*, notes Presbyterian membership ranged between eight thousand and ten thousand in the early decades of the twentieth century and settled out at about seven thousand in the 1920s, remaining there even though Native American population figures have continued to increase.

8. Eliza Spalding diary, March 20, 1837, in Drury, *First White Women*, 1:203.

9. Phillips, *Protestant America*, 7.

10. N. Whitman to C. Prentiss [mother], May 2, 1840, in Whitman, *Letters of Narcissa Whitman*, 93.

11. Phillips, *Protestant America*, 65.

12. Hutchison, *Errand to the World*, 62–65.

13. Webster, "ABCFM and the First Presbyterian Missions," 178.

14. Webster, "Oregon Mission," 26.

15. Drury, *Nine Years*, 124.

16. Whitman wrote of McLoughlin, "We cannot speak too highly of his kindness to us since we have been in this country." M. Whitman to D. Greene, March 12, 1838, cited in Drury, *Marcus and Narcissa Whitman*, 1:274.

17. Drury, *Marcus and Narcissa Whitman*, 1:249; Webster, "Oregon Mission," 26. Walker, however, was the only one who had been raised on a farm. Drury, *Nine Years*, 125.

18. N. Whitman to S. Prentiss [father], October 10, 1840, in Whitman, *Letters of Narcissa Whitman*, 101.

19. H. Jackson to E. E. Dye, January 11, 1893, cited in Drury, *Marcus and Narcissa Whitman*, 1:107. On the personality differences see also Jeffrey, *Converting the West*, 87, 88.

20. Dr. Marcus and Narcissa Whitman located among the Cayuses at Waiilatpu, the Rev. Henry and Eliza Spalding went among the Nez Perces at Lapwai, the Rev. Cushing and Myra Eells with the Rev. Elkanah and Mary Walker settled among the Spokans at Tshimakain, and the Rev. Asa Bowen and Sarah Smith lived briefly at Kamiah before leaving the mission. William and Mary Gray resided with the Spaldings for a brief period. The dissension among these groups that had such a disastrous effect on the mission is well recorded in their correspondence to the board and documented in Drury, *Marcus and Narcissa Whitman*.

21. Drury, *Marcus and Narcissa Whitman*, 1:239, 240, 356; Josephy, *Nez Perce Indians*, 180. Smith is credited with reducing the Nez Perce language to writing, Spalding's attempt proving inadequate. Walker had little help from Eells with the Spokan translation work and failed to complete even one of the gospels; Drury, *Nine Years*, 336.

22. Drury, *Presbyterian Panorama*, 114.

23. Drury, *Marcus and Narcissa Whitman*, 1:252, 253.

24. H. H. Spalding to D. Greene, April 21, 1838, cited in Drury, *Henry Harmon Spalding*, 182.

25. Drury, *Henry Harmon Spalding*, 170; Drury, *Presbyterian Panorama*, 115. Josephy, *Nez Perce Indians*, 225, claims that Spalding's secular education of the Nez Perces ultimately made him the most successful of the Northwest missionaries.

26. Drury, *Nine Years*, 128n., 525.

27. M. Whitman and H. H. Spalding to D. Greene, April 21, 1838, in Webster, "ABCFM and the First Presbyterian Missions," 181, citing Hulbert, 6:302–11; also cited in Drury, *Marcus and Narcissa Whitman*, 1:288, 289, 291. Drury notes that this unreasonable request may have been sparked by a sense of competition with the Methodist mission.

28. Webster, "ABCFM and the First Presbyterian Missions," 182. The board was suffering from a national depression begun in 1837 that put it over forty thousand dollars in debt. See Willand, *Lac Qui Parle*, 109.

29. Drury, *Marcus and Narcissa Whitman*, 1:255.

30. S. R. Riggs, *Mary and I*, 19.

31. S. R. Riggs to ABCFM, "A Sketch of the Missionary Labors among the Dakotas," January 2, 1862, American Board of Commissioners for Foreign Missions Papers, Minnesota Historical Society (hereafter cited as ABCFM Papers).

32. Ibid.

33. Folwell, *History of Minnesota*, 1:189. Folwell does note that the Rev. Jedediah Stevens, who arrived several months after T. S. Williamson, was the cause of some friction, resolved only with his resignation from the ABCFM in 1839. See Folwell, 1:190, 194, 195.

34. Pond, *Dakota*, 10, 11.

35. Meyer, *History of the Santee Sioux*, 49, 52, 62, 64.

36. Ibid., 183, 188; on the important contribution of the Pond brothers to the missionary endeavors, see also Gary Clayton Anderson's introduction in Pond, *Dakota*, vii–xxi.

37. Folwell, *History of Minnesota*, 1:199, 200; S. R. Riggs, *Mary and I*, 40, 41; Drury, *Presbyterian Panorama*, 110; on Renville's significant contribution to the mission, see G. C. Anderson, "Joseph Renville," 59–79.

38. Folwell, *History of Minnesota*, 1:200, 203; the *Iapi Oaye*, a Dakota-language paper written by Christian Dakotas and missionaries, was published at the Santee Normal Training School from 1871 to 1939. It carried local and national news, English and Bible lessons, and announcements of church meetings, weddings, funerals, and items of local interest. Within four years its Dakota circulation was twelve hundred. The English version,

the *Word Carrier*, was published from 1873 to 1939 and was used primarily to garner support in the East. It is now available on microfiche (New York: Clearwater Pub. Co., 1981). See also S. R. Riggs, *Mary and I*, 236, 237, 283; Meyer, *History of the Santee Sioux*, 178.

39. S. R. Riggs, *Mary and I*, 37.

40. On Narcissa Whitman's teaching career see Drury, *Marcus and Narcissa Whitman*, 1:108, 152; for Mary Walker's see, Drury, *Elkanah and Mary Walker*, 40; for Mary Riggs's see, S. R. Riggs, *Mary and I*, 4, 5;. for Sarah Smith's see Drury, *First White Women*, 3:34, 40; for Mary Gray's see, Drury, *First White Women*, 1:243; Margaret Williamson may also have been a teacher, but I could not establish that for certain, although she undoubtedly assisted her husband when not encumbered by family duties.

41. H. H. Spalding to E. White, undated, in W. H. Gray, *History of Oregon*, 236.

42. M. L. Riggs, *A Small Bit*, 51.

43. Willand, *Lac Qui Parle*, 152, 161, 162. According to Willand, Riggs was discouraged by the performance of Native teachers and in 1849, after ten years of hiring them for the outstations, largely discontinued the practice.

44. Willand, *Lac Qui Parle*, 153.

45. The school for the Cayuses gave way to one for the mixed-blood and white children living at the mission, and by 1844 a teacher had been hired for them. The Spaldings' school continued until 1847, when the Nez Perces stopped attending and then destroyed the building. For more on the closure of the Spalding school see Drury, *Henry Harmon Spalding*, 324–26; Josephy, *Nez Perce Indians*, 200, 238; on the Whitman school see Drury, *First White Women*, 1:147, 158–60.

46. M. L. Riggs, *A Small Bit*, 61.

47. Willand, *Lac Qui Parle*, 159.

48. G. Pond to S. B. Treat, February 20, 1852, in Willand, *Lac Qui Parle*, 167. S. R. Riggs, "A Sketch of Missionary Labors," 7, ABCFM Papers; Riggs claimed that number reached about 150 by the time of the Dakota war of 1862.

49. Drury, *Marcus Whitman, M.D.*, 354, 371. The Tshimakain mission school slowly came to an end by 1846 for lack of students; Drury, *Nine Years*, 335.

50. N. Whitman to C. Prentiss, December 5, 1836, in Drury, *Marcus Whitman, M.D.*, 174. See description according to John K. Townsend, scientist with the Wyeth party, in Ruby and Brown, *Cayuse Indians*, 64, 65.

51. Ruby and Brown, *Cayuse Indians*, 63; Josephy, *Nez Perce Indians*, 73, 74; Drury, *Marcus Whitman, M.D.*, 161.

52. Drury, *Marcus and Narcissa Whitman*, 1:196, 240.

53. Drury, *Nine Years*, 486.

54. Joseph was also known as Teutakas and Timothy as Timosa in Drury, *Marcus and Narcissa Whitman*, 1:336. They retained their Nez Perce names as last names on church roles (Joseph's spelled "Tuitakas"), 368. Timothy was called Ta-Moots-Tsoo in Alcorn, *Timothy*, 19.

55. M. Walker to E. Walker, February 12, 1839, in Drury, *Elkanah and Mary Walker*, 119; Drury, *Marcus and Narcissa Whitman*, 1:338. Narcissa noted this same behavior while camping with Timothy's camp in January 1839, commenting that he "spoke of his great wickedness, and how very black his heart was; how weak and insufficient he was of himself to effect his own salvation; that his only dependence was in the blood of Christ to make him clean and save his soul from sin and hell." She mentioned that he had "recently come from the meeting at Brother Spalding's;" Drury, *Henry Harmon Spalding*, 213, 214. Spalding noted after a service on December 23, 1838, "Before the sermon closed Timothy was before the stand in tears . . . overtaken with grief."

56. Drury, *Marcus and Narcissa Whitman*, 1:336.

57. Timothy and Joseph settled near the Spaldings and intervened on their behalf when James (Hin-mah-tute-ke-kaikt, or Thunder Eyes) objected to the Spaldings, Timothy, and Joseph all living on his land. See Alcorn, *Timothy*, 23; Drury, *Marcus and Narcissa Whitman*, 1:396; Josephy, *Nez Perce Indians*, 207.

58. Willand, *Lac Qui Parle*, 100–102; G. C. Anderson, "Joseph Renville," 73–75.

59. S. R. Riggs, *Mary and I*, 32.

60. G. C. Anderson, "Joseph Renville," 75.

61. M. L. Riggs to T. Longley and M. Longley [parents], March 22, 1839, in M. L. Riggs, *A Small Bit*, 92.

62. S. R. Riggs, *Mary and I*, 65. Riggs surmised that women were more apt to join the church because of their lower status among the Dakotas. He believed they had less to lose by making the changes required to become Christian. See Willand, *Lac Qui Parle*, 103; W. E. Strong, *Story of the American Board*, 48.

63. G. C. Anderson, *Little Crow*, 42. Anderson spells his name "Joseph Napesniduta."

64. S. R. Riggs, "A Sketch of Missionary Labors," 10–13, ABCFM Papers; S. R Riggs, *Mary and I,* 65–68, 88, 89; T. S. Williamson, "Indian Reminiscenes—Joseph Napeshnee," *Chicago Tribune,* April 26, 1871, Grace Lee Nute Collection, Minnesota Historical Society (hereafter cited as GLN); G. C. Anderson, *Little Crow,* 43.

65. Adams, Williamson, and Renville, *History of the Dakota Presbytery,* 9; S. R. Riggs, *Mary and I,* 204.

66. Drury, *Presbyterian Panorama,* 115. For a list of church members, see, McBeth, *Nez Perces,* 63, 64; "A True Copy," appendix 2.

67. Adams, Williamson, and Renville, *History of the Dakota Presbytery,* appendix; Willand, *Lac Qui Parle,* 236.

68. Drury, *Marcus and Narcissa Whitman,* 1:446.

69. Drury, *Marcus Whitman, M.D.,* 318; W. E. Strong, *Story of the American Board,* 50, 51.

70. Willand, *Lac Qui Parle,* 109, 110.

71. Drury, *Nine Years,* 485, 486.

72. N. Whitman to S. Prentiss, April 30, 1840, in Whitman, *Letters of Narcissa Whitman,* 92.

73. Ibid.

74. Drury, *Nine Years,* appendix 2, 517.

75. T. S. Williamson to D. Greene, May 10, 1837, in Willand, *Lac Qui Parle,* 114.

76. Drury, *Marcus and Narcissa Whitman,* 1:395. An indication of the animosity felt toward the missionaries appeared shortly after taking up residence in 1843 at the new station at Traverse des Sioux in Iowa Territory (in the area that would become Minnesota). Riggs noted the move "would not depend upon their [the Dakotas] giving us an invitation to stay." When Mary's brother, Thomas Longley, drowned, they were told that the Dakota water god, Oonktehe, "was displeased for us coming to build there. *He* had seized the young man." S. R. Riggs, *Mary and I,* 76, 84.

77. S. R. Riggs, *Mary and I,* 55.

78. M. L. Riggs to H. Longley [sister], June 14, 1839, in M. L. Riggs, *A Small Bit,* 99.

79. Drury, *Nine Years,* 380.

80. S. R. Riggs, *Mary and I,* 79.

81. Ibid., 94.

82. H. H. Spalding to D. Greene, February 3, 1847, in Drury, *Henry Harmon Spalding,* 326.

83. Drury, *Marcus Whitman, M.D.*, 259, 260; Ruby and Brown, *Cayuse Indians*, 81.

84. S. R. Riggs, *Mary and I*, 103, 104.

85. Josephy, *Nez Perce Indians*, 220, 221, 225.

86. Meyer, *History of the Santee Sioux*, 58, 59, 60.

87. Phillips, *Protestant America*, 86.

88. Bowden, "Native American Presbyterians," 240. See also, S. R. Riggs, *Mary and I*, 42. Riggs wrote: "The gospel of soap was indeed a necessary adjunct and outgrowth of the Gospel of Salvation."

89. Statistics were gathered from various Annual Reports of the Boards of Foreign Missions (1838–93), Home Missions (1894–1923), and National Missions (1924–50) of the Presbyterian Church in the U.S.A. See also, Coleman, *Presbyterian Missionary Attitudes*, 14; Drury, *Presbyterian Panorama*; and Adams, Williamson, and Renville, *History of the Dakota Presbytery*, appendix.

CHAPTER ONE

The epigraph source is Arthur and Motanic, "The Conversion of Fish Hawk," 3, in Indians, Vertical File, Pendleton Public Library, Pendleton, Ore.

1. McWhorter, *Hear Me, My Chiefs!* 85. According to McWhorter, "Spirit visions are invariably depicted with a superabundance of wondrous flowing hair, often of a golden-yellowish tinge."

2. Arthur and Motanic, "Fish Hawk," 3.

3. Ibid.

4. For background on Protestant missions to Indians, of which Presbyterians were an active part, see, Berkhofer, *Salvation and the Savage*; Phillips, *Protestant America*; Ronda and Axtell, *Indian Missions*; and Coleman, *Presbyterian Missionary Attitudes*. According to Coleman, Presbyterian missionaries saw culture as "outside" of a person so that one could be "extricated from his or her corrupting environment, almost like a nut from its shell," 173. On Catholic missions, see, Duratschek, *Beginnings of Catholicism*; Markowitz, "Catholic Mission and the Sioux," 113–37.

5. Comaroff and Comaroff, *Of Revelation and Revolution*, 249. The authors contend that conversion itself is an "ideologically saturated construct" of modern Protestantism and therefore not a "significant analytic category," but because it is the construct under which these missionaries operated, it must be explored in relation to building Native churches.

6. McWhorter, *Hear Me, My Chiefs!* 81.

7. Josephy, *Patriot Chiefs*, xiv.

8. Berkhofer, *Salvation and the Savage*, 69, 122. Ironically, he also notes that whites continued to view Christian Indians as Indians and, therefore, lesser Christians.

9. Ibid., 114.

10. Salisbury, "Red Puritans," 50, 54.

11. Axtell, "Some Thoughts," 38. See also, Meyer, *History of the Santee Sioux*, 53; Josephy, *Nez Perce Indians*, 421–23.

12. For example, see, Bowden and Ronda, *John Eliot's Indian Dialogues*, 95. Eliot says, in the guise of a Christian Indian, "I am a *praying Indian*. I have left our old *Indian* customs, laws, fashions, lusts, pauwauings." M. M. Crawford to Miss Voss, July 23, 1931, McB-C, box 6. Crawford wrote proudly, "I heard of one of our workers asking a company of older Nez Perce people at Talmaks, if heathenism had anything good to give the [C]hristian, and that fine body of older people answered as with one voice, 'NO, NOTHING, THROW IT ALL AWAY.'"

13. Ronda, "'We Are Well As We Are,'" 67. Ronda notes the variety of Indian responses to missionization, challenging the view that Indians who became Christians were no longer Indians. Miller, *Prophetic Worlds*, 116. Miller picks up on the theme that for the Plateau Indians, when the white world intruded, the Indian "world fell to pieces."

14. Ronda and Axtell, *Indian Missions*, 49; Axtell, *After Columbus*, 121.

15. For examples of the use of an ethnohistorical approach to missions, see, McNally, *Ojibwe Singers*; Kidwell, *Choctaws and Missionaries*; McLoughlin, *Cherokees and Christianity*; Merrell, *Indians' New World*.

16. Furniss, "Resistance," 232.

17. Treat, *Native and Christian*, 10.

18. White, *Middle Ground*, 26. Along these same lines, see also Clifton, *Being and Becoming Indian*, 31.

19. McLoughlin, *Cherokees and Missionaries*, 348; McLoughlin, *Cherokees and Christianity*, 189.

20. DeMallie, *Sixth Grandfather*, 14, 23.

21. Milner and O'Neil, *Churchmen*, xii.

22. See Whitehead, "Christianity, a Matter of Choice," 98; Bolt, *Thomas Crosby*, 106, 107; and the conversion of Black Elk related in Steltenkamp, *Black Elk*, 32–35.

23. Curtis, *North American Indian*, 8:66, 67. Curtis notes that among the Nez Perces the name "Fish Hawk" denotes a shaman with "power to see sickness in the body and to remove it, even as he himself takes the fish from the water." Because of the close relationship of the Cayuse with the Nez

Perces, including use of a common language (Nez Perce), it is not unrealistic to assume that this Fish Hawk was a former shaman, although there is no written evidence to support the assertion.

24. James R. Walker, anthropologist, noted that Lakota holy men "articulated new insights by expanding the meaning of traditional images." In the same way, Fish Hawk, working with traditional elements and ceremonies, conveyed new meanings. J. R. Walker, *Lakota Belief*, 65.

25. McLaren, "Living the Middle Ground," 290. McLaren identifies maintaining autonomy as a major goal of Indians seeking the "middle ground," a recurring theme in White's *Middle Ground.*

26. Church membership rolls available to the author for the Neah Bay Presbyterian Church, the Wellpinit Presbyterian Church, the First Presbyterian Church of Kamiah, and the Lapwai (Spalding) Presbyterian Church all indicate that in most cases individuals joined the church along with their families.

27. Contrary to Carol Devens's thesis that women were the most tied to defending traditional culture and therefore most reluctant to convert to Christianity, it was primarily full-blood Dakota women and mixed-blood men that composed the early Dakota churches. See S. R. Riggs, *Mary and I*, 32; T. S. Williamson to D. Greene, May 10, 1842 in Eklund, "Dakota Conversions"; Devens, *Countering Colonization.*

28. S. R. Riggs to ABCFM, "The Declaration of Paul Mazakootemane of the Dakota People," May 3, 1869, 1, GLN.

29. Ibid.

30. Ibid.

31. Ibid., 2.

32. Ibid., 4.

33. "Speech of Paul Mazakutemani (Walking Gun). Delivered before the Synod (Presbyterian) of Minnesota, at Rochester, Sept. 30. [1871]," 2, GLN.

34. "The Declaration of Paul Mazakootemane," 3, GLN.

35. Ibid.

36. James Dickson, untitled and undated manuscript, 1, McB-C, box 11.

37. Ibid.

38. Ibid. Date recorded in *Sessional Minutes of the First Presbyterian Church of Kamiah*, 1889–1944, 18.

39. James Dickson, untitled and undated manuscript, 1, McB-C, box 11.

40. Ibid.

41. Ibid.

42. Ibid.
43. Ibid., 2.
44. Ibid.
45. Ibid.
46. J. Dickson to K. C. McBeth, April 10, 1906, McB-C, box 2.
47. James Dickson, untitled and undated manuscript, 2, McB-C, box 11.
48. "Speech of Paul Mazakutemani," 3, GLN.
49. Anderson and Woolworth, *Through Dakota Eyes*, 195.
50. Ronda, "Generations of Faith," 391. See also McLoughlin, *Cherokees and Christianity*; Axtell, *The European and the Indian*, 73.
51. Mark Arthur, "The Story of Mark Arthur's Conversion" in undated manuscript entitled "Mark Arthur," 4, McB-C, box 11; also quoted in Crawford, *Nez Perces*, 60–64; and Morrill and Morrill, *Out of the Blanket*, 260, 261.
52. "Mark Arthur," 4, McB-C, box 11.
53. J. E. Brown, *Spiritual Legacy*, 26, 27; V. Deloria, "Establishment of Christianity," 111; Josephy, *Nez Perce Indians*, 23. For descriptions of personal vision quests by Nez Perces, see McWhorter, *Yellow Wolf*, 27–29; Thomas, *Pi-Lu²-Ye-Kin*, 27, 28; Hayes, *Called to Evangelize*, 3.
54. Most vision quests for both Nez Perces and Dakotas took place in just such a setting. See, for example, McWhorter, *Yellow Wolf*, 27, 28; Standing Bear, *My Indian Boyhood*, 158; E. C. Deloria, *Speaking of Indians*, 35; Curtis, *North American Indian*, 8:64, 3:62; Irwin, *Dream Seekers*, 106. Albert Moore, Nez Perce, equated the vision quest with the activities of biblical characters: "John the Baptist going to the mountains was the same thing as *we'yek* [vision quest]. Same thing with Moses; he trained. Bush was burning. Then he went back to his people." Thomas, *Pi-Lu²-Ye-Kin*, 28.
55. Artemas Ehnamani, "Matt. 4:16," undated, Artemas Ehnamani Sermons, Minnesota Historical Society (hereafter cited as AE). On visions as "a light of some kind or a cloud," see Lakota holy man George Sword's explanation on seeking a vision, J. R. Walker, *Lakota Belief*, 86.
56. For discussions of the role of visions in various Indian societies see J. E. Brown, *Spiritual Legacy*, 59, 60; J. R. Walker, *Lakota Belief*, 84–86; DeMallie, *Sixth Grandfather*, 83; Haines, *Nez Perces*, 57; Josephy, *Nez Perce Indians*, 22, 23; Irwin, *Dream Seekers*. For examples of biblical visions, see, Dan. 5:1–30; Acts 9:1–19, 10:1–23.
57. Tribal elders customarily instructed the youth. It would not have been unusual for Arthur to seek the counsel of the church elders. See, for example, McWhorter, *Yellow Wolf*, 34; Irwin, *Dream Seekers*, 66.
58. E. C. Deloria, *Speaking of Indians*, 15.

59. Ibid., 18. For further discussion on the elaborate kinship system of the Sioux, see J. R. Walker, *Lakota Society*; Lowie, *Indians of the Plains*; Landes, *Mystic Lake Sioux*.

60. DeMallie in J. R. Walker, *Lakota Society*, 6. DeMallie notes that according to Walker's explanation, "real kinship was not narrowly defined by the Lakotas in biological terms, but was defined, rather, by behavior . . . among the Lakotas, relatives are people who *act* like relatives and consider themselves to be related."

61. George Sword makes this clear in J. R. Walker, *Lakota Belief*, 199. Sword describes the Hunka ceremony in which the Oglalas could adopt any Indian or non-Indian thereafter to treat as a blood relative. His explanation of the proper behavior toward one's Hunka included caring for all of his needs, defending him in war, assisting him "if he wished to steal a wife," and, in general, treating him as if he were a real relative.

62. McBeth, *Nez Perces*, 209.

63. McBeth, "Notebook," 75, in the Allen and Eleanor Morrill Papers, University of Idaho Library, Moscow (hereafter cited as AEM). Also cited in Morrill and Morrill, *Out of the Blanket*, 68, 69.

64. E. C. Deloria, *Speaking of Indians*, 62.

65. P. Mazacutamanee [Mazakutemani] to S. R. Riggs, July 11, 1864, Stephen R. Riggs Papers, Minnesota Historical Society (hereafter cited as SRR).

66. P. Mazakutemani to S. R. Riggs, April 25, 1865, SRR.

67. Pine Ridge Indian trader Richard Nines recorded Lakota views on friendship in J. R. Walker, *Lakota Society*, 41.

68. E. C. Deloria, *Speaking of Indians*, 64.

69. Radin, "Autobiography," 381–473.

70. Roe Cloud, *From Wigwam to Pulpit*, 8.

71. Ibid., 9.

72. Ibid.

73. Ibid.

74. Ibid., 10.

75. Ibid.

76. Ibid., 10.

77. Ibid., 9.

78. Standing Bear, *My Indian Boyhood*, 151.

79. C. A. Eastman, *Old Indian Days*, 173.

80. Thomas, *Pi-Lu'-Ye-Kin*, 3.

81. The history of the Flandreau community can be found in Meyer, *History of the Santee Sioux*, 242–57; William L. Beane, ed., "Eastman, Cloud Man, Many Lightnings: An Anglo-Dakota Family," compiled for the Eastman family reunion, July 6, 1989, 44–56, in John Eastman Collection, William L. Beane Private Collection, Flandreau, S.Dak.; John Eastman, "Wakpaipaksan Wihdukcanpi" ("Bend of the River Reflections"), December 4, 1890, *Iapi Oaye*, [January 1891?], trans. Sidney H. Byrd. Eastman contends that it was the success of the Flandreau community that inspired the Dawes Act.

82. Solomon Flute (Wakaniskadmani), "Wowapi Maqupi," *Iapi Oaye*, April 1872, 3, trans. Doris Robertson.

83. J. T. Day (Tunkasaiciye), "Takusnisni" ("Small Articles"), *Iapi Oaye*, February 1874, 6, trans. Doris Robertson.

84. Geo. S. Westman, "Wan Wohdaka," *Iapi Oaye*, May 1879, 23, trans. Doris Robertson.

85. "Mrs. S. D. Hinman Te" ("Mrs. S. D. Hinman Died"), *Iapi Oaye*, April 1876, 1, trans. Doris Robertson.

86. E. C. Deloria, *Speaking of Indians*, 40.

87. Landes, *Mystic Lake Sioux*, 110.

88. J. Hayes, sermon in letter to M. M. Crawford, February 4, 1927, McB-C, box 5.

89. Ibid.

90. McLoughlin, *Cherokees and Christianity*, 17.

91. At the time of the Dakota war the three Presbyterian mission churches grouped along the Missouri River were Hazelwood (Umahu), Yellow Medicine (Pajutazee), and Lower Sioux Agency (Zoar), with a combined membership of about eighty. See Adams, Williamson, and Renville, *History of the Dakota Presbytery*, appendix.

92. Noted missionary accounts include S. R. Riggs, *Tah-koo Wah-kan*; Barton, *John P. Williamson*; Whipple, *Lights and Shadows*. See also, Folwell, *History of Minnesota*, 2:249–54.

93. Francis Frazier, "Gospel for the Modern Sioux," 3, address given before the South Dakota State Historical Convention, Chippewa–Lac qui Parle Mission State Park, June 14, 1933, Francis Frazier Address, Minnesota Historical Society, St. Paul.

94. Ehnamani, "Joh. 8:50, 51," AE.

95. Ehnamani, "1 Cor. 1:27–31," AE.

96. Ehnamani, "Matt. 4:16," AE.

97. Ehnamani, "1 Cor. 1:27–31," AE.

98. A. Ehnamani to S. R. Riggs (Tomakoce), undated [with 1862, 1864 papers], SRR, trans. Sidney Byrd.

99. While Ehnamani remained a pastor, in 1883 the Dakota mission was split between the Congregationalists and the Presbyterians; and the Pilgrim Church, along with Ehnamani, was transferred to the Yankton Congregational Conference of Dakota. See Adams, Williamson, and Renville, *History of the Dakota Presbytery*, 24.

100. Treat, *Native and Christian*, 9.

101. McLoughlin, *Cherokees and Christianity*, 33.

102. Treat, *Native and Christian*, 9; Axtell, *After Columbus*, 120.

103. Coleman notes the Presbyterians' pragmatism in their approach toward Native languages: they were viewed as necessary to reach a people who could not yet understand English, but ultimately the goal was to teach the Indians English. Thus there was a stronger emphasis on translation in the 1830s, when Williamson and Riggs worked with the Dakotas and Spalding with the Nez Perces, than in the 1870s, when the McBeths worked with the Nez Perces. As the Indian missions moved from the Foreign Board to the Domestic (Home) Board in 1893, teaching and translation were further deemphasized, as Indians were now considered an English-speaking field, comparable to the Chinese and other immigrants. Coleman, *Presbyterian Missionary Attitudes*, 14, 15, 116–19.

104. S. L. McBeth to J. C. Lowrie, February 2, 1878, AIC: 22(E)/18.

105. Drury, *Presbyterian Panorama*, 110.

106. Sidney H. Byrd, "The Ptaya Owoglake," unpublished manuscript, 9, Sidney H. Byrd Private Collection, Santa Fe, New Mexico.

107. Sidney H. Byrd, telephone interview by the author, March 10, 1995.

108. Axtell, *After Columbus*, 120.

CHAPTER TWO

The epigraph source is John P. Williamson, *Dakota Mission*, 7.

1. Haines, *Nez Perces*, 178, 179; James, *Nez Perce Women*, 12–17.

2. McBeth, *Nez Perces*, 77, 78.

3. According to Drury, *Henry Harmon Spalding*, 402, the Yakimas prepared the way for Spalding's return; Josephy, *Nez Perce Indians*, 423, and D. E. Walker, *Conflict and Schism*, 52, both claim Spalding "accelerated the work."

4. S. R. Riggs, *Mary and I*, 187; T. S. Williamson to S. R. Riggs, January 16, 1863, SRR.

5. T. S. Williamson to S. B. Treat January 20, 1863, GLN.

6. R. Hopkins to S. R. Riggs, August 20, 1864, SRR; trans: no. DL027, Dakota Letters Project.

7. T. S. Williamson to W. S. Griffith, April 10, 1863, GLN.

8. S. R. Riggs to S. B. Treat, March 26, 1863, GLN.

9. S. R. Riggs to S. B. Treat, November 7, 1863, GLN.

10. T. S. Williamson to S. B. Treat, January 20, 1863, GLN.

11. S. R. Riggs, *Mary and I*, 187.

12. T. S. Williamson to S. B. Treat, January 20, 1863, GLN.

13. S. R. Riggs to S. B. Treat, March 26, 1863, GLN. Emphasis in the original.

14. T. S. Williamson to W. S. Griffith, April 10, 1863, GLN.

15. Ibid., 187; T. S. Williamson to S. B. Treat, January 20, 1863, GLN.

16. In the last several decades, greater attention has been given to the power and impact of these revivals and awakenings from both a historical and a religious perspective, aided by interdisciplinary studies including anthropology, sociology, and gender studies. See, for example, McLoughlin, *Revivals,* and his use of A. F. C. Wallace's anthropological framework for viewing revivals as cultural revitalization movements; Smith's *Revivalism and Social Reform,* which firmly bases social reforms on the foundations of antebellum revivalism; Long's *Revival of 1857–58,* which considers the impact of revivalism and its various interpretations on the shaping of evangelical thought.

17. Miller, *Prophetic Worlds,* 42–45.

18. For a complete history of the Dreamers, see Relander, *Drummers and Dreamers;* Josephy, *Nez Perce Indians,* 424–26.

19. See, for example, Mooney, *Ghost-Dance Religion;* J. R. Walker, *Lakota Belief.*

20. Blumhofer and Balmer, *Modern Christian Revivals,* xii; McLoughlin, *Revivals,* 2

21. Barton, *John P. Williamson,* 48–50; Folwell, *History of Minnesota,* 2:232, 233.

22. McBeth, *Nez Perces,* 78.

23. Barton, *John P. Williamson,* 66, 67.

24. S. R. Riggs, *Mary and I*, 192.

25. McBeth, *Nez Perces,* 78.

26. S. R. Riggs to S. B. Treat, March 26, 1863, GLN.

27. T. S. Williamson to W. S. Griffith, April 10, 1863, GLN.

28. S. R. Riggs, *Mary and I,* 196.

218   NOTES TO PAGES 54–60

29. S. R. Riggs to S. B. Treat, March 26, 1863, GLN.

30. Ibid., 197.

31. Ibid.

32. "A True Copy," 265, 267.

33. Jesset, *Chief Spokan Garry*, 76, 172, 177; Ruby and Brown, *Spokane Indians*, 70, note Garry's reluctance may have had more to do with his reluctance to suffer growing ridicule among his people for his preaching.

34. Boyd and Brackenridge, *Presbyterian Women*, 14.

35. Ginzberg, *Women and the Work of Benevolence*, 172, 173. Ginzberg notes that the Civil War served to escalate a national trend toward a "'masculinization' of the ideology of benevolence," which valued patriotism, efficiency, and professionalism over the more feminine virtues of "charity and compassion."

36. J. P. Williamson to S. B. Treat, May 7, 1863, GLN.

37. Barton, *John P. Williamson*, 18.

38. Ibid., 45.

39. J. P. Williamson to S. B. Treat, November 5, 1862, GLN.

40. J. P. Williamson to S. B. Treat, May 7, 1863, GLN.

41. Ibid.

42. Barton, *John P. Williamson*, 116.

43. Ibid., 113.

44. Ibid.

45. Ibid., 117, 118; Adams, Williamson, and Renville, *History of the Dakota Presbytery*, 10.

46. Barton, *John P. Williamson*, 143.

47. J. P. Williamson to J. C. Lowrie, March 14, 1879, AIC: 22(E)/136.

48. Ibid.

49. Barton, *John P. Williamson*, 260.

50. Ibid.

51. Ahlstrom, *Religious History*, 444, 445, 641; Marsden, *Evangelical Mind*, 30.

52. Prucha, *American Indian Policy*, 266, 268, 269; S. R. Riggs, *Tah-koo Wah-kan*, 401, 402.

53. Sue McBeth had apparently suffered a stroke during the war years that left her partially paralyzed. Kate McBeth notes that "Miss McBeth seldom appeared among the people," in *Nez Perces*, 221; and in Crawford, *Nez Perces*, 40. See also Morrill and Morrill, *Out of the Blanket*, 144, 153.

54. Kate McBeth, "Miss Sue L. McBeth," *The Church at Home and Abroad*, January 1897, 18; McBeth, *Nez Perces*, 91.

55. S. L. McBeth to J. C. Lowrie, November 2, 1880, AIC: 21 (D)/327; Crawford, *Nez Perces*, 40.

56. "Foreign Missions," *The Church at Home and Abroad*, May 1893, 352.

57. Hoyle, "Teacher of Preachers," 478.

58. McBeth, "Miss S. L. McBeth," 19; McBeth, *Nez Perces*, 222.

59. Kate McBeth notes in her diary in 1881 that Sue's attempts to place the church leadership in a position to govern the tribe were opposed even by her students, who probably felt the approbation of the tribe. She wrote, "There is not the eagerness to attend S[chool] that there was last year." McBeth diary, New Year's 1881, AEM.

60. S. L. McBeth to J. C. Lowrie, February 2, 1878, AIC: 22 (E)/18.

61. J. P. Williamson to S. R. Riggs, July 26, 1864, SRR.

62. J. P. Williamson to T. S. Williamson, March 8, 1865, Thomas S. Williamson Papers, Minnesota Historical Society, St. Paul.

63. J. P. Williamson to T. S. Williamson, January 5, 1865, Thomas S. Williamson Papers.

64. J. P. Williamson to S. B. Treat, May 7, 1863, GLN; Riggs notes in *Tah-koo Wah-kan*, 374, 375, that the prison was made a "religious educational training school, that on their release, these men should be prepared to carry the gospel to the regions beyond."

65. "Extracts from (Published) Report of the ABCFM, p. 130–132, September, 1867," 3, GLN.

66. Barton, *John P. Williamson*, 120; Parker, *Founding Presbyterianism*, 22.

67. M. B. Riggs, *Early Days at Santee*, 64.

68. S. R. Riggs, *Mary and I*, 285; Barton, *John P. Williamson*, 136.

69. S. R. Riggs, *Mary and I*, 284.

70. "Annual Report of John P. Williamson of the Dakota Mission for the year 1886," AIC: 33 (P-1)/372.

71. John P. Williamson, "Annual Report on Yankton Agency, 1887," AIC: 33 (P-1)/383.

72. "Annual Report of John P. Williamson of the Dakota Mission for the year 1886," AIC: 33 (P-1)/372.

73. Barton, *John P. Williamson*, 195, 196; Parker, *Founding Presbyterianism*, 59, 61.

74. Leslie Lewis, "Native Ministers of the Dakota Presbytery to 1988," 3, Oahe Collection, Augustana College, Sioux Falls, S.Dak.

CHAPTER THREE

The epigraph source is J. Hayes to K. C. McBeth, November 30, 1903, McB-C, box 2.

1. McLoughlin, *Cherokees and Christianity*; Ronda, "Generations of Faith." See also, Hankins, "Solomon Briant and Joseph Johnson," 54; Kidwell, *Choctaws and Missionaries*, 179–80.

2. Missionaries as early as Puritan John Eliot recognized the efficacy of using Natives to reach Natives. See Bowden and Ronda, *John Eliot's Indian Dialogues*, 42; Naeher, "Dialogue in the Wilderness," 361. On the influence of Mohegan Samson Occom, one of the first ordained Presbyterian Indian ministers, see, Blodgett, *Samson Occom*; M. C. Szasz, *Indian Education*.

3. S. R. Riggs to S. B. Treat, June 15, 1865, GLN.

4. M. M. Crawford to C. L. Thompson, February 28, 1924, McB-C, box 6.

5. S. L. McBeth to J. C. Lowrie, September 23, 1880, AIC: 21(D)/320.

6. S. L. McBeth to J. C. Lowrie, November 9, 1880, AIC: 21(D)/329.

7. James Dickson, untitled manuscript, McB-C, box 11.

8. Prucha, *American Indian Policy*, 223, 224.

9. Note that the Nez Perces of the Wallowa Valley would have been even more destitute had they moved onto the northern Idaho reservation in 1863, having lost their entire land base. See Curtis, *North American Indian*, 8:11. The resistance of the Joseph people to Christianity stemmed largely from their antipathy toward Lawyer and his followers (Christian Indians), who, in signing the 1863 treaty, "sold his brother's birthright." For a valuable study of the nontreaty Nez Perces through the eyes of their biographer L. V. McWhorter, see Evans, *Voice of the Old Wolf*. See also, D. E. Walker, *Conflict and Schism*, 46–49.

10. T. S. Williamson to W. S. Griffith, April 10, 1863, GLN, "They have been deprived of their arms and implements for hunting. With a very few exceptions their horses cattle & wagons were lost or have been disposed of to supply their urgent wants, and they have nothing remaining except their cooking utensils tents and clothes on their backs which will soon be worn out."

11. Ehnamani, "1 Cor. 1:27–31," AE.

12. McWhorter, *Yellow Wolf*, 296. See also D. E. Walker, *Indians of Idaho*, 159, 160; Curtis, *North American Indian*, 8:62–64; Josephy, *Nez Perce Indians*, 23, 24; Slickpoo, *Noon Nee-Me-Poo*, 57.

13. McWhorter, *Yellow Wolf*, 296, quoting Many Wounds.

14. D. E. Walker, *Indians of Idaho*, 159. "Weyekin" is the preferred spelling for Curtis and D. E. Walker, alternately spelled "wy-ya-kin"

(McBeth), or "wyakin" (Josephy, McWhorter), and "wey-ya-kin" (Slickpoo, Evans).

15. Thomas Tyon uses the phrase in his narrative in J. R. Walker, *Lakota Belief*, 150, 154. "Wakan Tanka," according to Walker and his Lakota informants, was translated the "Great Spirit" and was adopted by missionaries to refer to "Jehova, or the Christian God." It seems to have derived from an older concept of the power of all gods, sometimes called "Taku Skanskan" or simply "Skan," 31, 32.

16. A description of the Kit Fox Society is found in D. E. Walker, *Lakota Belief*, 270.

17. C. A. Eastman, *Soul of the Indian*, 7, 8.

18. DeMallie and Parks, *Sioux Indian Religion*, 31; it also carries the connotation that the one being petitioned is a relative who would be both willing and able to assist.

19. Underhill, *Red Man's Religion*, 96, 98. The cutting off of extremities, lacerations, and self-torture reached its most intense expression in the Sun Dance ritual, which was outlawed by the government in 1883. On the Sun Dance see J. R. Walker, "The Sun Dance and Other Ceremonies," 50–221; J. R. Walker, *Lakota Belief*, 175–191; Densmore, *Teton Sioux Music*, 84–151.

20. Irwin, *Dream Seekers*, 83–104.

21. Underhill, *Red Man's Religion*, 102. See, also, Hultkrantz, *Religions of the American Indians*, 81; D. E. Walker, *Conflict and Schism*, 19.

22. Slickpoo, *Noon Nee-Me-Poo*, 54; Curtis, *North American Indian*, 8:65; Thomas, *Pi-Lu'-Ye-Kin*, 21, 25; on the Inipi and other Sioux practices see J. E. Brown, *Sacred Pipe*, 31–43; J. R. Walker, *Lakota Belief*, 83–86; DeMallie, *Sioux Indian Religion*, 34, 35.

23. Thomas, *Pi-Lu'-Ye-Kin*, 21.

24. An Omaha prayer cited in Herzog, "La Flesche Family," 225. Joseph La Flesche (Iron Eye), Omaha chief of the mid-nineteenth century was the father of the first Indian woman medical doctor, Susan La Flesche Picotte; the first professional Indian anthropologist, Francis La Flesche; and the Indian rights activist, Susette La Flesche Tibbles. Herzog cites the example of Iron Eye's philosophically Omaha orientation and its reverence toward nature, despite conversion to Christianity, when he instructed his young daughter, Susette, to take her pet bird aside to dedicate it, praying, "God, I give you back your little bird. Have pity on your bird."

25. J. R. Walker, *Lakota Belief*, 73.

26. D. E. Walker, *Conflict and Schism*, 35. Walker cites an informant who says, "The Indians knew of the one God, *hanyawa-t* [Creator or Maker], before

the Whites came." McWhorter calls him "Hunyawat, or Ahkinkenetkii [Man Above, Above all, Deity]" in *Hear Me, My Chiefs!* 67. It appears this may stem from the more recent Dreamer religion.

27. A. P. Sawyer [A. B. Lawyer], to G. L. Deffenbaugh, published under "A Christian Indians' Plea," in *The Church at Home and Abroad*, February 1889, 155.

28. Viola, *Diplomats in Buckskins*, 95.

29. Kip, *Indian Council*, 208.

30. Native Christian theologians have been influenced by this historic approach to God and the rise of theologies of liberation among the oppressed peoples particularly of Latin America in the 1960s and 1970s. See, for example, Treat's introduction in *Native and Christian*, 15–17. Warrior questions whether or not American Indians can look to the Christian faith for liberation; he sees them more closely identified with the Canaanites, whose lands were taken by the Israelites. See Robert Warrior's essay "Canaanites, Cowboys, and Indians," in Treat, *Native and Christian*, 93–104, with responses by William Baldridge and Jace Weaver.

31. Curtis, *North American Indian*, 3:16; Spinden, "Nez Perce Indians," 242.

32. Slickpoo, *Noon Nee-Me-Poo*, 54; see also Spinden, "Nez Perce Indians," 242; Curtis, *North American Indian*, 3:13.

33. Curtis, *North American Indian*, 3:16.

34. D. E. Walker, *Conflict and Schism*, 16, 17. Outsiders often commented on the generosity of both Nez Perces and Dakotas. See, for example, Lewis and Clark's description of the Nez Perces in Moulton, *Journals*, 7:238. The second wife of artist and Army Capt. Seth Eastman made the same observation of the Dakotas in M. Eastman, *Dahcotah*, xix.

35. S. L. McBeth to J. C. Lowrie, May 27, 1880, AIC: 21(D)/236.

36. S. L. McBeth to J. C. Lowrie, September 23, 1880, AIC: 21(D)/320.

37. J. B. Renville to S. B. Treat, February 6, 1871, GLN.

38. Ibid.

39. S. L. McBeth to F. F. Ellinwood, July 12, 1887, quoted in Morrill and Morrill, *Out of the Blanket*, 273.

40. G. L. Deffenbaugh to F. F. Ellinwood, July 18, 1887, AIC: 1-1/263.

41. Ibid.

42. M. A. Renville to S. B. Treat, October 13, 1866, GLN.

43. J. B. Renville to T. S. Williamson, January 21, 1868, GLN.

44. A. B. Lawyer to F. F. Ellinwood, October 20, 1885, AIC: 2-2/156.

45. A. P. Sawyer [A. B. Lawyer] to G. L. Deffenbaugh, "A Christian Indians' Plea," in *The Church at Home and Abroad*, February 1889, 155.

46. A. B. Lawyer to Dr. White, published under "The Indian's Response," in *The Church at Home and Abroad,* June 1889, 549.

47. J. B. Renville to S. B. Treat, August 10, 1869, GLN.

48. Beaver, *To Advance the Gospel,* 31, 106.

49. The effort to eradicate tribal leaders, seen as perpetrators of traditional practices, was part of what was behind the 1871 legislation to end treating with Indian tribes as independent nations. See Prucha, *American Indian Policy,* 329, 320. The missionary perspective was voiced by Sue McBeth, who believed tribal chiefs prevented progress on the reservations because they kept people tied to a band rather than allowing the "Indian man to feel his individuality"; McBeth, *Nez Perces,* 220. On agency policing see Hagan, *Indian Police;* Prucha, *American Indian Policy,* 201–209.

50. Fowler, *Arapahoe Politics,* 3.

51. Ibid., 291. See also, Patterson, "Kincolith, B.C.," 45–55.

52. Spinden, "Nez Perce Indians," 242, notes the importance of these qualities to Nez Perce chiefs.

53. Joseph P. Hillers, David Weston, William Jones, and Peter Robinson, "Rev. John Eastman Wopida Eciyapi" ("They Give Thanks to Rev. John Eastman"), *Iapi Oaye,* April 1887, 14, trans. Doris Robertson.

54. This was especially true among the Nez Perces, whose tribal organization was less firmly entrenched. See, for example, Spinden, "Nez Perce Indians," 242–44; D. E. Walker, *Conflict and Schism,* 15–18; Coleman, *Presbyterian Missionary Attitudes,* 123. On the Dakotas see Pond, *Dakota,* 14, 68; J. R. Walker, *Lakota Society,* 24, 25.

55. DeMallie, "'These Have No Ears'," 531, 532.

56. Josephy, *Nez Perce Indians,* 70.

57. Curtis, *North American Indian,* 8:23; see also, Josephy, *Patriot Chiefs,* 330.

58. Rufus Anderson, "The Theory of Missions to the Heathen, A Sermon at the Ordination of Mr. Edward Webb, as a Missionary to the Heathen. Ware, Mass., Oct. 23, 1845," in Beaver, *To Advance the Gospel,* 79.

59. Jules Bonnet, ed., *Letters of John Calvin,* 2:190, quoted in Leith, *Introduction to the Reformed Tradition,* 82.

60. S. L. McBeth to J. C. Lowrie, February 27, 1879, AIC: 22(E)/130.

61. J. Hayes to K. C. McBeth, June 3, 1907, McB-C, box 2.

62. Thomas Wakeman, "Wakpaipaksan Omaka Teca" ("River Bend New Year"), *Iapi Oaye,* January 1880, 3, trans. Doris Robertson.

63. John Eastman, "Wakpaipaksan Cagatipi" ("Bend in the River"), *Iapi Oaye,* January 1887, trans Doris Robertson.

64. J. R. Walker, *Lakota Society,* 26; Spinden, "Nez Perce Indians," 243; Slickpoo, *Noon Nee-Me-Poo,* 51.

65. Grace Eastman Moore, "Life of My Father, John Eastman," undated, speech for the Annual Meeting of the Flandreau Historical Society, John Eastman Collection, William L. Beane Private Collection, Flandreau, S.Dak.

66. Ronda, "Generations of Faith," 394.

67. S. L. McBeth to J. C. Lowrie, September 23, 1880, AIC: 21(D)/320.

68. The first Dakota pastor, John B. Renville, was ordained in 1865 at age thirty-four. Artemas Ehnamani was ordained two years later at the age of forty-one. Of the first dozen pastors or so, about a half dozen had been warriors prior to their incarceration following the Dakota war. About the same number had been associated with earlier churches or missions and had received some English education.

69. J. P. Williamson to T. S. Williamson, May 27, 1875, Thomas S. Williamson Papers.

70. J. R. Walker, Lakota Society, 61, 62; D. E. Walker, Conflict and Schism, 17, 26.

71. D. E. Walker, Conflict and Schism, 25; Josephy, Nez Perce Indians, 22.

72. Slickpoo, Noon Nee-Me-Poo, 45; D. E. Walker, Conflict and Schism, 26.

73. J. R. Walker, Lakota Belief, 73; George Sword, "Foundations," in Lakota Belief, 79, 94.

74. J. R. Walker, Lakota Society, 62.

75. McBeth, Nez Perces, 10.

76. Joseph Cook, "Sermon," April 14, 1927, Kate C. McBeth Letters and Papers, San Francisco Theological Seminary Library, San Anselmo, Calif.

77. Ibid.

78. See, for example, J. Hayes to K. C. McBeth, August 25, 1902; March 3, 1905; October 12, 1906; March 18, 1907, McB-C, box 2.

79. David Faribault and John Eastman, "Solomon Samson Faribault," Iapi Oaye, May, 1882, 35, trans. Doris Robertson.

80. Ibid.

81. S. R. Riggs, Tah-koo Wah-kan, 382, 383.

82. Sessional Records of the Lapwai Presbyterian Church, April 3, 1886. Private Collection, Lapwai, Idaho.

83. S. R. Riggs, Tah-koo Wah-kan, 383.

84. Dakota (Indian) Presbytery Minutes, September 21, 1882, 1:218. For this failing Rev. Titus Ichaduze was deposed from the ministry by vote of the presbytery at that meeting.

85. J. Hayes to K. C. McBeth, March 3, 1905, McB-C, box 2. Nez Perce warrior Yellow Wolf also notes, "Water is medicine for everything," in McWhorter, Yellow Wolf, 29.

86. G. L. Deffenbaugh to J. C. Lowrie, April 23, 1885, AIC: 2-2/64.

87. J. B. Renville to S. R. Riggs, January 13, 1868, GLN.

88. J. B. Renville to S. B. Treat, August 10, 1869, GLN.

89. "John Eastman Awaits Fulfillment of Bargain for Pettigrew's Defeat," December 25, [1917?], unidentified newspaper article, John Eastman Collection, William L. Beane Private Collection. On the Santee claims case, see Folwell, *History of Minnesota*, 2:438–39; Meyer, *History of the Santee Sioux*, 301, 302.

90. J. P. Hillers, D. Weston, W. Jones, and P. Robinson, "Rev. John Eastman Wopida Eciyapi" ("They Give Thanks to Rev. John Eastman"), *Iapi Oaye*, April 1887, 14, trans. Doris Robertson.

91. Ibid.

92. See, for example, M. C. Szasz, *Between Indian and White Worlds*, 20.

93. G. E. Moore, "Life of My Father, John Eastman."

94. Ibid.

95. S. L. McBeth to J. C. Lowrie, November 9, 1880, AIC: 21(D)/329.

96. J. Hayes to K. C. McBeth, June 13, 1904, McB-C, box 2.

97. *Constitution of the Presbyterian Church*, 1871, 435.

98. Ibid., 436, 437, 438.

99. *Minutes of the General Assembly of the Presbyterian Church in the U.S.A.*, 1854, 507; quoted in Moore, *New Digest*, 79. As early as 1792 it was debated in the church whether two or three years were desirable for the "study of Divinity," to prepare ministerial candidates adequately. By the turn of the century, three years were required, but allowances were made for fewer, with the permission of the presbytery; Moore, *New Digest*, 75. See also, Moore, *Presbyterian Digest of 1898*, 426. Note that this applied to men only. Women were not ordained as ministers in the Presbyterian Church until 1956. They could be ordained as deacons by 1906 and as ruling elders by 1930. See Rogers, *Presbyterian Creeds*, 227, 228.

100. Adams, Williamson, and Renville, *History of the Dakota Presbytery*, 10.

101. *Annual Report, 1924–1925*, Lapwai, Idaho, in letter from M. M. Crawford to Miss Voss, February 19, 1925, Kate C. McBeth Letters and Papers.

102. G. L. Deffenbaugh to F. F. Ellinwood, July 18, 1887, AIC: 1-1/263.

103. R. Williams to J. C. Lowrie, April 20, 1878, AIC: E/42.

104. Ibid.

105. Henry Venn, "Letter to the Bishop of Jamaica," January 1867, quoted in Beaver, *To Advance the Gospel*, 98.

106. M. M. Crawford to J. M. Somerndike, January 8, 1933, McB-C, box 6.

107. J. Hayes's sermon in letter to K. C. McBeth, February 4, 1927, McB-C, box 5.

108. Ibid.

CHAPTER FOUR

The source for the epigraph is John C. Wakeman (Unktomiska), "Wowiyuk-can Wanji" ("One [Understanding] Opinion"), *Iapi Oaye*, December 1874, 46, trans. Doris Robertson.

1. Phillips, *Protestant America*, 29, 30.

2. Curtis, *North American Indian*, 8:3, 4; J. R. Walker, *Lakota Society*, 58; Pond, *Dakota*, 6; D. E. Walker, *Indians of Idaho*, 128.

3. J. R. Walker, *Lakota Society*, 3, 8; on band formation, 24, 25.

4. Ibid., 26.

5. Carlson, *Plains Indians*, 67.

6. Spinden, "Nez Perce Indians," 242, notes that Nez Perce bands were based upon geographical location, and every village had its chief. Curtis, *North American Indian*, 8:3, 4, concurs. Ray, *Cultural Relations*, 11, citing Spinden, also notes that the Nez Perces, on the periphery of the Plateau tribes, were strongly influenced by the political organization of the Plains Indians, and therefore village autonomy was modified by the unified election of a war chief by a number of villages when threatened by outsiders. He comments that such unity was rather loose, and that "several villages were united to form a tribe, rather than that the tribe was divided." See also, D. E. Walker, *Conflict and Schism*, 10; Josephy, *Nez Perce Indians*, 16, 30.

7. D. E. Walker, *Conflict and Schism*, 14, 15.

8. Curtis, *North American Indian*, 8:48, 49; Spinden, "Nez Perce Indians," 242; Ray, *Cultural Relations*, 19.

9. Spinden, "Nez Perce Indians," 242; Ray, *Cultural Relations*, 10.

10. Curtis, *North American Indian*, 8:4, claims band divisions were most likely in a process of "decay and separation rather than of consolidation" during the "historical period." The policies of the U.S. government by the 1870s would have continued this process, but, nevertheless, band loyalties remained unusually strong.

11. On the Grant Peace Policy, see Keller, *American Protestantism*; Prucha, *American Indian Policy*; Utley, *Indian Frontier*. See also, DeMallie, *Sixth Grandfather*, 15; Josephy, *Nez Perce Indians*, 431.

12. McBeth, *Nez Perces*, 89, 220; Coleman, *Presbyterian Missionary Attitudes*, 122, 123.

13. McBeth, *Nez Perces*, 17, 115.

14. Ibid., 115.

15. D. E. Walker, *Conflict and Schism*, 53.

16. Ibid., 53, 55.

17. George L. Deffenbaugh, "Churches, Ministers and Missionaries Connected with the Nez Perce Mission, 1872–1888," unpublished manuscript transcribed by Drury, April 19, 1936, Drury Papers, EWSHS. The Second Presbyterian Church of Kamiah was founded in 1890, and the sixth Nez Perce church was founded at Stites, also in Idaho, in 1903.

18. D. E. Walker, *Conflict and Schism*, 48. Factionalism on the Nez Perce reservation was compounded by U.S. government enactment of a head-chief system that singled out one band leader of the northern bands to represent all of the Nez Perces. When missionaries settled in the north, they exacerbated the divisions between northern and southern bands. The Treaty of 1863, which excluded the land of the southern bands from the reservation and was signed only by northern bands, effectively divided the Nez Perces between treaty and nontreaty, Christian and non-Christian bands.

19. Ibid., 57.

20. By 1890, there were eight ordained Nez Perce pastors and only four Nez Perce churches. The three missionary churches supplied by the Nez Perces, two among the Spokans, and one among the Umatillas, provided additional pulpits. There were, however, too many ministers for too few pulpits. Kate McBeth questioned as early as 1881 the need for so many ministers. "What ever is to be done with all these ministers?" she wrote plaintively in her diary. In 1883 she noted no "lack of preachers but too many," causing much strife and jealousy among them. McBeth diary, Christmas 1880, AEM; December 28, 1883, AEM.

21. D. E. Walker, *Conflict and Schism*, 68; Morrill and Morrill, *Out of the Blanket*, 339. There is evidence Lawyer would have started his own church regardless of the approval of presbytery, and that body acted as much to put an end to internal feuding between the Williams and Lawyer parties and prevent Lawyer's joining another denomination as because it deemed justifiable the creation of another church in Kamiah. See McBeth, "Facts regarding the two Spokan churches Wellpinit and Spokane River: At the Spring meeting of the Walla Walla Presbytery in April 1890," undated manuscript, McB-C, box 4.

22. D. E. Walker, *Conflict and Schism*, 68.

23. D. E. Walker, *Conflict and Schism*, 70, 71. Walker does not name the individuals, but they are found in the "Sessional Records of the Lapwain Presbyterian Church," June 4, 1910, typescript by Drury, Clifford Drury

Papers, Oregon Historical Society. Conner was registered as a student at San Francisco Theological Seminary for the school year 1903–1904.

24. D. E. Walker, *Conflict and Schism*, 70, 71.

25. Ibid., 71, 72.

26. S. R. Riggs, *Mary and I*, 196.

27. Ibid.

28. Of the appointment of elders see S. R. Riggs to S. B. Treat, November 7, 1863, GLN; concerning the appointment of "a female helper from each band to watch over & instruct the women," see J. P. Williamson to T. S. Williamson, January 6, 1863, Thomas S. Williamson Papers.

29. A. Ehnamani to S. R. Riggs, not dated [by context, probably between 1862 and 1864], SRR.

30. S. R. Riggs to S. B. Treat, November 7, 1863, GLN; J. P. Williamson to T. S. Williamson, January 6, 1863, Thomas S. Williamson Papers.

31. Meyer, *History of the Santee Sioux*, 153, 154.

32. Barton, *John P. Williamson*, 110, claims 382 charter members; S. R. Riggs, *Tah-koo Wah-kan*, 421, cites nearly 400 members.

33. Barton, *John P. Williamson*, 110, 111.

34. For example, the Ascension (Iyakaptape) Church on the Sisseton Reservation in South Dakota was composed of a number of Renville families, and John B. Renville served as its pastor from 1879–99; S. R. Riggs, *Mary and I*, 233, 234; S. R. Riggs, "Synod of Minnesota," August 22, 1876, SRR. Solomon Tankansaiciye established Middle Hill Church (Pahacokamya) among his relatives near Fort Ellice in Manitoba, Canada, and served there from 1879 to 1889; S. R. Riggs, *Mary and I*, 339–44; A. B. Baird, *Foreign Missions*, 19–22.

35. Ehnamani, "1 Cor. 1:27–31," AE.

36. M. M. Crawford to friends, January 19, 1923, McB-C, box 6.

37. "The Declaration of Paul Mazakootemane of the Dakota People," GLN.

38. James Dickson, untitled manuscript, McB-C. box 11.

39. See, for example, Coleman, *Presbyterian Missionary Attitudes*, chap. 5.

40. See, for example, James Dickson, untitled manuscript, McB-C, box 11; Ehnamani, "Matt. 4:16," AE. Edward Marsden, Tsimshian minister from Metlakatla, Territory of Alaska, ordained in 1899, writes in the same manner. See Marsden, "The Gospel Abroad and Its Triumphs," speech delivered at the State Christian Endeavor Convention, Dayton, Ohio, June 10, 1897, Edward Marsden Papers, San Francisco Theological Seminary Library, San Anselmo, Calif.

41. Ehnamani, "Matt. 4:16," AE.

42. Ibid.

43. J. B. Renville to S. B. Treat, February 27, 1873, GLN.

44. *Dakota (Indian) Presbytery Minutes*, 1:161; also cited in Barton, *John P. Williamson*, 181. In the form of a petition addressed to the commissioner of Indian affairs and the Indian agent, it requested help to control the dance as "we are not able to put a stop to it among ourselves." On the significance of the Grass Dance and its practice see Densmore, *Teton Sioux Music*, 468–77. According to Densmore, it originated with the Omahas and was believed to promote bravery and valor.

45. Phrase used by James Hayes several times in letters to Kate McBeth. See, for example, November 28, 1907, and December 20, 1907, McB-C, box 2; August 29, 1908, Drury Papers, EWSHS.

46. E. Pond to K. C. McBeth, February 13, 1888, McB-C, box 1.

47. M. M. Crawford to family, June 14, 1919, McB-C, box 6.

48. Ibid.

49. Ibid.

50. E. Pond to K. C. McBeth, February 13, 1888, McB-C, box 1. Of the feast, see Curtis, *North American Indian*, 7:76.

51. Ibid.

52. McBeth, *Nez Perces*, 169; synodical missionary Gunn used a biblical injunction, "Come out from among them, and be ye separate, saith the Lord, and touch not the unclean thing," to encourage the Nez Perce Christians to stand against the "heathen" activities of the non-Christian Fourth of July celebrations.

53. T. L. Riggs, "The Hazelwood Republic," 3, SRR.

54. "The Declaration of Paul Mazakootemane of the Dakota People," 2, GLN.

55. J. Eastman, "Wakpaipaksan Wihdukcanpi" ("Bend of the River Reflections"), *Iapi Oaye*, [January 1891?], trans. Sidney Byrd. On this community see also S. R. Riggs, *Mary and I*, 238–41; Meyer, *History of the Santee Sioux*, 242–57.

56. J. P. Williamson to J. C. Lowrie, March 14, 1879, AIC: 22(E)/136; J. P. Williamson to J. A. Burbank, October 22, 1869, National Archives, RG 75, cited in Meyer, *History of the Santee Sioux*, 245.

57. Meyer, *History of the Santee Sioux*, 102–107, 257.

58. Morrill and Morrill, "Talmaks," 48.

59. Slickpoo, *Noon Nee-Me-Poo*, 209.

60. Crawford, *Nez Perces*, 24; McBeth, *Nez Perces*, 163; Slickpoo, *Noon Nee-Me-Poo*, 209.

61. McBeth, *Nez Perces*, 165.

62. Morrill and Morrill, "Talmaks," 49.

63. Slickpoo, *Noon Nee-Me-Poo*, 210; Morrill and Morrill, "Talmaks," 53. Christian Indians found a formidable ally in Special Agent Alice Fletcher and her companion, Jane Gay, who encouraged the Nez Perce church leaders to petition the U.S. commissioner in Washington, D.C., to put a stop to the "heathen goings-on" at the Nez Perce Fourth of July celebrations. The commissioner, Thomas J. Morgan, immediately ordered the Nez Perce agent to prevent any such activity on agency, school, or mission grounds, thus separating the two celebrations once again. See Gay, *With the Nez Perces*, 130–34.

64. "Sessional Records of the Lapwain Indian Presbyterian Church," September 22, 1897, Clifford Drury Papers, Oregon Historical Society; McBeth, *Nez Perces*, 169, 170.

65. Crawford, *Nez Perces*, 27.

66. Morrill and Morrill, "Talmaks," 55.

67. Ibid.; the 646 acres were deeded to the tribe by the government.

68. Ibid., 28; Mrs. C. F. Bough [sister of Mary Crawford], to friends, July 25, 1916, McB-C, box 5. Mrs. Bough notes, "The entire section has been fenced for the purpose of providing pasture for the more than 400 horses with the annual camp and then there is an inner circle fenced in and it is in this inclosure the people pitch their tents."

69. Drury, "The Beginnings of Talmaks," 46. The Nez Perce Presbyterians celebrated their hundredth anniversary of Talmaks in July 1997.

70. Kidwell, *Choctaws and Missionaries*, 201.

71. McBeth, *Nez Perces*, 250.

72. Ibid., 248.

73. McBeth diary, February 2, 1880, AEM; February 3, 1880, AEM; 3rd Sabbath, September 1880, AEM.

74. T. S. Williamson to S. R. Riggs, January 16, 1863, SRR; T. S. Williamson to W. S. Griffith, April 10, 1863, GLN, MHS; quotation from J. P. Williamson, *Dakota Mission*, 7.

75. Curtis, *North American Indian*, 8:54; Spinden, "Nez Perce Indians," 258.

76. S. R. Riggs, *Tah-koo Wah-kan*, 464.

77. See, for example, on the numerous ceremonies of the Sioux: Densmore, *Teton Sioux Music*; J. R. Walker, *Lakota Belief*; Mooney, *Ghost-Dance Religion;* on the Nez Perces: Curtis, *North American Indian*, 8:3–76; Spinden, "Nez Perce Indians."

78. M. M. Crawford to Mr. Tenney, et al., August 22, 1929, McB-C, box 6; S. R. Riggs, *Tah-koo Wah-kan*, 483; McBeth, *Nez Perces*, 182.

79. T. S. Williamson to S. R. Riggs, January 27, 18[63], SRR.

80. S. R. Riggs, *Tah-koo Wah-kan*, 482; Pond, *Dakota*, 82.

81. M. M. Crawford to Mr. Tenney, et al., August 22, 1929, McB-C, box 6; S. R. Riggs, *Tah-koo Wah-kan*, 483.

82. McBeth, *Nez Perces*, 182; Barton, *John P. Williamson*, 18, makes the same claim for the Dakotas.

83. Densmore, *Teton Sioux Music*, 22.

84. Ibid.

85. Ibid.

86. For examples of Ojibwa and Choctaw use of hymns for sustaining Native culture see McNally, *Ojibwe Singers*, 19; Kidwell, *Choctaws and Missionaries*, 180.

87. S. L. McBeth to Mrs. Perkins, February 5, 1879, AIC: 22(E), 117.

88. McBeth diary, December 1, 1882, AEM.

89. S. R. Riggs, *Mary and I*, 313.

90. Morrill and Morrill, *Out of the Blanket*, 370.

91. Barton, *John P. Williamson*, 251.

92. Williamson and Riggs, *Dakota Odowan*, 3.

93. Densmore, *Teton Sioux Music*, 24.

94. S. R. Riggs, *Tah-koo Wah-kan*, 483, 484.

95. Joseph R. Renville, "Dakota Odowan 141," 1842, "Many and Great, O God, Are Thy Things," trans. by R. Philip Frazier, 1953, *The Presbyterian Hymnal*, 271. For a 1993 translation see Sidney H. Byrd, "Great Spirit God," Sidney H. Byrd Private Collection, Santa Fe, N.Mex.:

> Great Spirit God, the things which are yours
>   are numerous and great.
> The heavens above you set in their place,
>   and earth received its form by your hands.
> The ocean depths respond to your will,
>   for you can do all things.
> Your plan for our salvation, O God,
>   grant to my sinful soul.
> Beyond the heavens is your great abode,
>   all goodness is secure in your hands.
> This life divine which you gave to me,
>   is one that has no end.

96. Sidney H. Byrd, "The Story Behind Dakota Odowan 141," unpublished manuscript, 4, Sidney H. Byrd Private Collection, Santa Fe, N.Mex. Note that Samuel Pond claimed they sang a traditional Dakota death song. He should have recognized the difference had he been there. Pond, *Dakota*, 82.

97. S. L. McBeth to J. C. Lowrie, February 2, 1878, AIC: 22(E)/18.

98. S. L. McBeth to A. L. Lindsley, January 10, 1885, AIC: 2-2/17.

99. J. Fraser to A. J. Ralston, 1904, in McBeth, *Nez Perces*, 181.

100. Although existing voting records from session minutes do not indicate gender, Riggs indicates that women voted in the election of the pastors of the Pilgrim Church in S. R. Riggs, *Tah-koo Wah-kan*, 424; and during a special meeting of the congregation, in S. R. Riggs, *Mary and I*, 255. A vote for elder in the Kamiah First Church indicated all 133 members voted, *Sessional Minutes of the First Presbyterian Church of Kamiah*, December 23, 1893, p. 26. However, session minutes for the Lapwai (Spalding) Church on two other occasions indicate only one-third or one-fourth of the members voted for elder or pastor, bringing into question whether or not the women were voting; "Sessional Records of the Lapwain Presbyterian Church," March 23, 1899, and March 30, 1917, Clifford Drury Papers, Oregon Historical Society.

101. It was apparently a number of years, however, before women were allowed to sing in the Dakota church choirs. See M. B. Riggs, *Early Days at Santee*, 13.

102. McBeth, *Nez Perces*, 123.

103. For the classic treatment of eighteenth- and nineteenth-century gender divisions, see, for example, Welter, "The Cult of True Womanhood"; Cott, *Bonds of Womanhood*; on gender divisions and missionary culture see Boyd and Brackenridge, *Presbyterian Women*; Robert, *American Women in Mission*; Rogers, *Presbyterian Creeds*, 227, 228.

104. *The Church at Home and Abroad*, November 1888, 402.

105. See, for example, Lillian A. Ackerman, "Complementary But Equal: Gender Status in the Plateau," and Daniel Maltz and JoAllen Archambault, "Gender and Power in Native North America: Concluding Remarks," in Klein and Ackerman, *Women and Power*; Bragdon, "Gender as a Social Category," 586.

106. Pond, *Dakota*, 140; Spinden, "Nez Perce Indians," 242; D. E. Walker, *Conflict and Schism*, 10; descriptions by Thomas Tyon and John Blunt Horn in J. R. Walker, *Lakota Society*, 29, 30; McBeth, *Nez Perces*, 120. Anthropologist Lillian Ackerman, among others, has posited that Plateau women had equal status with men, but this argument rests on the concept of separate roles and equal rights. That the major decision making was done primarily

by men, whose public role entitled them to a voice and leadership in the councils not usually given women, was actually not far different from the actual practice of Victorian Christians. See Ackerman, "The Effect of Missionary Ideals," 71; James, *Nez Perce Women*, 2. P. T. Strong, "Feminist Theory," 692. Strong notes that Indian women found in Catholicism a means of expanding their public voice and believes it was a "hybrid practice" drawing on both Indian culture and Christian. The same seems to be the case for both the Nez Perce and Dakota Presbyterian women.

107. Harkin, "Engendering Discipline," 654. Harkin notes that Heiltsuk women were also active in Methodist women's groups, especially the younger ones, in support of the "goals of material, physical, and spiritual improvement."

108. *The Church at Home and Abroad*, October 1894, 327.

109. Mary Jane Eastman, "Wotanin" ("Flandreau D.T. News"), *Iapi Oaye*, April 1879, 14, trans. Doris Robertson.

110. Ibid.

111. Ascension Church Women, *Iyopta or Advance Society Minutes*, 1874–1881, Presbyterian Historical Society, Philadelphia.

112. McBeth, *Nez Perces*, 195.

113. M. B. Riggs, *Early Days at Santee*, 50, 51.

114. McBeth, *Nez Perces*, 194.

115. Morrill and Morrill, "Talmaks," 56; D. E. Walker, *Conflict and Schism*, 57.

116. M. B. Riggs, *Early Days at Santee*, 50.

117. D. E. Walker, *Conflict and Schism*, 88. Walker notes that as church membership declined in the twentieth century, the number of offices increased.

118. Leith, *Introduction to the Reformed Tradition*, 153, 154.

119. 1 Timothy 3:2–4.

120. *Sessional Records of the Lapwai Presbyterian Church*, April 27, 1879.

121. *Dakota (Indian) Presbytery Minutes*, June 9, 1883, 1:233.

122. G. L. Deffenbaugh to J. C. Lowrie, June 21, 1880, AIC: D/238.

123. S. R. Riggs, *Mary and I*, 339, 341; A. B. Baird, *Foreign Missions*, 19, 20. Baird refers to him as Enoch Returning Cloud.

124. J. P. Williamson to S. B. Treat, May 7, 1863, GLN; in the spring of 1863 there were 322 prisoners at Mankato and 1,591 at Fort Snelling. Meyer, *History of the Santee Sioux*, 137.

125. J. P. Williamson to T. S. Williamson, October 26, 1869, Thomas S. Williamson Papers.

126. S. R. Riggs, *Mary and I,* 240.

127. Pond, *Dakota,* 69, 70; Spinden, "Nez Perce Indians," 244.

128. D. E. Walker, *Conflict and Schism,* 57.

129. Balmer and Fitzmier, *The Presbyterians,* 15.

130. J. Hayes to K. C. McBeth, December 12, 1907, McB-C, box 2.

131. *Sessional Records of the Willpinit Presbyterian Church,* July 1, 1888, Presbytery of the Inland Northwest, Spokane, Wash.

132. Gray and Tucker, *Presbyterian Polity,* 152.

133. "Sessional Records of the Lapwain Presbyterian Church," July 6, 1885, Clifford Drury Papers, Oregon Historical Society.

134. Ibid.

135. Ibid.

136. McBeth diary, March 19, 1882, AEM.

137. *Sessional Records of the Willpinit Presbyterian Church,* October 6, 1918.

138. D. E. Walker, *Conflict and Schism,* 64.

139. *Sessional Records of the Willpinit Presbyterian Church,* December 31, 1916.

140. S. R. Riggs, *Tah-koo Wah-kan,* 382.

141. Ibid., 381, 382.

142. Ibid., 382, 383.

143. *Sessional Records of the Willpinit Presbyterian Church,* June 26, 1897.

144. Ibid., July 6, 1885.

145. "Sessional Records of the Lapwain Presbyterian Church," October 25, 1884.

146. *Sessional Records of the Lapwai Presbyterian Church,* October 26, 1884 [this date appears to be a mistake, as it fits in sequence as December 26, 1884].

147. J. P. Williamson to T. S. Williamson, September 25, 1871, Thomas S. Williamson Papers.

148. Ibid.

149. *Sessional Records of the Willpinit Presbyterian Church,* August 25, 1901.

150. Ibid., 56.

151. D. E. Walker, *Conflict and Schism,* 66. See, for example, the church's confrontation with the Nez Perce agent over the 1891 Fourth of July celebration, in Gay, *With the Nez Perces,* 130–34.

152. J. P. Williamson to A. Mitchell, May 10, 1889, AIC: P-1/395.
153. J. P. Williamson to S. R. Riggs, November 30, 1865, SRR.
154. Barton, *John P. Williamson*, 152, 227.
155. McBeth, *Nez Perces*, 244, 245.
156. Ibid.

CHAPTER FIVE

The source for the epigraph is P. Ides to M. M. Crawford, November 18, 1925, McB-C, box 5.

1. R. Anderson, "Foreign Missions," in Beaver, *To Advance the Gospel*, 107.

2. Hutchison, *Errand to the World*, 80, 81.

3. Ginzberg notes that in the post–Civil War era women working in benevolent organizations "refashioned the ideology of benevolence itself from an analysis of gender to one of class." Emphasis on gender differences was becoming a liability for women as society moved toward valuing more masculine traits of "nationalism, discipline, centralization and efficiency" for achieving social change. A rising class-stratified and class-conscious society provided new categories around which women could gather to retain what power they had. See Ginzberg, *Women and the Work of Benevolence*, 5, 133, 212. On the effect of changing views of gender relations on mission work, see also, Pascoe, *Relations of Rescue*; Hill, *The World Their Household*.

4. Pascoe, *Relations of Rescue*, xvi, xvii.

5. Ibid.

6. Boyd and Brackenridge, *Presbyterian Women*, 160.

7. S. L. McBeth to J. C. Lowrie, August 21, 1878, AIC: 22(E)/77.

8. Harkin, "Engendering Discipline," 645.

9. Welter, "She Hath Done What She Could," 632; Bendroth, "Women and Missions," 50, 51; Boyd and Brackenridge, *Presbyterian Women*, 159, 160. According to Hill, *The World Their Household*, 60, "In undertaking a mission to women and children in other cultures, evangelical women did not venture out of the domestic sphere; they simply enlarged it."

10. Beaver, *All Loves Excelling*, 178.

11. McBeth, *Nez Perces*, 142, 222. Her sister, Kate, seems to have been given the title after her death. See Fraser's memoir of Kate McBeth, *Peaka Soyapu*.

12. Boyd and Brackenridge, *Presbyterian Women*, 60–62.

13. The theological premise upon which this was based came from Paul's injunction to the younger Timothy: "I suffer not a woman to teach, nor to usurp authority over the man, but to be in silence." (1 Timothy 2:12)

14. Drury, *Henry H. Spalding and Asa Bowen Smith*, 106.

15. McBeth, *Nez Perces*, 115.

16. Ibid., 88; S. L. McBeth to J. C. Lowrie, September 23, 1880, AIC: 21(D)/320.

17. S. L. McBeth to J. C. Lowrie, February 2, 1878, AIC: 22(E)/18.

18. Morrill and Morrill, *Out of the Blanket*, 34.

19. Ibid., 33–37.

20. S. L. McBeth to J. C. Lowrie, February 2, 1878, AIC: 22(E)/18.

21. S. L. McBeth to unknown, undated letter fragment, AIC: 23(F)/326.

22. S. L. McBeth to J. C. Lowrie, May 27, 1880, AIC: 20(D)/236.

23. S. L. McBeth to J. C. Lowrie, September 23, 1880, AIC: 21(D)/309.

24. S. L. McBeth to A. L. Lindsley, January 10, 1885, AIC: 2-2/17.

25. S. L. McBeth to J. C. Lowrie, May 27, 1880, AIC: 21(D)/236.

26. S. L. McBeth to J. C. Lowrie, September 23, 1880, AIC: 21(D)/320.

27. S. L. McBeth to J. C. Lowrie, May 27, 1880, AIC: 21(D)/236.

28. McBeth diary, Christmas 1879, AEM.

29. McBeth diary, December 5, 1880, AEM.

30. McBeth diary, New Year's 1881, AEM.

31. A. Lawyer to F. F. Ellinwood, September 4, 1884, AIC: 1/289.

32. G. L. Deffenbaugh to F. F. Ellinwood, July 18, 1887, AIC: 1-1/263.

33. Ibid.

34. K. C. McBeth, "Facts regarding the two Spokane Churches Wellpinit and Spokane River," McB-C, box 4.

35. D. E. Walker, *Conflict and Schism*, 68.

36. Ibid., 68.

37. See, for example, letters from S. L. McBeth to K. C. McBeth, June 7, 1890, and February 18, 1891, McB-C, box 4.

38. S. L. McBeth to J. C. Lowrie, April 3, 1875, cited in Morrill and Morrill, *Out of the Blanket*, 36.

39. S. L. McBeth to J. C. Lowrie, November 9, 1880, AIC: 21(D)/329.

40. S. L. McBeth to W. Rankin, May 23, 1887, AIC: 1/107.

41. Ibid.

42. A. Frost to Mrs. Young, December 6, 1906, copied in Kate McBeth's hand, McB-C, box 2.

43. H. M. Foster to K. C. McBeth, July 25, 1904, McB-C, box 2.

44. McBeth, *Nez Perces*, 214–16; J. Hayes to K. C. McBeth, Nov. 11, 1907, McB-C, box 2.

45. "The Jubilee at Walla Walla," *The Occident*, September 12, 1888, 2.

46. Ibid.

47. Helen Clark, "Chips from an Old Block," transcribed by Veda Forrest, unpublished manuscript, Neah Bay Presbyterian Church, Neah Bay, Wash.

48. For a short sketch of her work among the Spokans, see Ruby and Brown, *Spokane Indians*.

49. Of the twenty-one letters in the McBeth-Crawford Collection of Helen W. Clark to Kate McBeth and Mary Crawford, none bear full dates and most have no date so must be given approximate dates according to contents. The references to Indian needs and Chief Lot are from letters written from the Spokane Reservation about 1895. This reference is to a letter written shortly after arriving in Neah Bay, about 1900, McB-C, box 3.

50. H. Clark to K. C. McBeth, undated but probably written prior to leaving Spokane, McB-C, box 3.

51. H. Clark to K. C. McBeth, May 18, [1907?], McB-C, box 3.

52. Pascoe, *Relations of Rescue*, 122.

53. H. Clark to K. C. McBeth, February 13, [1905?], McB-C, box 3.

54. H. Clark to K. C. McBeth, undated [February 1906, by context], McB-C, box 3.

55. J. Hayes to K. C. McBeth, March 3, 1905, McB-C, box 2.

56. J. Hayes to K. C. McBeth, February 27, 1905, McB-C, box 2.

57. H. Clark to K. C. McBeth, [February 1906?], McB-C, box 3.

58. J. Hayes to K. C. McBeth, February 20, 1906, McB-C, box 2.

59. Ibid.

60. J. Hayes to K. C. McBeth, February 26, 1906, McB-C, box 2.

61. *Session Book of the Neah Bay Presbyterian Church*, February 26, 1906. Neah Bay Presbyterian Church, Neah Bay, Wash.

62. Ibid.

63. Ibid.

64. H. Clark to K. C. McBeth, March 15, [1906?], McB-C, box 3.

65. Ibid. The Indian Shaker Church is not to be confused with the Shaker sect begun by Ann Lee in the eastern United States and popular between the 1830s and 1850s. Although marked by similar movements in worship, the Indian Shakers began in 1881 when John Slocum, a Squaxin Indian, was believed dead and revived. He preached that God had sent him back to lead other Indians to Christianity. For general information on the

Indian Shakers see Mooney, *Ghost-Dance Religion*; Eells, *Indians of Puget Sound*; Barnett, *Indian Shakers*.

66. H. Clark to K. C. McBeth, March 15 [1906], McB-C, box 3.

67. J. Hayes to K. C. McBeth, February 27, 1905, McB-C, box 2.

68. Ibid.

69. H. Clark to K. C. McBeth, undated [by context, late 1890s, from Spokane], McB-C, box 3.

70. H. Clark to K. C. McBeth, March 15, [1906?], McB-C, box 3.

71. Barnett, *Indian Shakers*, 145. Mooney claimed that by 1896 the Presbyterian Church had given "official endorsement" to the Shakers. If their orthodoxy was in question, their "character and actions" were not, for the religion had noticeably beneficial effects, according to the Presbyterians, on the moral improvement of the Indians, condemning as it did, alcohol, gambling, and shamanism. See Mooney, *Ghost-Dance Religion*, 747, 751.

72. Noted Shaker leader Lans Kalapa (church session records spell the name "Kallappa") joined the church March 7, 1925. His brother, James Kalapa, came forward May 29, 1927, following an evangelistic meeting led by Nez Perce pastor James Dickson and Spokan pastor Daniel Scott (both schooled at McBeth mission). He did not join the church officially, though, until October 24, 1937. On the influence of the Kalapa brothers at Neah Bay, see Barnett, *Indian Shakers*, 63–65.

73. H. Clark to K. C. McBeth, undated [March 1906?], McB-C, box 3.

74. H. Clark to K. C. McBeth, November 9 [1906], McB-C, box 3.

75. Ibid.

76. Pascoe, *Relations of Rescue*, xvii. Pascoe notes that the nineteenth-century women's search for moral authority assumed "the primacy of Victorian female values and was sharply critical of male privilege," 50.

77. H. Clark to K. C. McBeth, November 9 [1906?], McB-C, box 3.

78. Ibid.

79. H. Clark to K. C. McBeth, May 12, [1902?], McB-C, box 2. References to Caroline Ladd's grandsons Harry and Elliot Corbett indicate that Clark's sponsor was Caroline Ladd, although Clark does not mention her first name.

80. Ibid.

81. "Neah Bay Presbyterian Church Observing Fiftieth Anniversary," Neah Bay Presbyterian Church, Neah Bay, Wash.

82. H. Clark to K. C. McBeth, May 18, [1907 or 1908?], McB-C, box 3.

83. H. Clark to K. C. McBeth, March 15 [1906], McB-C, box 3.

84. Helen Peterson, September 20, 1994, tape-recorded interview with author, Neah Bay, Wash.

85. *Session Book of the Neah Bay Presbyterian Church*, September 20, 21, 1924.

86. Ibid., 14. According to Barnett, Kalapa took his religion underground, was accused by detractors that he had left the Shaker faith and was "only a Presbyterian," but still "considered himself a good Shaker." See Barnett, *Indian Shakers*, 65.

87. S. L. McBeth to K. C. McBeth, July 16, 1892, McB-C, box 4.

88. M. M. Crawford to Miss Voss and the Women of the Board, May 16, 1928, unsigned, McB-C, box 6.

89. Barton, *John P. Williamson*, 115, 116.

90. On Flandreau see, Meyer, *History of the Santee Sioux*, 242–57; S. R. Riggs, *Mary and I*, 238–41; Beane, "Eastman"; J. Eastman, "Wakpaipaksan Wihdukcanpi."

91. Beane, "Eastman," 51.

92. S. R. Riggs, *Mary and I*, 239. Meyer, *History of the Santee Sioux*, 243, claims these Indians had acquired a "sizable measure of selfishness" and some were "no doubt . . . chronic malcontents." Selfish or not, both missionaries and historians seem to agree with Williamson that these Indians were led by "the same longing to 'be one's own,' or for freedom, as we say, which led the Puritans to Plymouth Rock," Barton, *John P. Williamson*, 144.

93. J. Eastman, "Wakpaipaksan Wihdukcanpi."

94. John Williamson and others believed the Flandreau Indians deserved to benefit, along with other tribesmen, from the sale of their lands in Minnesota. Therefore, Congress voted in 1873 to include the Flandreau Indians in the appropriations given to the Santees for land cessions. See Meyer, *History of the Santee Sioux*, 246–48.

95. Beane, "Eastman," 53.

96. John Williamson, despite his location at Yankton, was made "special agent" for Flandreau to deal with government regulations and subsidies. J. P. Williamson to J. C. Lowrie, March 14, 1879, AIC: 22(E)/136. With the support of the Flandreau community, he continued to lobby for their independence from government supervision, but in 1879 Flandreau was placed under the authority of the Santee Agency. See Meyer, *History of the Santee Sioux*, 248, 253.

97. Barton, *John P. Williamson*, 260.

98. J. Eastman to A. Mitchell, July 21, 1887, AIC: 33(P)/1. Emphasis in the original.

99. Ibid.

100. Ibid.

101. Barton, *John P. Williamson*, 260. Eastman referred to "Brother Williamson" in his letter to the board July 21, 1887, AIC: 33(P)/1.

102. McBeth, *Nez Perces*, 244.

CHAPTER SIX

The epigraph source is M. M. Crawford, quoting Joseph Cook, to J. Fraser, Dec. 11, 1932, McB-C, box 6.

1. M. M. Crawford to her family, Aug. 5, 1936, Kate C. McBeth Letters and Papers.

2. For a full description of Presbyterian Church polity, see also Gray and Tucker, *Presbyterian Polity*. To understand church polity in its historical context, see Smylie, *Brief History*.

3. Adams, Williamson, and Renville, *History of the Dakota Presbytery*, 22.

4. Morrill and Morrill, *Out of the Blanket*, 330–32, 364; McBeth, *Nez Perces*, 209.

5. For example, according to the *Minutes of the Presbytery of Spokane*, 5, 108, 109, 128, Silas Whitman was a member of the Church Erection Committee for 1890, 1891, and on the committee to review the session records of Kettle Falls Church in northeastern Washington for the year 1895. The Wellpinit Church hosted the presbytery June 9, 1925, at the ordination of Daniel Scott.

6. McBeth, *Nez Perces*, 198; Barton, *John P. Williamson*, 144–49.

7. Crawford, *Nez Perces*, 29, 30.

8. M. M. Crawford to U.S. Board of Indian Commissioners, Dec. 26, 1924, unsigned, McB-C, box 6.

9. Unfortunately, Walla Walla Presbytery records for this era could not be located. However, according to the *Minutes of the Spokane Presbytery*, Presbytery of the Inland Northwest, Nez Perce ministers serving the Spokane River (Deep Creek) and Wellpinit Churches were regularly assigned to standing committees. M. M. Crawford to C. M. Blair, November 18, 1927, McB-C, box 6.

10. M. M. Crawford to J. M. Somerndike, Nov. 11, 1932, McB-C, box 6.

11. McBeth, "Facts regarding the two Spokane Churches," 1, McB-C, box 4. Historians continue to be divided over the issue of Williams's guilt,

but the fact remains that factions sought the power of the presbytery to bolster their own positions. See, D. E. Walker, *Conflict and Schism*, 68; Morrill and Morrill, *Out of the Blanket*, 289–91; 307–10. Not surprisingly, the McBeth sisters and friends believed Williams's claim of innocence and stood by him. See, for example, S. L. McBeth to K. C. McBeth, April 29, 1890, McB-C, box 4; McBeth, *Nez Perces*, 116, 117; Gay, *With the Nez Perces*, 87–89.

12. K. C. McBeth to S. Woods, August 24, 1892, McB-C, box 4; Samuel Woods, "To Elders of Meadow Creek Church," McB-C, box 1.

13. *Constitution of the Presbyterian Church, U.S.A., Part 2*, 1995, G-14.0513.

14. "Stated supply" referred to a pastor who, if not serving a church, was available at the call of a church session to serve for up to a year at a time.

15. D. O. Ghormley to K. C. McBeth, March 25, 1897, McB-C, box 1.

16. T. M. Gunn to the session and congregation of the Lapwai Presbyterian Church, May 18, 1897, McB-C, box 1.

17. Ibid. The Presbyterian Board of National Missions regularly contributed to the salaries of Native ministers.

18. D. O. Ghormley to K. C. McBeth, March 25, 1897, McB-C, box 1.

19. "Sessional Records of the Lapwain Presbyterian Church," May 30, 1897, Clifford Drury Papers, Oregon Historical Society.

20. McBeth, *Nez Perces*, 202.

21. Ibid., 201.

22. Letter from M. M. Crawford, Nov. 17, 1916, unsigned, McB-C, box 6.

23. McBeth, "Facts regarding the two Spokane Churches," McB-C, box 4.

24. Goodman, "Nez Perce Indians," 1; D. E. Walker, *Conflict and Schism*, 59.

25. M. M. Crawford to the Joint Session of the Nez Perce Churches, April 26, 1927, unsigned, McB-C, box 6.

26. M. M. Crawford, Nov. 17, 1916, unsigned, McB-C, box 6.

27. M. M. Crawford to Mark [Arthur], March 5, 1931, McB-C, box 6.

28. Draft of letter to Rev. John M. Somerndike from Joint Session and Campmeeting Committee of the Nez Perce churches, April 25, 1938, unsigned, Kate C. McBeth Letters and Papers. The request concerning the placement of the young missionary Miss Gillette was ignored. M. M. Crawford to L. C. McEwan, June 7, 1938, McB-C, box 6.

29. M. M. Crawford to Miss Voss, July 23, 1931, unsigned, McB-C, box 6.

30. M. M. Crawford to Mark [Arthur], March 5, 1931, McB-C, box 6.

31. D. E. Walker, "Recommendations Regarding Certain Problems Concerning Nez Perce Presbyterianism," undated, Department of Anthropology, University of Oregon, Eugene, Oregon, in the Deward Walker Collection, Washington State University, Pullman. See also Goodman, "Nez Perce Indians," 1, quoting Walker, who also claimed that the founding of the Joint Session "was as much a result of white exclusiveness as it was a desire of the Nez Perces to escape from Presbytery control."

32. Goodman, "Nez Perce Indians," 1.

33. Barton, *John P. Williamson*, 117, 118.

34. Adams, Williamson, and Renville, *History of the Dakota Presbytery*, 9, 10; *Dakota (Indian) Presbytery Minutes*, September 30, 1867, 1:1.

35. Hunter Keen, "Papers on Dakota Indians," unpublished manuscript written at Princeton, New Jersey, May 1968, 93, Hunter Keen Private Collection, Spokane, Wash.; Adams, Williamson, and Renville, *History of the Dakota Presbytery*, 9, 10.

36. There was a Choctaw Presbytery for several decades until it merged with other presbyteries in the 1950s. Dakota Presbytery successfully fended off the church's attempt to merge it with other presbyteries in the 1970s. In 1994 a presbytery was established for Korean Presbyterians in the United States, also a nongeographical presbytery. See *Mission Yearbook for Prayer and Study*, 1996, 132.

37. Adams, Williamson, and Renville, *History of the Dakota Presbytery*, 7.

38. Keen, "Papers," 106.

39. See, for example, *Dakota (Indian) Presbytery Minutes*, August 31, 1868, 1:18; November 8, 1870, 1:63; June 14, 1873, 1:99.

40. Barton, *John P. Williamson*, 178. For examples of entries written in Dakota, see *Dakota (Indian) Presbytery Minutes*, June 20, 1874, 1:116, 117, and April 23, 1896, 2:202–204.

41. T. L. Riggs quoted in S. R. Riggs, *Mary and I*, 295.

42. *Dakota (Indian) Presbytery Minutes*, April 1, 1875, 1:122.

43. Ibid.

44. S. R. Riggs, *Mary and I*, 284; Barton, *John P. Williamson*, 149, 150.

45. S. R. Riggs, *Mary and I*, 294, 295; Barton, *John P. Williamson*, 149–51.

46. J. P. Williamson, *Dakota Mission*, 26, 27.

47. Barton, *John P. Williamson*, 152, 188.

48. Adams, Williamson, and Renville, *History of the Dakota Presbytery*, 21, 24.

49. Keen, "Papers," 105.

50. *Dakota (Indian) Presbytery Minutes*, April 5, 1869, 1:28.

51. Ibid., April 27, 1889, 59; Adams, Williamson, and Renville, *History of the Dakota Presbytery*, 19, 30. Barton, *John P. Williamson*, 179, also mentions this propensity.

52. See, for example, *Dakota (Indian) Presbytery Minutes*, August 31, 1868, 1:14; September 16, 1876, 1:144; September 27, 1889, 2:67; April 16, 1909, 3:144.

53. *Dakota (Indian) Presbytery Minutes*, September 27, 1889, 2:67.

54. Ibid.

55. *Dakota (Indian) Presbytery Minutes*, April 1891, 2:98, 99.

56. Joseph Blacksmith, "Wotanin Waste Wasamhdepi" ("They Put Up a Good Sign"), *Iapi Oaye*, February 1885, 1, trans. Doris Robertson.

57. Language is taken from *Constitution of the Presbyterian Church*, 1911, 376. An explication of the regulation is found in *Digest of the Acts and Deliverances*, 1938, 513.

58. *Digest of the Acts and Deliverances*, 1923, 323. Note a misprint of the citation from the *Digest* of "1923."

59. The decisions of the General Assembly are summarized in *Digest of the Acts and Deliverances*, 1938, 509, 510.

60. Leslie Lewis, "Native Ministers of the Dakota Presbytery to 1988," 3, in the collection of Miscellaneous Papers, Augustana College, Sioux Falls, S.Dak.

61. M. M. Crawford to L. B. Hillis, Oct. 27, 1926, Kate C. McBeth Letters and Papers.

62. M. M. Crawford to W. A. Stevenson, D.D., Jan. 17, 1927, unsigned, McB-C, box 6.

63. M. M. Crawford to Mrs. Bennett, Aug. 3, 1936, Drury Papers, EWSHS.

64. Meyer, *History of the Santee Sioux*, 296, 297.

65. M. M. Crawford to Friends, Jan. 10, 1935, Drury Papers, EWSHS.

66. "Petition," unsigned and undated, Kate C. McBeth Letters and Papers.

67. Although the bill was defeated initially, in 1948 the Nez Perces adopted a tribal government ruled by a tribal council and the Nez Perce Tribal Executive Committee. See D. E. Walker, "Nez Perce," 437.

68. M. M. Crawford to Friends, Jan. 10, 1935, Drury Papers, EWSHS.

69. M. M. Crawford to Mrs. Bennett, Aug. 3, 1936, Drury Papers, EWSHS.

70. M. M. Crawford to J. Fraser, Aug. 17, 1932, McB-C, box 6.

71. M. M. Crawford to Dr. Hare, July 20, 1932, Drury Papers, EWSHS.

72. Ibid.

73. M. M. Crawford to Mr. Thompson, February 28, 1924, McB-C, box 6.

74. W. W. McHenry to M. M. Crawford, April 23, 1925, Kate C. McBeth Letters and Papers.

75. P. Ides to M. M. Crawford, April 23, 1925, Kate C. McBeth Letters and Papers.

76. W. W. McHenry to M. M. Crawford, April 23, 1925, Kate C. McBeth Letters and Papers.

77. "Quotation from letter from Perry Ides," April 29, 1925, Kate C. McBeth Letters and Papers.

78. Ibid.

79. Ibid.

80. *Session Book of the Neah Bay Presbyterian Church,* November 17, 1935.

81. M. M. Crawford to Mrs. Bennett, July 14, 1938, Kate C. McBeth Letters and Papers.

82. According to Thorndike's daughter, Gertrude Stock, her father was horrified when he arrived to replace an existing pastor who had not been informed by the presbytery that he was, in effect, being replaced. Interview by the author with Gertrude Stock, fall 1994, Sekiu, Wash.

83. *Session Book of the Neah Bay Presbyterian Church,* April 8, 1937.

84. Ibid., December 5, 1937, p. 76.

85. Ibid., December 8, 1937, p. 77.

86. Mary Ann Gehres, "Isolated but Integrated," 8. Gehres also cites failing eyesight as the reason for his retirement, indicating that was the "official" word given by the church.

87. M. M. Crawford to Miss Scott, July 26, 1932, Drury Papers, EWSHS.

88. M. M. Crawford to J. Fraser, May 4, 1937, Kate C. McBeth Letters and Papers; M. M. Crawford to Mrs. Bennett, August 3, 1936, Drury Papers, EWSHS.

89. M. M. Crawford to Mrs. Bennett, August 3, 1936, Drury Papers, EWSHS.

90. See M. M. Crawford to L. C. McEwan, Nov. 20, 1929, McB-C, box 6, in presbytery's attempt to put a white minister over the Kamiah churches; see M. M. Crawford to J. Fraser, Feb. 13, 1925, McB-C, box 6, in the struggle to allow the Nez Perces to host the Synod of Washington for the entire week when some thought the synod members would not be comfortable; see M. M. Crawford to C. M. Drury, Nov. 20, 1933, unsigned, McB-C, box

6, concerning the slight to Nez Perce ministers ignored at a presbytery meeting.

91. M. M. Crawford to Mrs. Bennett, July 14, 1938, SFTS.

92. M. M. Crawford (unsigned) to the white ministers of the Northern Idaho Presbytery, n.d., Kate C. McBeth Letters and Papers.

93. Ibid.

94. The language concerning these requirements of the ordained remained fairly consistent until the late 1960s and amendments of the early 1970s, when it was changed in order to recognize women candidates through the use of more inclusive language—to allow "strong and worthy persons" to receive "more effective training" for the ministry. The requirements and the process also became more defined and stringent, although there has always remained latitude for presbyteries to bypass them with cause. See, for example, *Constitution of the Presbyterian Church (U.S.A.), Part 2,* 1995.

95. Barton, *John P. Williamson,* 178.

96. See appendixes attached for list of Dakota and Nez Perce pastors.

CHAPTER SEVEN

The source for the epigraph is John Eastman, "Wakpaipaksan Cagatipi" ("The Ice House"), *Iapi Oaye,* January 1887, trans. Doris Robertson.

1. McBeth, *Nez Perces,* 209.

2. J. Hayes, sermon in letter to M. M. Crawford, February 4, 1927, McB-C, box 5.

3. White, "Race Relations," 400, 401; Harmon, *Indians in the Making,* 8.

4. Berkhofer, *White Man's Indian,* 55, 57.

5. Ibid., 59; Persons, *American Minds,* 297.

6. Harmon, "Lines in Sand," 435.

7. Persons, *American Minds,* 304.

8. Ibid.; Berkhofer, *White Man's Indian,* 51, 52.

9. G. C. Anderson, "Joseph Renville and the Ethos of Biculturalism," in Clifton, *Being and Becoming Indian,* 60.

10. S. R. Riggs, *Tah-koo Wah-kan,* 421.

11. Ibid., 422.

12. M. A. Renville to S. R. Riggs, January 23, 1863, SRR.

13. M. A. Renville to S. B. Treat, October 13, 1866, GLN.

14. J. B. Renville to S. B. Treat, February 24, 1866, GLN.

15. J. B. Renville to S. B. Treat, August 10, 1869, GLN.

16. J. B. Renville to S. B. Treat, January 7, 1868, GLN.

17. J. B. Renville to S. B. Treat, February 6, 1871, GLN.

18. 1 Cor. 9:22.

19. J. B. Renville to S. B. Treat, February 6, 1871, GLN.

20. Ibid.

21. M. C. Szasz, *Between Indian and White Worlds.* Szasz's introduction and conclusion to this book on cultural brokers provides an excellent overview of the scholarship on these individuals living in more than one world, as well as insightful analysis of their particular roles and challenges.

22. Ibid.

23. S. B. Treat to J. B. Renville, March 31, 1871, GLN.

24. J. B. Renville to S. B. Treat, February 6, 1871, GLN; on citizenship and its tie to allotment, see Prucha, *Great Father,* 2:681–86; Meyer, *History of the Santee Sioux,* 165, 166, 180–83, 194.

25. J. B. Renville to S. B. Treat, February 6, 1871, GLN.

26. J. B. Renville to S. B. Treat, February 27, 1873, GLN.

27. Ibid.

28. J. Eastman, "Wakpaipaksan Wihdukcanpi."

29. "His Sioux Civilized in One Generation," *Washington Times,* December 15, 1903.

30. J. Eastman to H. Welsh, February 25, 1893, *The Indian Rights Association Papers, 1864–1973,* 3:A5088.

31. Ibid.

32. Ibid.

33. J. Eastman, "Wakpaipaksan Cagatipi."

34. J. Eastman, "Wakpaipaksan Wihdukcanpi."

35. Ibid.

36. John Eastman's father, Tawakanhdiota, or Many Lightnings (Jacob Eastman), was descended from a line of Wahpeton chiefs including Scarlet Plume and Shakes the Earth When He Walks. He served as a war chief of Wabasha's band during the Dakota war. John Eastman's mother, Wakantankawin, or Great Spirit Woman (Mary Nancy Eastman), was the granddaughter of the Mdewakanton Chief Mahpiyawicasta, or Cloudman of Lake Calhoun, an early convert to farming and Christianity. See Beane, "Eastman," 46, 47; Wilson, *Ohiyesa,* 11, 12.

37. J. Eastman, "Wakpaipaksan Wihdukcanpi."

38. Ibid.

39. "His Sioux Civilized in One Generation," *Washington Times*, December 15, 1903.

40. Ibid.

41. J. Eastman, "Wakpaipaksan Wihdukcanpi."

42. Ibid.

43. For more on the Dreamers see Mooney, *Ghost-Dance Religion*, 716–31; Relander, *Drummers and Dreamers*; Josephy, *Nez Perce Indians*, 424, 425.

44. Thomas, *Pi-Lu'-Ye-Kin*, 64.

45. Ibid., 66.

46. Ibid.; Moore, however, returned to the church in his last years and was buried at the Lapwai (Spalding) Presbyterian Church in 1965. "Oldest Nez Perce Dies at 103," *Lewiston Morning Tribune*, Sunday, October 10, 1965, p. 20.

47. J. Hayes's sermon in a letter to M. M. Crawford, February 4, 1927, McB-C, box 5.

48. Treat, *Native and Christian*, 9. See, for example, Noley, *First White Frost* and Weaver, *Native American Religious Identity*.

49. Axtell, *The European and the Indian*, 42, 43.

50. Weaver, *Native American Religious Identity*, 6. Johnstone, *Operation World*, 566, claims 17 percent of Native Americans are Christians. More conservative figures include Twiss, *One Church Many Tribes*, 55, who claims only 3 to 5 percent are "born-again Christians" after five hundred years of missionary effort.

51. Treat, *Native and Christian*, 22.

52. Ibid., 9.

53. By action of General Assembly, 1995. For an example of earlier studies, see, Schusky, *Dakota Indians in Today's World*; Corbett and Kush, *Mending the Hoop*; for a general history, see Beaver, *Introduction to Native American Church History*.

54. Annual Report of John P. Williamson of the Dakota Mission, 1886, AIC: 33(P-1)/372.

55. J. Eastman to A. Mitchell, July 21, 1887, AIC: 33(P)/1.

Bibliography

ARCHIVAL SOURCES

American Board of Commissioners for Foreign Missions Papers, BA10. A512. Minnesota Historical Society, Division of Archives and Manuscripts, St. Paul. Typescripts. Cited in the notes as ABCFM Papers.

American Indian Correspondence: The Presbyterian Historical Society Collection of Missionaries' Letters, 1833–1893. Westport, Conn.: Greenwood Press, 1979. Microfilm. Cited in the notes as AIC.

Artemas Ehnamani Sermons, P150. Minnesota Historical Society, Division of Archives and Manuscripts, St. Paul. Cited in the notes as AE.

Ascension Church Women, *Iyopta or Advance Society Minutes*, 1874–1881. Presbyterian Historical Society, Department of History, Presbyterian Church, U.S.A., Philadelphia.

Miscellaneous Papers, Augustana College, Center for Western Studies, Sioux Falls, S.Dak.

Board of Foreign Missions, Presbyterian Church in the U.S.A., Department of Missionary Personnel, 1832–1952, RG 360. Presbyterian Historical Society, Department of History, Presbyterian Church, U.S.A., Philadelphia.

Personal Papers, Sidney H. Byrd Private Collection, Santa Fe, N.Mex.

Helen Clark, "Chips from an Old Block: Notes by Helen Clark." Neah Bay Presbyterian Church, Neah Bay, Wash.

James Cornelison Papers, MSS 687. Oregon Historical Society, Portland.

Henry T. Cowley Letters. Presbyterian Historical Society, Department of History, Presbyterian Church, U.S.A., Philadelphia.

Dakota (Indian) Presbytery Minutes, 1868–1951. 5 vols. Presbyterian Historical Society, Department of History, Presbyterian Church, U.S.A., Philadelphia.

Clifford Drury File. Washington State Historical Society, Tacoma.

Clifford Drury Papers, MSS 2430. Oregon Historical Society, Portland.

Clifford M. Drury Papers, MS 17. Eastern Washington State Historical Society, Spokane. Cited in the notes as Drury Papers, EWSHS.

Clifford M. Drury Papers. San Francisco Theological Seminary Library, San Anselmo, Calif.

Clifford Merrill Drury Collection of Research, Manuscripts, and Correspondence, MS 437. Idaho State Historical Society Library and Archives, Boise.

John Eastman Collection. William L. Beane Private Collection, Flandreau, S.Dak.

Francis Frazier Address, FE99.D1F8. Division of Archives and Manuscripts, Minnesota Historical Society, St. Paul.

The Indian Rights Association Papers, 1864–1973. Glen Rock, N.J.: Microfilming Corporation of America, 1974.

Indians, Vertical File. Pendleton Branch Library, Pendleton, Ore.

Personal Papers, Hunter Keen Private Collection, Spokane, Wash.

Edward Marsden Papers. San Francisco Theological Seminary Library, San Anselmo, Calif.

Kate C. McBeth Letters and Papers. San Francisco Theological Seminary Library, San Anselmo, Calif.

McBeth-Crawford Collection, MS 370. Idaho State Historical Society Library and Archives, Boise. Cited in the notes as McB-C.

Minutes of the Presbytery of Spokane, 1890–1972. Presbytery of the Inland Northwest, Spokane, Wash. Microfilm.

Allen and Eleanor Morrill Papers, AG 113. University of Idaho Library, Moscow. Cited in the notes as AEM.

"Neah Bay Presbyterian Church Observing Fiftieth Anniversary." Pamphlet. Neah Bay Presbyterian Church, Neah Bay, Wash.

Grace Lee Nute Papers, CBX.9.N976. Minnesota Historical Society, Division of Archives and Manuscripts, St. Paul. Typescripts. Cited in the notes as GLN.

Oahe Collection. Augustana College, Center for Western Studies, Sioux Falls, S.Dak.

Samuel and Gideon Pond Papers, P437. Minnesota Historical Society, Division of Archives and Manuscripts, St. Paul.

Presbyterian Church, Washington Territory, 1882–1937. Presbytery of the Inland Northwest, Spokane, Wash. Microfilm.

Protestant Missionaries Collection, MSS 1225. Oregon Historical Society, Portland.

Stephen R. Riggs Papers, P727. Minnesota Historical Society, Division of Archives and Manuscripts, St. Paul. Cited in the notes as SRR.

Stephen R. Riggs Papers, RG 238. Presbyterian Historical Society, Department of History, Presbyterian Church, U.S.A., Philadelphia.

Session Book of the Neah Bay Presbyterian Church, Neah Bay, Washington, 1922–. Neah Bay Presbyterian Church, Neah Bay, Wash.

Sessional Minutes of the First Presbyterian Church of Kamiah, 1889–1944. Private Collection, Lapwai, Idaho. Microfilm.

Sessional Records of the Lapwai Presbyterian Church, 1876–1894. Private Collection, Lapwai, Idaho. Microfilm.

"Sessional Records of the Lapwain Presbyterian Church," 1884–1948. Excerpts typescripted by C. M. Drury, Clifford Drury Papers, Oregon Historical Society, Portland.

Sessional Records of the Willpinit Presbyterian Church, 1882–1937. Presbytery of the Inland Northwest, Spokane, Wash. Microfilm.

Deward Walker Collection, Washington State University, Pullman.

Thomas S. Williamson Papers, P726. Minnesota Historical Society, Division of Archives and Manuscripts, St. Paul.

PERIODICALS AND NEWSPAPERS

The Church at Home and Abroad. Philadelphia: Presbyterian Board of Publication, 1887–1898.

Iapi Oaye. Santee, Nebr.: Santee Normal Training School, 1871–1939. Microfiche.

Lewiston Morning Tribune

The Occident

Washington Times

Word Carrier. Santee, Nebr.: Santee Normal Training School, 1873–1939. Microfiche.

DISSERTATIONS AND THESES

Dawson, Deborah Lynn. "'Laboring in My Savior's Vineyard': The Mission of Eliza Hart Spalding." Ph.D. diss., Bowling Green State University, 1988.

Eklund, Allison Fabyanske. "Dakota Conversions to Christianity, 1834–1862: An Exercise in Multiple Interpretations." Master's thesis, United Theological Seminary, St. Paul, 1994.

Hamilton, John M. "A History of the Presbyterian Work among the Pima and Papago Indians of Arizona." Master's thesis, University of Arizona, 1948.

Higham, Carol Lee. "The Savage and the Saved: Protestant Missionaries, the Image of the Indian, and National Policy in the U.S. and Canada, 1830–1900." Ph.D. diss., Duke University, 1993.

McCoy, Genevieve. "Sanctifying the Self and Saving the Savage: The Failure of the ABCFM Oregon Mission and the Conflicted Language of Calvinism," Ph.D. diss., University of Washington, 1991.

Mensel, Ernst Jerome. "John, Charles, and Elaine Goodale Eastman: Their Story—A Contribution to the American Indian." Master's thesis, Dartmouth College, 1954.

Widder, Keith Robert. "Together as Family: Métis Children's Response to Evangelical Protestants at the Mackinaw Mission, 1823–1837." Ph.D. diss., Michigan State University, 1989.

BOOKS AND ARTICLES

Ackerman, Lillian A. "The Effect of Missionary Ideals on Family Structure and Women's Roles in Plateau Indian Culture." *Idaho Yesterdays* 31 (spring/summer 1987): 64–73.

Adams, Moses N., John P. Williamson, and John B. Renville. *The History of the Dakota Presbytery of the Presbyterian Church in the United States of America.* Good Will, S. Dak.: Good Will Mission Indian Industrial Training School Press, 1892.

Ahlstrom, Sydney E. *A Religious History of the American People.* New Haven: Yale University Press, 1972.

Alcorn, Rowena, L. *Timothy, A Nez Perce Chief, 1800–1891.* Fairfield, Wash.: Ye Galleon Press, 1985.

Anderson, Gary Clayton. "Joseph Renville and the Ethos of Biculturalism." In *Being and Becoming Indian: Biographical Studies of North American Frontiers,* edited by James A. Clifton. Chicago: Dorsey Press, 1989.

———. *Little Crow: Spokesman for the Sioux.* St. Paul: Minnesota Historical Society Press, 1986.

Anderson, Gary Clayton, and Alan R. Woolworth, eds. *Through Dakota Eyes: Narrative Accounts of the Minnesota Indian War of 1862.* St. Paul: Minnesota Historical Society Press, 1988.

Anderson, Owanah. *Jamestown Commitment: The Episcopal Church and the American Indian.* Cincinnati: Forward Movement Press, 1988.

Axtell, James. *After Columbus: Essays in the Ethnohistory of Colonial North America.* New York: Oxford University Press, 1988.

———. *The European and the Indian: Essays in the Ethnohistory of Colonial North America.* New York: Oxford University Press, 1981.

———. *The Invasion Within: The Contest of Cultures in Colonial North America.* New York: Oxford University Press, 1985.

———. "Some Thoughts on the Ethnohistory of Missions." *Ethnohistory* 29 (1982): 35–41.

Baird, Andrew Browning. *Foreign Missions of the Presbyterian Church in Canada: The Indians of Western Canada.* Toronto: Press of the Canada Presbyterian, 1895.

Baird, Samuel J. *A History of the Early Policy of the Presbyterian Church in the Training of Her Ministry and the First Years of the Board of Education.* Philadelphia: Presbyterian Board of Education, 1865.

Balmer, Randall, and John R. Fitzmier. *The Presbyterians.* Westport, Conn.: Greenwood Press, 1993.

Banker, Mark T. *Presbyterian Missions and Cultural Interaction in the Far Southwest, 1850–1950.* Urbana: University of Illinois Press, 1993.

Barnett, H. G. *Indian Shakers: A Messianic Cult of the Pacific Northwest.* Carbondale: Southern Illinois University Press, 1957. Reprint, Arcturus Books, 1972.

Barton, Winifred W. *John P. Williamson, A Brother to the Sioux.* New York: Fleming H. Revell Co., 1919. Reprint, Clements, Minn.: Sunnycrest Publishing, 1980.

Beattie, William Gilbert. *Marsden of Alaska: A Modern Indian.* New York: Vantage Press, 1955.

Beaver, R. Pierce. *All Loves Excelling: American Protestant Women in World Mission.* Grand Rapids, Mich.: William B. Eerdmans, 1968.

———. *Introduction to Native American Church History.* Edited by David Keller. Tempe: Cook College and Theological School, 1983.

———. *The Native American Christian Community: A Directory of Indian, Aleut, and Eskimo Churches.* Monrovia, Calif.: MARC, A Division of World Vision International, 1979.

———, ed. *Pioneers in Mission: The Early Missionary Ordination Sermons, Charges, and Instructions.* Grand Rapids, Mich.: William B. Eerdmans, 1966.

———. *To Advance the Gospel: Selections from the Writings of Rufus Anderson.* Grand Rapids, Mich.: William B. Eerdmans, 1967.

Bendroth, Margaret L. "Women and Missions: Conflict and Changing Roles in the Presbyterian Church in the United States of America, 1870–1935." *American Presbyterians* 65 (spring 1987): 49–59.

Berkhofer, Robert F., Jr. *Salvation and the Savage: An Analysis of Protestant Missions and American Indian Response, 1787–1862.* Lexington: University of Kentucky Press, 1965.

———. *The White Man's Indian: Images of the American Indian from Columbus to the Present.* New York: Random House, 1978; Vintage Books, 1979.

Blegen, Theodore C. *Minnesota: A History of the State.* Minneapolis: University of Minnesota, 1963.

Blodgett, Harold. *Samson Occom.* Hanover, N.H.: Dartmouth College Publications, 1935.

Blumhofer, Edith L., and Randall Balmer, eds. *Modern Christian Revivals.* Urbana: University of Illinois Press, 1993.

Bolt, Clarence. *Thomas Crosby and the Tsimshian: Small Shoes for Feet Too Large.* Vancouver: University of British Columbia Press, 1992.

Bosch, David J. *Transforming Mission: Paradigm Shifts in Theology of Mission.* New York: Orbis, 1991.

Bowden, Henry Warner. *American Indians and Christian Missions: Studies in Cultural Conflict.* Chicago: University of Chicago Press, 1981.

———. "Native American Presbyterians: Assimilation, Leadership, and Future Challenges." In *The Diversity of Discipleship: The Presbyterians and Twentieth Century Christian Witness,* edited by Milton J. Coalter, John Mulder, and Louis B. Weeks. Louisville: Westminster/John Knox Press, 1991.

Bowden, Henry Warner, and James P. Ronda, eds. *John Eliot's Indian Dialogues: A Study in Cultural Interaction.* Westport, Conn.: Greenwood Press, 1980.

Boyd, Lois A., and R. Douglas Brackenridge. *Presbyterian Women in America: Two Centuries of a Quest for Status.* Westport, Conn.: Greenwood Press, 1983.

Bragdon, Kathleen, "Gender as a Social Category in Native Southern New England." *Ethnohistory* 43 (fall 1996): 573–92.

Brown, G. Thompson. *Presbyterians in World Mission: A Handbook for Congregations.* Rev. ed. Decatur, Ga.: CTS Press, 1988, 1995.

Brown, Joseph Epes, ed. *The Sacred Pipe: Black Elk's Account of the Seven Rites of the Oglala Sioux.* Norman: University of Oklahoma Press, 1953. Reprint, New York: Penguin Books, 1971.

———. *The Spiritual Legacy of the American Indian.* New York: Crossroad Publishing Co., 1991.

Cannon, Miles. *Waiilatpu: Its Rise and Fall, 1836–1847.* Boise, Idaho: Capital News Job Rooms, 1915.

Carlson, Paul H. *The Plains Indians.* College Station: Texas A&M University Press, 1998.

Chance, Norman A. "Acculturation, Self-Identification, and Personality Adjustment." In *The Emergent Native Americans: A Reader in Culture Contact,* edited by Deward E. Walker, Jr. Boston: Little, Brown, 1972.

Clifton, James A., ed. *Being and Becoming Indian: Biographical Studies of North American Frontiers.* Chicago: Dorsey Press, 1989.

Coale, George L. "Ethnohistorical Sources for the Nez Perce Indians, Part 1." *Ethnohistory* 3 (summer 1956): 246–55.

———. "Ethnohistorical Sources for the Nez Perce Indians, Part 2." *Ethnohistory* 3 (fall 1956): 346–60.

Coates, Lawrence G. "The Spalding-Whitman and Lemhi Missions: A Comparison." *Idaho Yesterdays* (spring/summer 1987): 38–46.

Coleman, Michael C. *Presbyterian Missionary Attitudes toward American Indians, 1837–1893.* Jackson: University Press of Mississippi, 1985.

Collier, John. *Indians of the Americas: The Long Hope.* Slightly abridged. New York: Mentor Books, 1947.

Comaroff, Jean, and John Comaroff. *Of Revelation and Revolution: Christianity, Colonialism, and Consciousness in South Africa.* Vol. 1. Chicago: University of Chicago Press, 1991.

Constitution of the Presbyterian Church in the United States of America. Philadelphia: Presbyterian Board of Publication, 1871, 1911.

Constitution of the Presbyterian Church (USA), Part 2: Book of Order. Louisville: Office of the General Assembly, 1995.

Corbett, Cecil, and Gary Kush. *Mending the Hoop: A Comprehensive Report of the Indian Church Career Research and Planning Project.* Native American Consulting Committee, 1974.

Cott, Nancy F. *The Bonds of Womanhood: "Woman's Sphere" in New England, 1780–1835.* New Haven: Yale University Press, 1977.

Crawford, Mary M. *The Nez Perces Since Spalding: Experiences of Forty-one Years at Lapwai, Idaho.* Berkeley: Professional Press, 1936.

Curtis, Edward S. *The North American Indian: Being a Series of Volumes Picturing and Describing the Indians of the United States and Alaska.* 20 vols. Cambridge: Cambridge University Press, 1907–1930. Reprint, New York: Johnson Reprint Corp., 1970.

Deloria, Ella C. *Speaking of Indians.* New York: Friendship Press, 1944. Reprint, Vermillion: University of South Dakota Press, 1992.

Deloria, Vine, Jr. "The Establishment of Christianity Among the Sioux." In *Sioux Indian Religion: Tradition and Innovation,* edited by Raymond J. DeMallie and Douglas R. Parks. Norman: University of Oklahoma Press, 1987.

DeMallie, Raymond J. "Sioux until 1850." In *Handbook of North American Indians,* vol. 13, edited by William Sturtevant. Washington, D.C.: Smithsonian Institution, 2001.

————, ed. *The Sixth Grandfather: Black Elk's Teachings Given to John G. Neihardt.* Lincoln: University of Nebraska Press, 1984.

————. "'These Have No Ears': Narrative and the Ethnohistorical Method." *Ethnohistory* 40 (fall 1993): 515–38.

DeMallie, Raymond J., and Douglas R. Parks, eds. *Sioux Indian Religion: Tradition and Innovation.* Norman: University of Oklahoma Press, 1987.

Dennis, James S. *Native Agents and Their Training: A Paper Read at the Fifth General Council of the Alliance of the Reformed Churches, held at Toronto, Sept. 21–30, 1892.* Reprint, *The Magazine of Christian Literature* (November 1892).

Densmore, Frances. *Teton Sioux Music.* Smithsonian Institution. Bureau of American Ethnology, Bulletin 61. Washington: Government Printing Office, 1918.

Devens, Carol. *Countering Colonization: Native American Women and Great Lakes Missions, 1630–1900.* Berkeley: University of California Press, 1992.

Digest of the Acts and Deliverances of the General Assembly of the Presbyterian Church in the United States of America. Vol. 1. Philadelphia: Office of the General Assembly, 1923, 1930, 1938.

Drury, Clifford Merrill. "The Beginnings of Talmaks: 'Galloping Over the Butte.'" Craigmont, Idaho: Rev. David H. Crawford, 1958. In *Seventy Five Years Presbyterian Camp Meetings of the Nez Perce Indians,* edited by Henry Sugden. N.p., n.d.

————. *Chief Lawyer of the Nez Perce Indians, 1796–1876.* Glendale, Calif.: Arthur H. Clark Co., 1979.

————. *Elkanah and Mary Walker: Pioneers Among the Spokanes.* Caldwell, Idaho: Caxton Printers, Ltd., 1940.

————. *Henry Harmon Spalding.* Caldwell, Idaho: Caxton Printers, Ltd., 1936.

————. *Marcus and Narcissa Whitman and the Opening of Old Oregon.* 2 vols. Glendale, Calif.: Arthur H. Clark, 1973. Reprint, Vol. 1, Seattle: Pacific Northwest National Parks and Forests Assoc., 1986.

————. *Marcus Whitman, M.D.: Pioneer and Martyr.* Caldwell, Idaho: Caxton Printers, Ltd., 1937.

————. *Nine Years with the Spokane Indians: The Diary, 1838–1848, of Elkanah Walker.* Glendale, Calif.: Arthur H. Clark Co., 1976.

————. *Presbyterian Panorama: One Hundred and Fifty Years of National Missions History.* Philadelphia: Board of Christian Education, Presbyterian Church in the U.S.A., 1952.

———, ed. *Diaries and Letters of Henry H. Spalding and Asa Bowen Smith Relating to the Nez Perce Mission, 1838–1842.* Glendale, Calif.: Arthur H. Clark Co., 1958.

———. *First White Women over the Rockies: Diaries Letters, and Biographical Sketches of the Six Women of the Oregon Mission Who Made the Overland Journey in 1836 and 1838.* 3 vols. Glendale, Calif.: Arthur H. Clark, 1966.

———. "The Spalding-Lowrie Correspondence." *Journal of the Department of History (The Presbyterian Historical Society) of the Presbyterian Church in the U.S.A.* 20 (March–June–September 1942): 1–114.

Duratschek, M. Claudia. *The Beginnings of Catholicism in South Dakota.* Washington, D.C.: Catholic University of America Press, 1943.

Eastman, Charles A. (Ohiyesa). *Old Indian Days.* New York: McClure Co., 1907. Reprint, Lincoln: University of Nebraska Press, 1991.

———. *The Soul of the Indian, An Interpretation.* Boston: Houghton Mifflin, 1911. Reprint, Lincoln: University of Nebraska Press, Bison Book, 1980.

Eastman, Mary. *Dahcotah; or, Life and Legends of the Sioux around Fort Snelling.* New York: Thomas B. Smith, 1849. Reprint, Minneapolis: Ross & Haines, Inc., 1962.

Edmunds, R. David. "Native Americans, New Voices: American Indian History, 1895–1995." *American Historical Review* (June 1995): 717–40.

Eells, Myron. *The Indians of Puget Sound: The Notebooks of Myron Eells.* Edited by George Pierre Castile. Seattle: University of Washington Press, 1985.

Evans, Steven Ross. *Voice of the Old Wolf: Lucullus Virgil McWhorter and the Nez Perce Indians.* Pullman: Washington State University Press, 1996.

Fisher, Robin. *Contact and Conflict: Indian-European Relations in British Columbia, 1774–1890.* Vancouver: University of British Columbia Press, 1977.

Folwell, William Watts. *A History of Minnesota.* 2 vols. St. Paul: Minnesota Historical Society, 1924.

Forbes, Bruce David. "'And Obey God, Etc.': Methodism and American Indians." In *Perspectives on American Methodism: Interpretive Essays,* edited by Russell E. Richey, Kenneth E. Rowe, and Jean Miller Schmidt. Nashville: Kingswood Books, 1993.

Fowler, Loretta. *Arapahoe Politics, 1851–1978: Symbols in Crises of Authority.* Lincoln: University of Nebraska Press, 1982.

Fraser, Julia. *Peaka Soyapu: The White Mother of the Nez Perces: Kate Christine McBeth, A Memoir.* Unpublished.

Furniss, Elizabeth. "Resistance, Coercion, and Revitalization: The Shuswap Encounter with Roman Catholic Missionaries, 1860–1900." *Ethnohistory* 42 (spring 1995): 231–63.

Gay, E. Jane. *With the Nez Perces: Alice Fletcher in the Field, 1889–1892.* Edited by Frederick E. Hoxie and Joan T. Mark. Lincoln: University of Nebraska Press, 1981.

Geertz, Clifford. *The Interpretation of Cultures: Selected Essays.* New York: Basic Books, 1973.

Gehres, Mary Ann. "Isolated But Integrated: At Neah Bay, Northwest Corner of the U.S.A., Makah Indians are Active Citizens and Churchmen." *Presbyterian Life* (November 10, 1956): 7–9.

Ginzberg, Lori D. *Women and the Work of Benevolence: Morality, Politics, and Class in the Nineteenth-Century United States.* New Haven: Yale University Press, 1990.

Goodman, Grace Ann. "Nez Perce Indians and Presbyterian Churches." Institute of Strategic Studies. New York: Board of National Missions, United Presbyterian Church in the U.S.A., Oct. 1966.

Gray, Joan S., and Joyce C. Tucker. *Presbyterian Polity for Church Officers.* 2d ed. Louisville: Westminster/John Knox Press, 1986.

Gray, W. H. *A History of Oregon, 1792–1849, Drawn from Personal Observation and Authentic Information.* Portland, Oreg.: Harris & Holman, 1870.

Hagan, William T. *Indian Police and Judges: Experiments in Acculturation and Control.* New Haven: Yale University Press, 1966.

Haines, Francis. *The Nez Perces: Tribesmen of the Columbia Plateau.* Norman: University of Oklahoma Press, 1955.

Handy, Robert T. "The American Religious Depression, 1925–1935." In *Religion in American History: Interpretive Essays,* edited by John M. Mulder and John F. Wilson. Englewood Cliffs, N.J.: Prentice-Hall, 1978.

Hankins, Jean F. "Solomon Briant and Joseph Johnson: Indian Teachers and Preachers in Colonial New England." *Connecticut History* 33 (November 1992): 38–60.

Harkin, Michael. "Engendering Discipline: Discourse and Counterdiscourse in the Methodist-Heiltsuk Dialogue." *Ethnohistory* 43 (fall 1996): 643–61.

Harmon, Alexandra. *Indians in the Making: Ethnic Relations and Indian Identities around Puget Sound.* Berkeley: University of California Press, 1998.

———. "Lines in Sand: Shifting Boundaries between Indians and Non-Indians in the Puget Sound Region." *Western Historical Quarterly* 26 (winter 1995): 429–53.

Harrod, Howard L. *Becoming and Remaining a People: Native American Religions on the Northern Plains.* Tucson: University of Arizona Press, 1995.

Hayes, James. *Called to Evangelize.* New York: Board of National Missions of the Presbyterian Church in the U.S.A., 1928.

Herzog, Kristin. "The La Flesche Family: Native America Spirituality, Calvinism, and Presbyterian Missions." *American Presbyterians: Journal of Presbyterian History* 65 (fall 1987): 222–232.

Hill, Patricia R. *The World Their Household: The American Woman's Foreign Mission Movement and Cultural Transformation, 1870–1920.* Ann Arbor: University of Michigan Press, 1985.

Hinckley, Ted C. "Sheldon Jackson College: Historic Nucleus of the Presbyterian Enterprise in Alaska." *Journal of Presbyterian History* 49 (spring 1971): 59–79.

Hoxie, Frederick E. *A Final Promise: The Campaign to Assimilate the Indians, 1880–1920.* Lincoln: University of Nebraska Press, 1984.

Hoyle, Lydia Huffman. "Teachers of Preachers: Sue McBeth and Her Mission to the Nez Perces." *Missiology* (October 1999): 475–80.

Hulbert, Archer Butler, and Dorothy P. Hulbert, eds. "Marcus Whitman, Crusader." Vols. 6–8, *Overland to the Pacific,* 8 vols. Denver: Stewart Commission of Colorado College, 1932–41.

Hultkrantz, Ake. *The Religions of the American Indians.* Translated by Monica Setterwall. Berkeley: University of California Press, 1979.

Hunn, Eugene S. *Nch'i-Wa'na, "The Big River": Mid-Columbia Indians and Their Land.* Seattle: University of Washington Press, 1990.

Hunter, Jane. *The Gospel of Gentility: American Women Missionaries in Turn-of-the-Century China.* New Haven: Yale University Press, 1984.

Hutchison, William R. *Errand to the World: American Protestant Thought and Foreign Missions.* Chicago: University of Chicago Press, 1987.

Irwin, Lee. *The Dream Seekers: Native American Traditions of the Great Plains.* Norman: University of Oklahoma Press, 1994.

James, Caroline. *Nez Perce Women in Transition, 1877–1990.* Moscow: University of Idaho Press, 1996.

Jeffrey, Julie Roy. *Converting the West: A Biography of Narcissa Whitman.* Norman: University of Oklahoma Press, 1991.

Jessett, Thomas E. *Chief Spokan Garry, 1811–1892: Christian, Statesman, and Friend of the White Man.* Minneapolis: T. S. Denison & Co., 1960.

Johnstone, Patrick. *Operation World.* 6th ed. Waynesboro, Ga.: Paternoster U.S.A., 2001.

Josephy, Alvin M., Jr. *The Nez Perce Indians and the Opening of the Northwest.* Abridged ed. New Haven: Yale University Press, 1971. Reprint, Lincoln: University of Nebraska Press, Bison Book, 1979.

———. *The Patriot Chiefs: A Chronicle of American Indian Resistance.* New York: Viking Press, 1958.

Keller, Robert H., Jr. *American Protestantism and United States Indian Policy, 1869–82.* Lincoln: University of Nebraska Press, 1983.

Kidwell, Clara Sue. *Choctaws and Missionaries in Mississippi, 1818–1918.* Norman: University of Oklahoma Press, 1995.

Kidwell, Clara Sue, Homer Noley, and George E. "Tink" Tinker. *A Native American Theology.* New York: Orbis, 2001.

Kip, Lawrence. *The Indian Council in the Valley of the Walla-Walla.* San Francisco: Whitton, Towne & Co., 1855. Reprint, Tarrytown, N.Y.: William Abbatt, 1915.

Klein, Laura F., and Lillian A. Ackerman, eds. *Women and Power in Native North America.* Norman: University of Oklahoma Press, 1995.

Kosmin, Barry A., and Seymour P. Lachman, eds. *One Nation Under God and Religion in Contemporary American Society.* New York: Crown Trade Paperbacks, 1993.

Kraft, Charles H. *Christianity in Culture: A Study in Dynamic Biblical Theologizing in Cross Cultural Perspective.* New York: Orbis Books, 1979.

Landes, Ruth. *The Mystic Lake Sioux: Sociology of the Mdewakantonwan Santee.* Madison: University of Wisconsin Press, 1968.

Leith, John H. *Introduction to the Reformed Tradition: A Way of Being the Christian Community.* Rev. ed. Atlanta: John Knox Press, 1977.

Limerick, Patricia Nelson. *The Legacy of Conquest: The Unbroken Past of the American West.* New York: W. W. Norton, 1987.

Loewenberg, Robert J. *Equality on the Oregon Frontier: Jason Lee and the Methodist Mission 1834–43.* Seattle: University of Washington Press, 1976.

Long, Kathryn Teresa. *The Revival of 1857–58: Intrepreting an American Religious Awakening.* Oxford: Oxford University Press, 1998.

Longfield, Bradley J. *Presbyterian Controversy: Fundamentalists, Modernists, and Moderates.* New York: Oxford University Press, 1991.

Lowie, Robert H. *Indians of the Plains.* New York: McGraw-Hill, 1954.

Mark, Joan. *A Stranger in Her Native Land: Alice Fletcher and the American Indians.* Lincoln: University of Nebraska Press, 1988.

Markowitz, Harvey. "The Catholic Mission and the Sioux, A Crisis in the Early Paradigm." In *Sioux Indian Religion: Tradition and Innovation,* edited by Raymond J. DeMallie and Douglas R. Parks. Norman: University of Oklahoma Press, 1987.

Marsden, George M. *The Evangelical Mind and the New School Presbyterian Experience: A Case Study of Thought and Theology in Nineteenth-Century America.* New Haven: Yale University Press, 1970.

Martin, Joel W. *The Land Looks After Us: A History of Native American Religion.* Oxford: Oxford University Press, 1999.

McBeth, Kate. *The Nez Perces Since Lewis and Clark.* New York: Fleming H. Revell Co., 1908. Reprint, Moscow: University of Idaho Press, 1993.

McLaren, Darcee. "Living the Middle Ground: Two Dakota Missionaries, 1887–1912." *Ethnohistory* 43 (spring 1996): 278–305.

McLaughlin, James. *My Friend The Indian.* 1910. Reprint, Lincoln: University of Nebraska Press, 1989.

McLoughlin, William G. *Champions of the Cherokees: Evan and John B. Jones.* Princeton, N.J.: Princeton University Press, 1990.

———. *The Cherokees and Christianity, 1794–1870: Essays on Acculturation and Cultural Persistence.* Edited by Walter H. Conser, Jr. Athens: University of Georgia Press, 1994.

———. *Cherokees and Missionaries, 1789–1839.* New Haven: Yale University Press, 1984.

———. *Revivals, Awakenings, and Reform: An Essay on Religion and Social Change in America, 1607–1977.* Chicago: University of Chicago Press, 1978.

McNally, Michael D. *Ojibwe Singers: Hymns, Grief, and a Native Culture in Motion.* Oxford: University of Oxford Press, 2000.

McWhorter, Lucullus Virgil. *Hear Me, My Chiefs! Nez Perce Legend and History.* Caldwell, Idaho: Caxton Printers, 1952; reprint, 1992.

———. *Yellow Wolf: His Own Story.* Caldwell, Idaho: Caxton Printers, 1940; reprint, 1991.

Merrell, James H. *The Indians' New World: Catawbas and Their Neighbors from European Contact through the Era of Removal.* New York: W. W. Norton, 1989.

Merritt, Jane T. "Dreaming of the Savior's Blood: Moravians and the Indian Great Awakening." *William and Mary Quarterly* 3d ser., 54 (October 1997).

Meyer, Roy W. *History of the Santee Sioux: United States Indian Policy on Trial.* Rev. ed. Lincoln: University of Nebraska Press, 1967; Bison Book, 1993.

Miller, Christopher L. *Prophetic Worlds: Indians and Whites on the Columbia Plateau.* New Brunswick, N.J.: Rutgers University Press, 1985.

Milner, Clyde A., II, and Floyd A. O'Neil, eds. *Churchmen and the Western Indians, 1820–1920.* Norman: University of Oklahoma Press, 1985.

Mission Yearbook for Prayer and Study, 1996. Louisville: Presbyterian Distribution Service, 1996.

Mooney, James. *The Ghost-Dance Religion and the Sioux Outbreak of 1890.* Edited by Raymond J. DeMallie. Washington, D.C.: Government Printing Office, 1896. Reprint, Lincoln: University of Nebraska Press, Bison Book, 1991.

Moore, William E. *A New Digest of the Acts and Deliverances of the General Assembly of the Presbyterian Church in the United States of America.* Philadelphia: Presbyterian Publication Committee, 1861.

––––––. *The Presbyterian Digest of 1886. A Compend of the Acts and Deliverances of the General Assembly of the Presbyterian Church in the United States of America.* Philadelphia: Presbyterian Board of Publication, 1886.

––––––. *The Presbyterian Digest of 1898. A Compend of the Acts, Decisions, and Deliverances of the General Presbytery General Synod and General Assembly of the Presbyterian Church in the United States of America 1706–1897.* Philadelphia: Presbyterian Board of Publication, 1898.

Morrill, Allen Conrad, and Eleanor Dunlop Morrill. *Out of the Blanket: The Story of Sue and Kate McBeth, Missionaries to the Nez Perces.* Moscow: University Press of Idaho, 1978.

––––––. "Talmaks." *Idaho Yesterdays* 8 (fall 1964). In *Seventy Five Years Presbyterian Camp Meetings of the Nez Perce Indians,* edited by Henry Sugden. N.p., n.d.

Moses, L. G., and Margaret Connell Szasz. "'My Father, have pity on me!': Indian Revitalization Movement of the Late Nineteenth Century." *Journal of the West* 23 (January 1984): 5–15.

Moulton, Gary E., ed. *The Journals of the Lewis and Clark Expedition, March 23–June 9, 1806.* Vol. 7. Lincoln: University of Nebraska Press, 1991.

Naeher, Robert James. "Dialogue in the Wilderness: John Eliot and the Indian Exploration of Puritanism as a Source of Meaning, Comfort, and Ethnic Survival." *New England Quarterly* (September 1989): 346–68.

Neihardt, John G., ed. *Black Elk Speaks: Being the Life Story of a Holy Man of the Oglala Sioux.* New York: William Morrow, 1932. Reprint, Lincoln: University of Nebraska Press, 1979; Bison Book, 1988.

Noley, Homer. *First White Frost: Native Americans and United Methodism.* Nashville: Abingdon Press, 1991.

O'Connell, Barry, ed. *On Our Own Ground: The Complete Writings of William Apess, A Pequot.* Amherst: University of Massachusetts Press, 1992.

Parker, Donald Dean. *Founding Presbyterianism in South Dakota.* N.p., 1963.

Pascoe, Peggy. *Relations of Rescue: The Search for Female Moral Authority in the American West, 1874–1939.* New York: Oxford University Press, 1990.

Patterson, E. Palmer. "Kincolith, B.C.: Leadership Continuity in a Native Christian Village, 1867–1887." *Canadian Journal of Anthropology/Revue Canadienne d'Anthropologie* 3 (fall 1982): 45–55.

––––––. "Native Missionaries of the North Pacific Coast: Philip McKay and Others." *The Pacific Historian* 30 (spring 1986): 22–37.

Persons, Stow. *American Minds: A History of Ideas.* 2d ed., rev. Malabar, Fla.: Robert E. Krieger Publishing Company, 1983.

Phillips, Clifton Jackson. *Protestant America and the Pagan World: The First Half Century of the A.B.C.F.M., 1810–1860.* Cambridge: Harvard University Press, 1969.

Pond, Samuel W. *The Dakota or Sioux in Minnesota as They Were in 1834.* Minnesota Historical Collections, vol. 12, 1908. Reprint, St. Paul: Minnesota Historical Society, 1986.

The Presbyterian Hymnal. Louisville: Westminster/John Knox Press, 1990.

Prucha, Francis Paul. *American Indian Policy in Crisis: Christian Reformers and the Indian, 1865–1900.* Norman: University of Oklahoma Press, 1976.

————. *The Great Father: The United States Government and the American Indians.* 2 vols. Lincoln: University of Nebraska Press, 1984.

Radin, Paul. "The Autobiography of a Winnebago Indian." *American Archaeology and Ethnology* (April 15, 1920): 381–473.

Ray, Verne F. *Cultural Relations in the Plateau of Northwestern America.* Los Angeles: Southwest Museum, 1939.

Relander, Click. *Drummers and Dreamers: The Story of Smowhala the Prophet and His Nephew Puck Hyah Toot, the Last Prophet of the Nearly Extinct River People, the Last Wanapums.* Caldwell, Idaho: Caxton Printers, 1986.

Riggs, Maida Leonard, ed. *A Small Bit of Bread and Butter: Letters from the Dakota Territory, 1832–1869.* South Deerfield, Mass.: Ash Grove Press, 1996.

Riggs, Mary B. *Early Days at Santee: The Beginnings of Santee Normal Training School.* Santee, Neb.: Santee Normal Training School Press, 1928.

Riggs, Stephen R. *A Dakota-English Dictionary.* Edited by James Owen Dorsey. Washington, D.C.: Government Printing Office, 1890. Reprint, St. Paul: Minnesota Historical Society, 1992.

————. *Mary and I: Forty Years with the Sioux.* Chicago: W. G. Holmes, 1880. Reprint, Williamstown, Mass.: Corner House Publishers, 1971.

————. *Tah-koo Wah-kan; or, the Gospel among the Dakotas.* Boston: Congregational Publishing Soc., 1869. Reprint, New York: Arno Press, 1972.

Robert, Dana L. *American Women in Mission: A Social History of Their Thought and Practice.* Macon, Ga.: Mercer University Press, 1996.

Roe Cloud, Henry. *From Wigwam to Pulpit, A Red Man's Story of His Progress from Darkness to Light.* New York: Woman's Board of Home Missions of the Presbyterian Church in the U.S.A., n.d.

Rogers, Jack. *Presbyterian Creeds: A Guide to the Book of Confessions.* Philadelphia: Westminster Press, 1985.

Ronda, James P. "Generations of Faith: The Christian Indians of Martha's Vineyard." *William and Mary Quarterly* 3d ser., 38 (July 1981): 369–94.

———. *Lewis and Clark among the Indians*. Lincoln: University of Nebraska Press, 1985.

———. "'We Are Well As We Are': An Indian Critique of Seventeenth-Century Christian Missions." *William and Mary Quarterly* 3rd ser., 34 (January 1977): 66–82.

Ronda, James P., and James Axtell. *Indian Missions: A Critical Bibliography*. Bloomington: Indiana University Press, 1978.

Ruby, Robert H., and John A. Brown. *The Cayuse Indians: Imperial Tribesmen of Old Oregon*. Norman: University of Oklahoma Press, 1972.

———. *Half-Sun on the Columbia: A Biography of Chief Moses*. Norman: University of Oklahoma Press, 1965.

———. *The Spokane Indians: Children of the Sun*. Norman: University of Oklahoma Press, 1970.

Salisbury, Neal. "Red Puritans: The 'Praying Indians' of Massachusetts Bay and John Eliot." *William and Mary Quarterly* 3rd ser., 31 (January 1974): 27–54.

Saum, Lewis O. *The Popular Mood of America, 1860–1890*. Lincoln: University of Nebraska Press, 1990.

Schultz, Paul, and George Tinker. *Rivers of Life: Native Spirituality for Native Churches*. Edited by George Tinker. Minneapolis: Augsburg Publishing/Fortress Press, 1988.

Schusky, Ernest L. *Dakota Indians in Today's World: A Study of Dakota Indians' Needs in Relation to United Presbyterian U.S.A. Work*. New York: Board of National Missions, United Presbyterian Church in the U.S.A., 1962.

Schwantes, Carlos. *The Pacific Northwest: An Interpretive History*. Lincoln: University of Nebraska Press, 1989.

Sheehan, Bernard W. *Seeds of Extinction: Jeffersonian Philanthropy and the American Indian*. Chapel Hill: University of North Carolina Press, 1973.

Simmons, William S. "Red Yankees: Narragansett Conversion in the Great Awakening." *American Ethnologist* 10 (May 1983): 253–71.

Slickpoo, Allen P., Sr. *Noon Nee-Me-Poo (We, the Nez Perce)*. Lapwai: Nez Perce Tribe of Idaho, 1973.

Smith, Timothy L. *Revivalism and Social Reform in Mid-Nineteenth Century America*. Nashville: Abingdon Press, 1957. Reprint, Baltimore: Johns Hopkins University Press, 1980.

Smylie, James H. *A Brief History of the Presbyterians*. Louisville: Geneva Press, 1996.

Spicer, Edward H., ed. *Perspectives in American Indian Culture Change.* Chicago: University of Chicago Press, 1961.

Spinden, Herbert Joseph. "The Nez Perce Indians." *Memoirs of the American Anthropological Association* 2, pt. 3 (November 1908): 165–274.

Standing Bear, Luther. *My Indian Boyhood.* Boston: Houghton Mifflin, 1931. Reprint, Lincoln: University of Nebraska Press, Bison Book, 1988.

Steltenkamp, Michael F. *Black Elk: Holy Man of the Oglala.* Norman: University of Oklahoma Press, 1993.

Strong, Pauline Turner. "Feminist Theory and the 'Invasion of the Heart' in North America." *Ethnohistory* 43 (fall 1996): 683–711.

Strong, William E. *The Story of the American Board: An Account of the First Hundred Years of the American Board of Commissioners for Foreign Missions.* Boston: Pilgrim Press, 1910.

Szasz, Ferenc Morton. *The Protestant Clergy in the Great Plains and Mountain West, 1865–1915.* Albuquerque: University of New Mexico Press, 1988.

Szasz, Margaret Connell, ed. *Between Indian and White Worlds: The Cultural Broker.* Norman: University of Oklahoma Press, 1994.

———. *Indian Education in the American Colonies, 1607–1783.* Albuquerque: University of New Mexico Press, 1988.

Thomas, Anthony E. *Pi-Lu꞉-Ye-Kin: The Life History of a Nez Perce Indian.* Ann Arbor: University Microfilms, 1970.

Tinker, George E. *Missionary Conquest: The Gospel and Native American Cultural Genocide.* Minneapolis: Fortress Press, 1993.

Treat, James. *Native and Christian: Indigenous Voices on Religious Identity in the United States and Canada.* New York: Routledge, 1995.

"A True Copy of the Records of the First Presbyterian Church in the Territory of Oregon, Organized in 1838." *Fourteenth Annual Session of Synod of Washington* 2 (October 1–4, 1903): Appendix 2.

Twiss, Richard. *One Church Many Tribes: Following Jesus the Way God Made You.* Ventura, Calif.: Regal Books, 2000.

Underhill, Ruth M. *Red Man's Religion: Belief and Practices of the Indians North of Mexico.* Chicago: University of Chicago Press, 1965.

Utley, Robert M. *The Indian Frontier of the American West 1846–1890.* Albuquerque: University of New Mexico Press, 1984.

Van Lonkhuyzen, Harold W. "A Reappraisal of the Praying Indians: Acculturation, Conversion, and Identity at Natick, Massachusetts, 1646–1730." *New England Quarterly* (September 1990): 396–428.

Vibert, Elizabeth. "'The Natives Were Strong to Live': Reinterpreting Early-Nineteenth-Century Prophetic Movements in the Columbia Plateau." *Ethnohistory* 42 (spring 1995): 197–229.

Viola, Herman J. *Diplomats in Buckskins: A History of Indian Delegations in Washington City*. Washington, D.C.: Smithsonian Institution Press, 1981. Reprint, Bluffton, S.C.: Rivilo Books, 1995.

Walker, Deward E., Jr. *Conflict and Schism in Nez Perce Acculturation: A Study of Religion and Politics*. Pullman: Washington University Press, 1968.

———. *Indians of Idaho*. Moscow: University of Idaho Press, 1978.

———. "Nez Perce." In *Handbook of North American Indians*, vol. 12, edited by William Sturtevant. Washington, D.C.: Smithsonian Institution, 1998.

Walker, James R. *Lakota Belief and Ritual*. Edited by Raymond J. DeMallie and Elaine A. Jahner. Lincoln: University of Nebraska Press, 1980; Bison Book, 1991.

———. *Lakota Society*. Edited by Raymond J. DeMallie. Lincoln: University of Nebraska Press, 1982; Bison Book, 1992.

———. "The Sun Dance and Other Ceremonies of the Oglala Division of the Teton Dakota." *Anthropological Papers*, American Museum of Natural History, 16, pt. 2 (1917).

Weaver, Jace, ed. *Native American Religious Identity: Unforgotten Gods*. Maryknoll, N.Y.: Orbis, 1998.

Webster, Jonathan Howes. "The ABCFM and the First Presbyterian Missions in the Northwest." *American Presbyterians* 65 (fall 1987): 174–85.

———. "The Oregon Mission and the ABCFM." *Idaho Yesterdays* 31 (spring/summer 1987): 24–34.

Welter, Barbara. "The Cult of True Womanhood: 1820–1860." *American Quarterly* 18 (summer 1966): 151–74.

———. "She Hath Done What She Could: Protestant Women's Missionary Careers in Nineteenth-Century America." *American Quarterly* 30 (winter 1978): 624–38.

White, Richard. *Middle Ground; Indians, Empires, and Republics in the Great Lakes Region, 1650–1815*. Cambridge: Cambridge University Press, 1991.

———. "Race Relations in the American West." *American Quarterly* 38 (1986): 396–416.

Whitehead, Margaret. "Christianity, a Matter of Choice: The Historic Role of Indian Catechists in Oregon Territory and British Columbia." *Pacific Northwest Quarterly* (July 1981): 98–106.

Whipple, Henry B. *Lights and Shadows of a Long Episcopate*. New York: Macmillan Co., 1899.

Whitman, Narcissa. *The Letters of Narcissa Whitman*. Fairfield, Wash.: Ye Galleon Press, 1986.

Willand, Jon. *Lac Qui Parle and the Dakota Mission*. Madison, Minnesota: Lac qui Parle County Historical Society, 1964.

Williamson, John P. *An English-Dakota Dictionary*. New York: American Tract Society, 1902. Reprint, St. Paul: Minnesota Historical Society Press, 1992.

———. *The Dakota Mission: Past and Present*. Minneapolis: Tribune Job Printing Co., 1886.

Williamson, John P., and Alfred L. Riggs, eds. *Dakota Odowan. Dakota Hymns*. The Dakota Mission of the American Missionary Association and the Presbyterian Board of Foreign Missions, 1879. Reprint, American Tract Society, 1944.

Wilson, Raymond. *Ohiyesa: Charles Eastman, Santee Sioux*. Urbana: University of Illinois Press, 1983.

Yohn, Susan M. *A Contest of Faiths: Missionary Women and Pluralism in the American Southwest*. Ithaca, N.Y.: Cornell University Press, 1995.

Index

CPSIA information can be obtained
at www.ICGtesting.com
Printed in the USA
LVHW031953110422
715892LV00007B/1331

9 780806 190013